Fences, Decks, and Other Backyard Projects

3rd Edition

Dan Ramsey

TAB Books
Division of McGraw-Hill, Inc.
New York   San Francisco   Washington, D.C.   Auckland   Bogotá
Caracas   Lisbon   London   Madrid   Mexico City   Milan
Montreal   New Delhi   San Juan   Singapore
Sydney   Tokyo   Toronto

© 1992 by **TAB Books**.
TAB Books is a division of McGraw-Hill, Inc.

pbk 4 5 6 7 8 9 10 11 12 FGR/FGR 9 9 8 7 6 5
hc   1 2 3 4 5 6   7   8   9 FGR/FGR 9 9 8 7 6 5 4 3 2

Library of Congress Cataloging-in-Publication Data

Ramsey, Dan, 1945 –
    Fences, decks, and other backyard projects / Dan Ramsey. — 3rd
ed.
        p.   cm.
    Includes index.
    ISBN 0-8306-3494-0 (h)   ISBN 0-8306-3493-2 (p)
    1. Fences.   2. Decks (Architecture, Domestic)   3. Garden
structures.
TH4965.R35   1992
631.2'7—dc20   91-47022
                                                           CIP

Acquisition Editor: Kimberly Tabor
Book Editor: Debra Marshall
Director of Production: Katherine G. Brown
Book Design: Jaclyn J. Boone
Cover Design: Holberg Design, York, Pa.
Cover Photo: The producers of Wolmanized® lumber. Project   HT3
  designed and built by Archadeck®.   4071

Contents

Acknowledgments

Many people in the fence industry contributed to this and earlier editions of this book. They include Mike O'Brien, manager of product publicity for the Western Wood Products Association; Huck DeVenzio, public relations for Hickson Corporation (Wolmanized pressure-treated lumber); Ginny Blair, director of public relations of the Chain Link Fence Manufacturers Institute; Jan Bradford, membership manager of the International Fence Industry Association; Robin F. Pendergrast, the Aluminum Association; Charles N. Farley, director of marketing assistant of the Brick Institute of America; Doug McNeill, product sales manager of Weyerhaeuser Company; Western Red Cedar Lumber Association; Colleen G. Goidel and Stacey Graham Wilson, Building Products, of Georgia-Pacific Corporation; James Moran and Gerald B. Wellner, Koppers Company, Inc.; Bonnie Meister, Patricia Young, and Pamela Allsebrook of the California Redwood Association; Builders Fence Company, Inc.; the U.S. Department of Agriculture; Dean R. Presterman, Cooperative Extension Service, Iowa State University; Washington State Cooperative Extension Service; Cliff Pluard of Pluard & Sons Fence Service, Inc., Ken Downing and Jerry O'Dell of The Fenceman Fence Co., and Paul Larison of Parr Lumber Company, all of Vancouver, Washington; and especially to Val Ramos for his excellent photography.

I also want to thank Heather Ramsey for her many hours of accurately typing the manuscript for this third edition. And I thank Byron Ramsey for his work preparing the more than 350 illustrations in this book.

Introduction

Robert Frost reminds us that "Good fences make good neighbors." The corollary is also true: good neighbors make good fences . . . and decks . . . and gazebos . . . and outdoor structures.

Fences come in all shapes, sizes, colors, and purposes—from the Great Wall of China to the little white picket fence around the roses. Fences are built from wood, metal, wire, iron, steel, glass, fiberglass, plastic, clay, brick, and scrap. They can be simple or ornate, functional or aesthetic.

Gazebos and other outdoor structures are the answer to similar needs. Decks are outdoor rooms, where families cook, eat, and relax in the shade. Storage sheds protect outdoor furniture and equipment from the elements.

Fences, Decks and Other Backyard Projects—3rd Edition is a fully illustrated book that explains how to choose, design, prepare, build, and maintain all types of fences for many purposes. First-time and veteran fence builders alike will find practical and useful information about tools, posts and framing, corners and ends, braces, gates, maintenance and repair, landscaping, and dozens of other important subjects, together with step-by-step how-to instructions and hundreds of illustrations.

You'll also find chapters about designing and building other outdoor structures: decks, sunshades, gazebos, engawas, aeries, tree houses, greenhouses, and much more. The section on landscaping will help you enhance the beauty and function of your fence. Special sections show you how to choose the right fence materials.

This latest edition includes new ideas, plans, and information to make your backyard a more liveable and enjoyable place for you and your family.

To the memory of my father,
Clarence Allen Ramsey.
And to the future of my children,
Heather, Byron, and Brendon Ramsey.

1
All about fences

In our efforts to define our own space, the human race has dug moats, hand-built a 1500-mile wall over mountains, and planted a flag on the moon. Psychologists say we do these things because of primordial territorial instincts. Whatever the reason, we're building more fences today than ever before—and we're putting them to work for us in new ways.

A fence is a barrier enclosing or bordering a field, yard, or other area. It prevents entrance, confines animals or people, or marks a boundary. A newer function of fences is to control the environment. The effects of the sun, wind, and earth, can be controlled with fences and walls.

History of fences

No one knows when the first fence was built, but the largest is still in place. The Great Wall of China was begun during the third century B.C., and many sections still stand. Its base was 15 to 30 feet thick, and its height averaged 25 feet. Its length was approximately 1500 miles.

Fences during biblical times were actually walls built around cities for protection. A dozen or more feet thick, these walls were built to withstand almost any encroachment by human or environmental sources.

Fences took on a new function during the Victorian era: beauty. Fences short enough to step over included ornate whorls and arabesques meant to impress the passerby. In America, the desire to live near centers of commercial activity reduced the size of property on which homes were built. Individuality was expressed through the art of landscaping, and in the design of fences. Fences became elements of the landscape and structures of beauty and expression (FIG. 1-1).

Fences retained their original purposes down on the farm: to keep people out and animals in. Innovations such as barbed wire, woven wire, and electric fences were a great help to farmers.

Fig. 1-1 *Fences are as creative as their designers.* California Redwood Association

Uses for fences

Let's look at the reasons people build fences—all of which can be lumped together under the phrase "environmental control." Specifically people build fences to:

- Mark property boundaries.
- Mark area boundaries.
- Keep people in or out.
- Keep animals in or out.
- Control visibility for privacy.
- Control the sun.
- Control the wind.
- Control snow.
- Control water.
- Control erosion.

- Reduce or control noise.
- Define landscape.
- Create a visual effect.

Most fences serve several purposes. A chain-link fence may mark boundaries, keep some people and animals in and keep others out, define the landscape, and improve the home's visual effect. The fence also adds value to the property by making the home a better place to live.

Property boundary

Fences can define the boundaries of a property. As homesteads become smaller and smaller, many people nonaggressively express their territorial rights by marking property lines with a fence.

Property boundary fences need not be large or expensive. Many are simple rail or picket fences erected along the front and sides of the property. These fences can also define the landscape by shunting traffic away from lawns, shrubs, and flowers. A boundary fence can also be a privacy fence, shielding the vision of others from private areas of a yard, or shielding the sight of unattractive areas from the homeowner. In rural areas, simple property boundary fences also serve as animal control fences.

Area boundary

Small properties must be efficient. Yards must serve as recreation areas, service areas, and storage and garden areas. Efficiency can be achieved by segmenting a yard with specially designed fences. A pool area may be fenced by a movable security fences. A garden area will need a security fence that doesn't block the sun's rays. A privacy area needs a large opaque fence to block visual access. A dog run can be fenced for security and visibility.

Exterior security

Fences can reduce or eliminate the opportunities of intruders entering your property. Some fences might simply slow intruders down. Others by reducing visibility into the yard, make it less likely that a stranger will venture into an unknown area. Still other fences can be wired to set off an alarm whenever someone tries to enter.

Interior security

Fence builders may want to keep others, primarily children, on the property or within a defined area. Interior security fences can be anything from a 4-foot-high chain-link fence to a 2-foot-thick concrete wall—depending on your needs, budget, and skills.

An interior security fence for children or animals must be high enough, as well as difficult to scale. If you're building a fence to keep your 2-year-old child out of the street, make it high enough to retain a 10-year-old child. Build it from materials such as large-weave chain-link or basket-weave wood. These same rules apply if you're building a prison fence.

Animal control

Fences can also keep animals in or out. A two-strand wire fence will contain cattle. A pet owner will build an enclosure to keep his animal away from cars and postmen. A proud gardener might build a fence to keep neighborhood dogs from damaging plants.

Visual control

Privacy is the primary reason many suburban fences are built. The easiest way to achieve total privacy is to rim your property with a high, solid fence. Once the fence is up, you might discover that you've created a rigid environment with a confined, boarded-up feeling. You might also have alienated yourself from your neighbors.

An alternative is to use a combination of plants, screens, and opaque and semiopaque fences to control visibility. You can install a solid board or panel fence in areas where complete privacy is desirable, and low rail fences where visibility isn't as important as property boundary definition.

In areas where you want to ensure privacy, do your best to make the solid fence handsome on both sides (FIG. 1-2). Remember: your neighbor has to look at it, too. It can either be a pleasant view or an unpleasant suggestion of your unfriendliness. Be a good neighbor with your "good neighbor" fence.

A privacy fence doesn't have to be at the

Fig. 1-2 This fence offers privacy and beauty. California Redwood Association

edge of your property line. You can build an 8-foot-high privacy fence round your pool or patio much more easily and less expensively, and it will seem more neighborly than a full 6-foot perimeter fence (FIG. 1-3). You can also use translucent glass or plastic to obscure vision while allowing light into your yard.

Sun control

Your fence can control the sun's heat and glare in many ways. Shade can be produced with solid wood, masonry, or other fence materials. Glare can be reduced with plastic or glass panels. Your choice of design and materials will depend on any other uses the fence will have. If it must also screen an area from winds, a solid fence material is preferred. If light breezes are desired, a louvered fence will be best.

Other structures can help control the sun's effects within your yard. Chapter 14 will show you how to choose and build decks, chapter 15 provides information about gazebos, while

chapter 16 offers plans for other sun controls, including the gazebo, pavilion, sun trap, screens, and arbors.

Wind control

The wind is not as easy to control as the sun, because its behavior is less predictable. Before building a fence for wind control, study the wind's behavior in your yard. The direction of the prevailing wind is not necessarily the direction it will blow across the patio. Your house, trees, and other structures change the direction of the wind, just as you can divert and direct the wind with a fence.

To discover the wind's direction at your proposed fence location, simply attach colored yarn or strips of cloth to stakes set in the ground. As the prevailing wind blows, the yarn or cloth strips will indicate how structures in your yard deflect the wind. Plan your fence to capture or release the wind as you desire (FIG. 1-8).

Fig. 1-3 *Fences are often built to enclose pools for safety and privacy.* International Fence Industry Association

Snow control

If you're building a fence in Florida, you can pass over this section. Most areas of the country get at least some snow each year. In northern climates snow can be a headache to the fence builder. Snow drifts against solid fences and piles up, producing a fence's two greatest enemies: moisture and pressure.

The solution is made in planning and design. You need to know the direction of the prevailing winter wind and how any nearby structures change its direction. Snow will accumulate quickly where it's stopped by a fence or wall. In most cases this is undesirable but can be reduced or eliminated by a fence that doesn't block wind flow. A snow-stopping fence might be desirable in areas where the snow would otherwise drift onto plants or patios. A solid, well-constructed fence will do the job.

Water control

Fences can control rainwater, standing water, or running water. Livestock ranchers build water fences across creeks to dam up or control water flow. Homeowners in areas of high wind and heavy rains can divert rain away from doorways, windows, and other areas. Fences can keep standing water away from lawns, flowers, etc.

Soil control

Fences and walls can reduce erosion and control soil. A solid fence can divert water runoff and help protect the root systems of trees and plants. Larger fences used to hold back earth are called *retaining walls*; these can be built from heavy timbers, brick, concrete, blocks, or stone.

When you build any fence or wall on a slope, carefully consider the direction, path, and amount of drainage. A fence or wall cannot stop drainage, it can only divert it safely. Retaining walls should have "weep holes" every few feet to allow moisture in the retained dirt to drain off. Dammed water can freeze and damage a wall. Walls of brick, concrete, and stone, suitable for soil control, are discussed in chapter 9.

Noise control

Fences can be physical and psychological barriers to noise. In an area where noise is a problem, such as near a major highway or factory, a tall, thick fence can actually reduce the noise level by absorbing and reflecting the sound. Living fences—such as hedges, trees, and climbing vines—are also effective noise barriers.

Psychologists say that removing a sound from sight can seem to reduce the noise. It isn't actually reduced, but the noise often becomes a less-irritating background noise if it's removed from the line of sight. This phenomenon can be used by homeowners bothered by highway traffic, industrial plants, and noise from nearby schools.

Landscape control

Fences can separate your outdoor living area into rooms (FIG. 1-4). You can then use them to develop moods through landscaping. A recrea-

Fig. 1-4 *A decorative outdoor room is formed by this unusual wood fence.*
Western Wood Products Association

tion area could have open fencing and low-maintenance plants. The garden area would have a security fence protecting the vegetables and fruits from animals. A sunbathing area can be contained with a solid high fence surrounding grass. A flower garden might be separated from the recreation area with a louvered board fence or picket fence.

Fences can also serve as vertical gardens for climbing plants and flower boxes. Ivy or sweet peas can be crisscrossed on strings attached to wooden, chain-link, or brick fences. Fences can be a natural backdrop for flowers.

Decoration

Fences can be completely decorative (FIG. 1-5). They can serve as outdoor canvases for a variety of colors and designs. Fences can be constructed and painted to blend in with the color and design of your home or another structure. They can highlight fountains, wood designs, or unique planters. They can serve primarily as art.

Types

Fences have been designed in every imaginable form with every possible material. Fences have been built from lumber, railroad ties, plywood, hardboard, aluminum, iron, steel, logs, wire, brick, stone, poured concrete, split wood, glass, plastic, bamboo, canvas, fiberglass, bottles, cans, adobe, dirt, clay, living plants, and many other natural and man-made materials.

Solid fences, built to stop things, are mostly made of wood or masonry, such as brick or stone.

Open fences, designed to reduce vision, elements, or entry, or to enhance the beauty of property, are made of a wide variety of build-

Fig. 1-5 *Fences can be decorative.* Western Red Cedar Lumber Association

ing materials, including nearly all types of wood, metal, stone, and larger plants.

Walls are simply solid strong fences. Walls hold back dirt or other elements, or add security. Walls are also built solely for beauty.

Screens are short-width fences designed to shield an area from view or the elements. Screens are used to separate a property into areas or rooms.

Fences can be a low fence of 4 feet or shorter, or a high fence of 5 feet or more (FIG. 1-6). The sizing is general; a high picket fence might only be 4 feet high, and a short board fence can be 5 feet high.

To simplify things, this book separates fences, walls, and screens into seven categories: rail fences, picket fences, board fences, chain-link fences, livestock fences, masonry fences, and other fence materials. These fences are covered in chapters 4 through 10. Chapters 2 and 3 explain how to plan and build fences. Later chapters cover decks, outdoor structures, gates, maintenance, and landscaping.

Rail fences

The so-called "rail" fence is actually a "post and rail" fence: the post is the vertical member

Fig. 1-6 *Fences come in all sizes and shapes.* California Redwood Association

and the rails run horizontally. Rail fences are as varied as their applications.

Most rail fences are low—2 to 4 feet—and open. They were originally built by pioneers to contain livestock, and were constructed of small logs and split wood. The first rail fence was the zigzag, or snake, fence built by early settlers from available timber. The fence was simple to construct and maintain, but it used more wood than today's rail fences.

As fence materials became scarce and property lines needed to be better-defined, the post and rail fence evolved to the two- and three-rail fence. The two-rail fence is used as a landscaping element, while the three-rail fence can serve as a livestock security fence.

Modern rail fences are usually constructed of 4-×-4-foot-long rails of logs, split rails, 4×4 board rails (FIG. 1-7). You'll learn more about how to design and build rail fences in chapter 4.

Picket fences

Picket fences are rail fences with evenly-spaced horizontal pickets attached to the rails. Picket fences are practical and decorative (FIG. 1-8). Nearly all picket fences are no higher than 4 feet high.

The picket fence has many advantages over other types of fences. First, it defines a property line without obstructing vision or eliminating the feeling of openness. Second, the picket fence has become an art form and so suggests a friendly owner. Pickets are simply boards that have had their tops cut to a uniform design. Third, picket fences are practical control fences for children and small pets, the natural enemies of all growing things. Fourth, picket fences are easy to construct and maintain. Picket fences can be purchased in 4- and 6-foot sections, painted and ready to install.

Picket fences seem to look best with older homes on small city lots. Chapter 5 shows how to design your own picket fence and build it with basic tools.

Board fences

Board fences comprise all types of high wood fence designs, from board-on-board to slat,

Fig. 1-7 A rail fence of 4×4 posts. Western Wood Products Association

Fig. 1-8 *A ''fence'' means a picket fence for many people.*

louver, and grape-stake fences. Construction of the post and rails is basically the same in any of these fences; the difference is in the "siding" placed on the fence (FIG. 1-9).

Board fences are useful and easy to build, but they use lots of wood and can be expensive. Careful planning can overcome the cost factor and many design problems.

Most board fences are designed for security and privacy. They are the most common "backyard" fences, and isolate your yard from the view of others. Some good neighbors build a modified board fence, shorter or more open, to reduce visibility without eliminating friendliness (FIG. 1-10).

Planning, material selection, construction

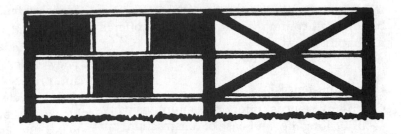

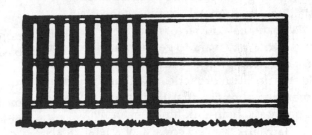

Fig. 1-9 *There are many ways to "side" a board fence.*

Fig. 1-10 *A good neighbor fence.* Western Wood Products Association

techniques, and step-by-step instructions for building all common board fences are offered in chapter 6.

Chain-link fences

Chain-link fences offer maximum visibility, security, long life, and ease of construction, but don't offer privacy. Privacy can be attained by installing wood, metal, or plastic inserts.

Wire fence contractors are very competitive, so you may want to get several bids before you tackle the project yourself—they might be able to do it more cheaply than you can. Remember, though, that there's a wide range of quality in chain-link fence materials.

Chain-link fences consist of metal posts, fabric, tension bars and bands, top rails, and fittings. The posts are set in concrete. The chain-link fabric is stretched between posts and attached with the tension bar and bands. Gates are hung separately. Chapter 7 includes complete instruction on how to select and install chain link fences.

Livestock fences

Livestock fences, which contain valuable animals, must be both efficient and economical. Livestock fences include those made with barbed wire, woven wire, poultry netting, cable, electrified stringers, and wood.

Productive farmland is often fenced with woven wire or a combination of woven wire and barbed wire. Marginal, cutover, or other less productive land is usually fenced with less expensive materials, such as single-strand wire. Woven wires are used to confine livestock. Electric fencing is convenient when more permanent fencing would be too expensive or perhaps undesirable.

Chapter 8 tells how to design and build wire and wood livestock fences.

Masonry fences

Fences and walls can also be built with masonry materials: brick, concrete, stone, etc. They enclose outdoor space and offer security and privacy.

Concrete masonry walls are built with blocks of Portland cement, graded rock, and water. Blocks with a quarter or more of their cross-sectional area open are called "hollow" blocks. They are easy to use in fence construction even by builders with minimal tools and basic knowledge.

Bricks are solid masonry, often colored red by the inclusion of clay. Bricks usually require more skill to lay, but the technique can be quickly learned by the do-it-yourselfer.

Stone is more difficult to work with because stones are varied in size and shape. Selection and placement are important. The results are more natural and decorative than fences and walls of man-made materials.

Chapter 9 includes step-by-step instructions in how to build masonry fences, and walls (FIG. 1-11). It gives you information about buying the basic materials and tools, how to pour footings, how to mix mortar, and how to cut brick.

Decks, gazebos, and other outdoor structures

Decks are horizontal platforms, usually of wood, that are built as flooring for outdoor rooms (FIG. 1-12). Deck-building is extremely popular among do-it-yourselfers, partly because construction is simple.

Chapter 14 illustrates many plans and ideas that will fit nearly all deck uses.

A gazebo is a freestanding structure, sometimes with a touch of wall (like wainscoting) or an attractive railing, sometimes with full walls on two or three sides built out of fancy lattice-

Fig. 1-11 *Brick fences can also be used as retaining walls.* Brick Institute of America

Decks, gazebos, and other outdoor structures **13**

Fig. 1-12 *A fence can be combined with a deck.* California Redwood Association

work. Whatever materials are used, gazebos are always sturdy, light, and airy (FIG. 1-13).

You'll find additional information about gazebos in chapter 15.

There are many outdoor structures that will complement your fence and increase the usefulness of your property. You can build decks, railings and fences, walks and engawas, screens, enclosures, arbors and treillage, pavilions, aeries, tree houses, planters, green-

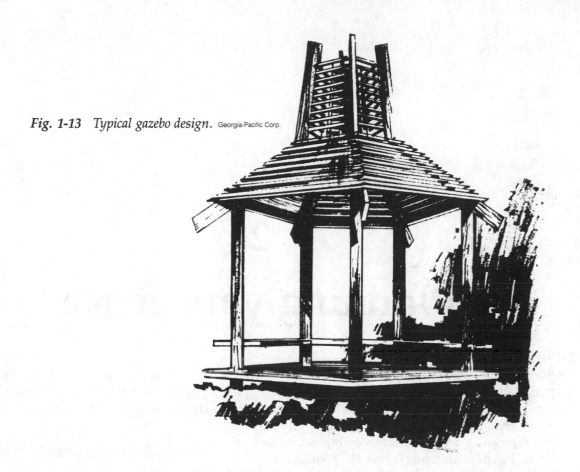

Fig. 1-13 *Typical gazebo design.* Georgia-Pacific Corp.

houses, storage rooms, and dozens of other useful structures with basic skills and tools. That's what chapter 16 is all about.

Chapter 11 explains gates. Chapter 12 describes fence maintenance. Chapter 13 illustrates how to use your fence as a landscaping element to increase the beauty of your property.

2

Planning your fence

Every good fence is built twice—once on a paper and once on the ground. Fence building would be simple if everyone lived on a perfectly level 100-×-100 lot. But most property is not typical; slopes have to be descended; trees must be passed; soils must be considered; styles must be chosen.

The first thing to do when planning your fence is to study your property: size, shape, soil, drainage, trees, ground cover, utilities, local weather conditions, and appropriateness of your fence design.

Next, draw up simple plans (FIG. 2-1). Review as many ideas as possible, learn about local building regulations, consider height and length requirements, locate the fence, talk with neighbors, and then pick your fence.

Choose the best type of fence to solve your problem: closed, tall, short, wood, masonry, etc. Pick the style, list the materials you'll need, and consider the gates and related hardware. Review your plans for function and appropriateness. Finally, solve any special problems: slopes, trees, curves, banks, water,

soils, and strength. If your fence is first built on paper, problems can be easily solved and errors corrected before you build.

Studying property

Before you decide which fence is best, take a good look at the property you're going to fence. Make a rough measurement of the fence line. If possible, plant a few stakes and run a string showing the proposed fence. Write down your measurements, and special requirements or angles.

Make a rough sketch of the shape; a full drawing isn't necessary yet. If your lot is rectangular, you don't have to draw it to scale, just make two sides longer than the others.

Mark north on your rough sketch and note or draw in nearby properties and fences. Draw in any grades, banks, berms, trees, or other elements that might affect your fence. Pay special attention to topography. Wind direction, sun orientation, and shade from outside property lines should be put on your map.

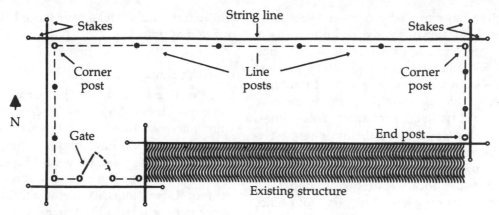

Fig. 2-1 Typical fence plan.

The soil is important to the fence builder for two reasons: Soil type indicates how the ground will drain, and some soils are easier to dig for postholes and wall footings. You can have your soil tested at little or no cost through the local cooperative extension service (refer to the phone book) or a soil laboratory. They will analyze the soil and make recommendations about digging and trenching, post materials, hole or footing depth, and digging equipment. They can also tell you whether concrete or gravel will be the most efficient hole filler for your fence. Make sure you take soil samples from along your proposed fence line. In some areas soil types are mixed and can be found in ribbons just a few feet wide.

How water drains at the site will also be important to your plan. It's usually best to plan your fence along the highest elevations to allow water to run away from it. Fences built in low spots, especially wood post fences, quickly deteriorate and must be replaced more often. If necessary, you can change the direction of natural drainage and keep standing water away from fences and walls with catch basins, contouring, and dry wells.

Plants are also important in your plan. If your landscape is already established, you'll probably want to disturb as little as possible. If you haven't landscaped yet, you can use your fence as a part of your landscaping plan. What type of ground cover do you plan—grass (what type), ivy, sandwort, juniper, or potentilla? Are there shrubs or plants you want to keep? How will they be affected by your fence? How about hedges? Can you integrate them into your fence?

Trees can be a point of beauty or a source of trouble for fence builders. You may be able to blend existing trees into your fence plans. Don't try to move them, because most won't survive the change. Work around them or cut them down. Be careful not to damage the root systems of trees you are leaving; especially in rainy parts of the country the roots are probably near the surface and can easily be damaged.

There's a man-made element to planning your fence that many builders often forget until it's too late: utilities. Newer subdivisions may have underground utilities—phone, gas, water, and electrical lines. For convenience, many of these lines run along a utility easement on the property lines—just where you want to build your fence. To make sure you won't damage these lines, check with local utilities before digging. In many areas the utilities offer a single telephone number that may be used to get information about underground utility location. They have property maps available and can quickly locate your parcel and notify you of any underground hazards. Some utility companies will place stakes over utility lines to help you plan your fence or wall. Rural fence builders should also use this service, because primary utility lines run along fence lines, roads, and even through fields where easements have been purchased.

As you study your property and plan your fence, consider local weather conditions and what part your new fence will play. Your fence can deflect or stop winds, soften or eliminate sunshine, or deflect rains. Questions to ask yourself include:

Will this fence throw a shadow? Will it give too much shade to nearby plants?

What change will this fence have on the wind? Will it break it up and send it off in another direction? Which direction? Will it affect another landscaping element?

How will this fence affect and be affected by rain and snow? Is there proper drainage?

Does this fence need special preservatives or treatment to combat adverse sun or weather conditions in your yard?

Finally, how appropriate is this fence? Will it serve its intended purpose? Will it be an integral part of your landscaping, or will it detract?

A short brick wall could be an attractive addition to your yard, but it might not offer the security and privacy you need. A barbed wire fence might be efficient for containing animals, but could detract from the beauty of your landscaped yard. A tall fence to keep animals out of your azaleas might make your neighbors feel you're unfriendly. Make your fence both effective and appropriate.

Drawing plans

Once you've studied your property and have some good ideas about how to place and build your fence, it's time to get serious. Most stationery stores will have graph paper to help you draw a diagram of your property and amenities to scale. The best scale is one square per foot. If your lot is 100 feet wide, find graph paper with at least a 100-square width. Whatever scale you decide upon, make it consistent.

Find a map of your property if possible. Check the title insurance policy you received when you purchased your property. The map may be called a plat map, subdivision map, or section map, depending on the type of land and the part of the country you're in. If you can't find your map, request one from a local title insurance company or from the county courthouse. The map might even have a legal description on it such as "Lot 42, Mill Plain Acres" or "SW $1/4$, SE $1/2$ of Section 16" to help you locate lines.

With your drawing of your property in hand, talk over your fence plans with others. You can hold a family conference to decide what type and location would be best. Consult with neighbors to see if you can share fences or tie into another fence. Speak with local officials about fencing regulations.

Fence laws

There's a law for just about everything, and fences are no exception. Fence laws are usually practical: don't build a fence on someone else's property, don't build a fence where it will obstruct the safe view of drivers, and don't build a fence that will detract from the value of neighboring properties.

The problem is that laws involving fence

construction are not standard. They vary from state to state, city to city, and even neighborhood to neighborhood. Here's how to find out what laws govern the construction of fences in your area:

- Check your title insurance policy to see if there are any restrictions or reservations that might apply, such as "No fences shall be built in the area in front of the home." Check for easements for utilities or roads. Fences can't be built on most easements without written permission from the holder.
- Contact the county or city building department to see what regulations they might have about building fences. Some have basic regulations and a small fee based on the fence's value. Others have specific and detailed requirements.
- Make sure other regulations aren't violated. Your area might restrict fences on corner lots to a height of 4 feet for traffic visibility. Other local governments might not allow you to build your fence within a specific distance of a sidewalk. Your county courthouse or city hall can direct you to any departments that have jurisdiction.
- Talk with a government official or land title officer in your area to find out how close you can locate your fence and other structures to property lines. If you're building a common fence, you may be able to straddle the line. If lines aren't clear, you may offset your fence a foot or two inside the probable line location.

One problem that some fence builders face can be easily solved. Local codes might not allow a fence taller than 6 feet at the property line. That's a problem if your house sets high and you need at least an 8-foot fence for privacy. The solution is often the 45-degree rule. That is, a higher fence can be built within the property as long as it isn't higher than a 45-degree angle from a point 6 feet above the property line. You can simply build a taller fence a few feet inside your property line as long as it doesn't break this rule. Check if your area has the 45-degree rule.

As you draw your fence plans, consider the length of your fence, both sectional and overall. The overall length of your fence should be checked to make sure it will be structurally sound. Solid fences of more than 30 or 40 feet in length often need extra bracing in windy areas, depending on the design, components, and height. The length of fence sections is also important for the planning of post locations. Posts can be separated by 4, 6, 8, 10, or 12 feet of rail and siding or other cover, depending on the height of the fence, the weight of the materials, and the strength of the posts and the rails. Most board fences have 8-foot center-to-center posts. Chain-link fence posts are often spaced 10 feet apart, and picket fences are built with a typical 4-foot spread between posts. This should be reflected in your plan drawings.

You might be able to save plenty of time, labor, and money by tying your fence into that of a neighbor. The problems to overcome are few: an agreement of ownership, style, maintenance, and location. You may have a written agreement to attach your fence to his at a corner. You still own and maintain your fence, or you could build a common fence along the property line. You'll want a written agreement stating that you are "tenants in common," that you will share the erection and maintenance costs equally, and that the style of the fence will be one agreeable to both parties. Keep this agreement with your important papers and let subsequent owners know about it.

Choosing your fence

You can also use your plans to draw out the specific type of fence or fences you'll be building. You might decide to use one kind of fence around your garden area, another as a dog run, and a third for privacy around your patio. You could simply run a perimeter fence around your property to retain livestock, pets, and children.

Among solid wood fences you can choose a basket weave, panel, board, board-on-board, diagonal board, plastic, or other style fence (FIGS. 2-2 through 2-9). You can then draw a construction diagram or elevation of your fence to scale dimensions, the width between posts, the size of materials used in the construction, and you can even include a materials list.

Your materials list will help you estimate the cost of construction. A partial list of materials you may need to build your fence is included. You'll also need a list of tools for the job, listed in chapter 3 and in the chapters on each type of fence. Many of the tools you'll have on hand, while others may be purchased, rented, or borrowed.

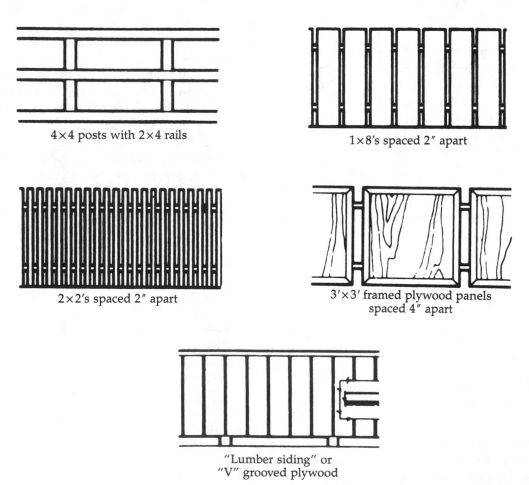

4×4 posts with 2×4 rails

1×8's spaced 2" apart

2×2's spaced 2" apart

3'×3' framed plywood panels spaced 4" apart

"Lumber siding" or "V" grooved plywood

Fig. 2-2   There are many types of siding you can install on a wood fence.

Fig. 2-3 *"Dog-eared" board fence.* <small>Val Ramos</small>

Fig. 2-4 *Alternate board fence.* <small>Val Ramos</small>

Fig. 2-5 *Post and rail fence.* <small>Val Ramos</small>

Fig. 2-6 *Horizontal board fence.* <small>Val Ramos</small>

Choosing your fence **21**

Fig. 2-7 Split rail fence. Val Ramos

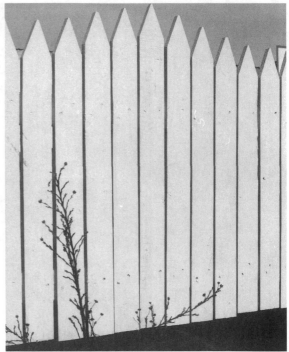

Fig. 2-8 Picket fences can become more decorative with height variations. Val Ramos

Fig. 2-9 Decorative slat fence. Val Ramos

Wood fences

- Posts: 3-×-4, 4-×-4, or 4-×5-inch milled or split wood; 5-, 6-, or 7-foot-long steel position L, T, or U shape.

- Stringers: 2-×-3 or 2-×-4 rails in 4-, 5-, 6-, or 8-foot lengths.

- Siding: 1-×-4, 1-×-6, 1-×-8 boards, of 4-, 5-, 6-, or 8-foot lengths; 1-×-1, 1-×-2, or 1-×-3 pickets of 3-, 4-, or 5-foot grape stakes; $3/8$×2×4, 6, or 8-foot lath for battens of lattice; $1/4$-to-$3/4$-inch exterior plywood in 4-×-8-foot sheets; other solid panels (tempered hardboard, aluminum, galvanized steel, fiberglass, acrylic plastic, plastic-filled screening, reed screen, plate glass, wire glass, etc.).

Wire fences

- Posts: (same as wood fences, above).

- Stringers: (same as wood fences, above).

- Fabric: 9-, 11-, $12^{1}/2$-, $14^{1}/2$-gauge galvanized strand or woven field wire, $12^{1}/2$- to $15^{1}/2$-gauge barbed wire; $1/2$, 1, 2, 3- by-4 mesh wire; poultry netting or fence, etc.

Chain-link fences

- Posts: $1^{3}/8$ to $2^{3}/8$-inch outside diameter galvanized steel posts, 2 to 3 feet longer than the wire height.

- Top rail: $1^{3}/8$-inch outside diameter galvanized steel rail (usually in 21-foot lengths)

- Fabric: $1^{1}/2$- to 9-gauge in widths of 3, $3^{1}/2$, 4, 5 and 6 feet, standard length of 50 feet per roll.

- Miscellaneous: Post caps, rail ends, top rail sleeves, brace bands, eye-tops, tension bars, tension bands, tie wires, post hinges, nuts, bolts, scrolls, gates, gate latch, etc., as needed.

Masonry fences

- Brick: standard, normal, SCR, Roman.

- Block: cinder, concrete, cement.

- Mortar: Portland cement, Sakrete concrete, other.

Planning the gate

Nearly every fence needs a gate. For practical purposes, the gate allows entrance to the fenced area. Aesthetically, a gate can also be a design element.

The first consideration in planning your gate is its location. You might decide to install a "good neighbor" gate for a friend living in an adjoining house, or your gate could be located so you can back your trailer into a fenced area. A gate can be the "door" from one part of your yard to another, such as from the recreation area to the garden. A gate can allow easy access to a pet area. The gate for a livestock fence can allow the vehicles to pass or animals to enter an adjoining pasture. Take a look at your design and review the purposes of your fence and the areas it serves.

Your gate should be an integral part of your fence. You can design it to blend in with your fence—such as in a solid board fence gate—or be decorative, such as in a short picket fence with overhead trellis. It can be built of similar or contrasting materials. A chain-link gate can be installed in a wooden fence. A wooden gate can complement a brick wall. A rail gate can break a woven wire fence.

Another gate design consideration is how it will open and close. You might want a left or right swinging gate, one that opens in or out from the primary area, or a double door gate.

Chapter 11 is devoted entirely to building and installing gates. You might want to look ahead to this chapter for some ideas on how to plan the best gate for your fence.

Reviewing your fence plans

Now that you've drawn your fence plans to scale, set them aside for awhile and take a look at other fences. This will sell you on your plan or give you ideas for improving it.

You have probably noticed that whenever you get a new interest, it opens your eyes to its commonness. If you buy a Hotzinger automobile because you want to be unique, you'll probably see four of them as you drive home from the dealer. You might take up coin collecting and learn that, to your surprise, half your friends are numismatists. It's the same with fences: as you seriously consider planning and building a fence, you will see hundreds of fences you never noticed before.

Look for fences and consider them as possible solutions to your fencing challenge. You might have your heart set on a 6-foot board-on-board fence, but look at how other homeowners have used concrete walls, grape stake siding, and even chain-link fences to achieve the same purposes. Your study of other fences will help you refine your own fence plan and give you design ideas that can improve the value of your property or reduce construction costs.

Your fence might be a large investment, costing $500 or more to construct. If so, you might want to invest $20 to $30 in the services of a landscape architect before you settle on a final plan. The architect can review your plans and make design and construction suggestions that can increase your fence's efficiency and value. He or she might suggest that you replace a section of your solid concrete block fence with a decorative concrete block screen or colored concrete section. The landscape architect might be able to suggest unusual picket designs or give you the address of a local home with a fence similar to the one you're constructing. If you're using a fence contractor, the architect might be able to give an opinion of his or her work, or suggest an alternative contractor.

You can find professional help through personal recommendations or listings in the Yellow Pages of the phone book under "Landscape Designers," "Landscape Architects," and "Architect." Get a fee quotation over the phone, then make an appointment with the one most experienced in designing fences. Make up two lists of questions: important and not as important. Cover the important ones first. If you still have time, get answers to the less important questions. Get your money's worth.

Solving fence problems

As you designed and planned your fence, you might have run into problems that must be solved before you build: problems such as going around a tree, descending a slope, edging a bank, making your fence curve, or crossing water. It's much cheaper to solve these problems on paper rather than in the field. Let's take them one at a time and see how other fence builders have turned a problem into a solution.

Trees

Fence layout can be complicated by one or more trees growing right on the proposed fence line. If the tree is small, it can be moved or removed. If it's large, you'll probably have to work around it. You can bring the fence right up to it and stop a couple inches short of the trunk, then begin the fence a couple inches away on the other side. The tree becomes part of the fence. Don't place the last post so close to the tree that you injure the root system when you dig the posthole. The fence should also be designed so that its edge next to the tree can be remodeled occasionally to accommodate the growth of the tree trunk.

Don't use the tree as a fence post, if you can avoid it. It might be injured by nails and boards. The nails usually don't do any damage to the tree, but they do make holes in the outer skin of the trunk that permit disease and bacteria to enter. If too many nails are embedded in the bark, or if wire mesh restricts growth, the tree's sap flow might be stopped, which can injure or kill the tree.

If you live in a high wind area allow more space between the tree and adjoining fence. The wind will make the trunk sway and twist, possibly damaging the fence.

Slopes

A sloping hillside stops many fence builders: they think hillside fencing is just too difficult to design and build. This is not true. The small extra effort and planning it takes to run your fence down the slope will be compensated by its additional beauty and design (FIGS. 2-10 and 2-11).

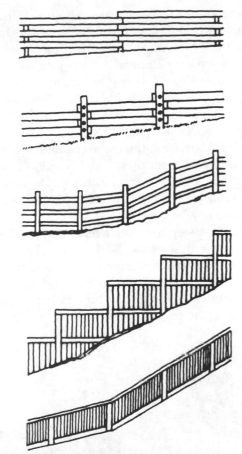

Fig. 2-10 *There are many ways to take a fence down a slope.*

Fig. 2-11 *Careful planning and construction can result in a beautiful sloping fence.* Weyerhaeuser Co.

There are two basic ways to build a hillside fence: contoured or stepped. Some fences look better built one way rather than the other, so your choice may depend on the purpose and materials (FIG. 2-12). Loose fencing such as post and rail, picket, and chain-link is often used as contour fencing. Solid boards are more commonly used as stepped fencing.

Less flexible are the more geometric forms, such as solid board, plywood, fiberglass panel, louver, and basket weave. These can be canted to fit a hillside, but they require careful cutting and fitting.

The first step in laying a fence along a slope is to figure how steep is the rise. There are many ways to do this, but the easiest is probably to use a line level and a chalk line. Run the string from a stake at the high point in your fence line. Tie the string to the stake at ground level and stretch it to a tall stake at the lowest point. Draw the string taut, hang the line level on the center of the string, and shift the string up or down on the tall stake until the bubble is centered. Then you can calculate the slope's drop by dividing the height of the string above the grade on the tall stake into the length of the line between the stakes.

To plan fence steps along the slope, simply divide the drop by the number of fence sections you have between the top and bottom of the slope. Therefore, if your sloping sections of fencing cover 24 feet in a drop of 6 feet, and you plan to build your fence in 8-foot sections, each section must drop 2 feet.

Banks

Fences built along, or to contain, banks need some engineering because of the natural stresses presented by the earth. It's best to have a landscape architect or engineer draw up your plans. The problem is that berms or banks are unstable ground, subject to shifting and erosion. Any structure built on a bank is subject to the same elements.

An engineer will suggest that footings and posts be installed deeper than normal to counter the erosion and shifting of earth around them (FIGS. 2-13 and 2-14). Bank erosion can also be slowed down or stopped by planting ground covers that have thick root systems.

Curves

If your fence plan calls for a curve, there are a couple of ways to build. You can build the fence in a true arc, or build in angled sections.

To plot a true arc curve, simple place a stake where the curve begins, one where it ends, and a pivot stake at a 90-degree angle from that point halfway between the two end stakes. Tie a string to the pivot stake, run the other end out to one of the end stakes, and attach a pointed stick. Make sure that the pivot

Fig. 2-12 Typical slope fence. Val Ramos

Fig. 2-13 *This fence is built on a concrete foundation to reduce soil movement.* Val Ramos

stake is the same distance from the other stake. Finally, use the pointed stick to scribe a line on the ground in an arc between each end stake. That's your curved fence line.

You can set posts and rails along this line and make the curve in short angles, or use a pliable fence siding, such as thin hardboard or basket weave, to make a true curve (FIG. 2-15).

Fig. 2-14 *Short banks can be controlled with stone walls.* Val Ramos

Fig. 2-15 *A rail fence can easily make the turn.* Val Ramos

Water

Sometimes a fence, especially a livestock fence, must cross standing or running water. This can present a problem for the fence builder, but not one that can't be overcome.

When fences cross ditches, streams, or dry washes that flood in winter, the problem is that the fence must serve its primary purpose of security or control without creating a barrier that can become choked with debris and cause a flood. One solution is to install a floodgate. This is a simple, rugged device that opens automatically at flood stage. It pivots on posts at each side of the stream, and swings upward as the water rises. Floodgates can also be slung on cables. Chapter 8 covers floodgates and livestock fences.

3

Building your fence

Thousands of miles of fence are built each year by people who have never before driven a nail, dug a posthole, or set a block. The required skills are easy to learn and apply.

Whether you decide to build your own fence or have an experienced contractor do it, you should talk with a contractor who can give you an estimate of costs, and possibly some pointers. Also, consider the tools you'll need to build your fence: basic building tools, tools for working the ground, woodworking tools, tools for metal and wire, and concrete-masonry tools.

You also need to know how to select and buy fencing materials: lumber, boards, chain-link fabric and posts, woven wire, brick, stone, concrete, nails, and other supplies. The basics of fence construction are important: how to locate your fence, dig holes and set posts, run rails and stringers, attach siding, and preserve and coat your fence.

Choosing a contractor

Price must be an important consideration in choosing a fence contractor, but there are shysters in every industry. You want to be sure that the contractor you select can and will deliver and, just as important, that he will be around later to back up his promises. There are points to consider when selecting a reliable fence contractor.

Beware of claims for unbelievable discounts. It may be a setup for the "bait-and-switch" routine where you'll hear: "Sorry, we're all out of that, but let me show you this." Read the small print in the ad. You might get the discount on the material, then find yourself paying an inflated price for labor or other items necessary to build the fence.

There is no such thing as "something for nothing." Business can't continue to exist without profits. The reputable contractor deserves a reasonable profit. He can't stay reputable without it.

Ask for and check the information on the contractor's business card. Check out his firm's reputation with the Chamber of Commerce or Better Business Bureau. A long-time operator will honor his guarantees. Be wary if a firm's name has been changed several times.

Ask about other fences his firm has installed nearby, and ask for the names of satisfied customers. Request samples of materials to be used. Ask for the names of suppliers, banks, credit references, and professional business associations.

Be wary of an estimate given over the telephone, or one by a salesman who doesn't personally inspect and measure the job. Fear tactics, price threats, knocking competitors, and sudden large price cuts are practices that should arouse your suspicions.

Get everything in writing. Most reputable firms use a printed estimate form that gives all the details of the contract and often serves as a contract when signed by both parties.

Don't settle for a mere mention of dimensions on the contract. Get all the specifications—the number and size of gates, the gauge or quality of materials to be used, heights, maximum post spacings, number of gate and corner posts, size and depth of postholes, whether concrete or other stabilizing materials will be used, and whether the fence will be level or will follow the contour of the yard.

You might want to ask for a copy of published industry standards to give you some basis for comparison. When comparing price, be sure the specifications are also comparable. Appendix A includes specifications for grading lumber, and appendix C outlines chain-link fence material specifications.

The contract should state who (you or the contractor) is responsible for clearing the fence line before the job and who will clean up afterwards. It should also state who will pay for any required permits.

If local and state licensing is required, has the contractor complied? If not, he might be legally lacking in the area of adequate insurance. You could be liable.

The contract should state the starting and completion dates, even though weather and other factors will cause understandable delays.

The contractor is obligated to advise you of your rights. You generally have three days to change your mind, and this should be in the contract.

Warranties and guarantees might be important to you. If so, ask for them in writing.

Compare every aspect of the estimates and contracts. Look at one or more fences that each firm has installed.

Finally, make your decision based on your confidence in the firm, built on the information you have in hand. But even if you decide to have a contractor build your fence, this book will help you understand how and why fences are built, so you can get your money's worth.

Deciding to do it yourself

You might decide to build your own fence. Finances might rule out the hiring of a contractor, or perhaps you simply have the urge to create and build it yourself.

If you have a feeling for tools and a capacity for doing reasonably careful work, you should be able to erect a fence that's as sturdy and attractive as any professional job. Fence building is not one of the most difficult skills to learn. Materials are easy to obtain. Standard lumber can be used to build many types of fences. Masonry work is simple to learn.

The only really tough part of building a fence is digging the postholes and setting the posts so they are firmly embedded and precisely aligned. You can do this by renting a posthole digger or hiring a worker who enjoys exercise. Your helper might even be available for "Tom Sawyer" work once the fence is up.

To decide whether it's worth your while to build your own fence, make an estimate of costs and compare it with an estimate from a contractor. The following explains how to go about a do-it-yourself cost estimate:

Lumber Using your fence plan, count the number of posts, rails, and pieces of siding you'll need and figure their lengths. Make sure the posts are long enough. Then add 10 percent to your total to allow for waste and error.

Hardware Fencing hardware includes gate hinges and latches, stringer brackets, fasteners, screws, bolts, and nails (TABLE 3-1).

Masonry Estimate the number of blocks, bricks, or stones you'll need for your fence or wall, along with the size and grade.

Concrete Posthole concrete requirements

**Table 3-1. Fence Plan and
Materials Sheet for a Chain-link Fence**

Posts	O.D. size	Length	Kind
			Corner posts
			End posts
			Gate posts
			Line posts

Amount	Size	Fence line sketch			
Tension bands					
Brace bands					
Rail ends					
Post caps					
Nuts and bolts					
Eye-tops					
Top rail					
Top rail sleeves					
Chain-link fabric					
Tension bars					
Tie wires		_____Gates_____			
Post hinge		Width	Height	Width	Height

depend on the width and depth of the hole. Estimate two tight 2-foot-deep holes per 90-pound bag of ready mix—one loose 3-foot-deep hole per bag.

Stain Estimate square footage of coverage, then check against the coverage table on the can.

To order your fencing materials, find the dealer with the lowest overall prices and purchase them through him. Larger orders often earn discounts of 10 percent or more, or credit is given towards related materials: tools, paint, and hardware. Cash also earns a discount with some dealers. Don't be afraid to ask for a discount: it could mean a savings of $50 or more.

Basic tools

A carpenter's level should be at least 24 inches long and contain three vials, so it can be used to check both horizontal and vertical planes. Some have a special vial on one end intended for checking 45-degree angles and slopes.

Chalk line is 50 to 100 feet of strong string encased with a quantity of chalk dust (FIG. 3-1). Stretch the string tightly between the two points, then snap it. The chalk on the string leaves a line mark. Better chalk line tools can be refilled with chalk dust and do double duty as a plumb bob, which is useful for making vertical lines.

A combination square is used to check corners and cuts for squareness and lay out lines for 45-degree cuts. Use it as a depth gauge and as a bench rule.

Flexible tapes are useful. Both a short (6 to 12 feet) and long (50 to 100 feet) tape should be in your toolbox. They come in different widths. A ³/₄-inch tape is a good choice, even though it's bulkier than others, because it has the rigidity to span openings without buckling. Better tapes have locks. Longer tapes should be thinner and more pliable.

Screwdrivers should include both straight

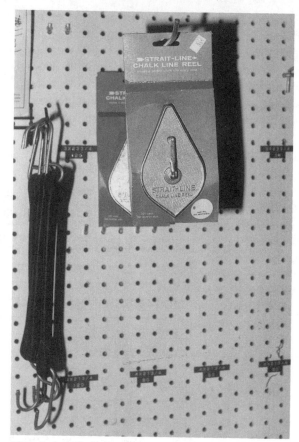

Fig. 3-1 *Chalk line for marking a fence or cutting fence tops.* Val Ramos

tip and Phillips-head in many sizes.

A claw hammer is an important tool to the wood fence builder, for driving and pulling nails. The striking surface should be slightly convex (ball-faced) and allow you to drive a nail flush without damage to adjacent surfaces. The handle may be hardwood or rubber-sheathed fiberglass or steel. Some prefer wood because it doesn't get cold to the touch. Others prefer steel because the head is more securely attached.

A crosscut saw has small teeth with knife-like points. The saw is designed for cutting across the grain of lumber, but it's also good for sawing all types of plywood. A saw that's "taper ground," which usually indicates a quality product, has 8 or 10 teeth per inch and is 26 inches long.

A keyhole saw has a narrow blade that tapers to a small point. The saw is useful for sawing curved lines. A single handle with three different blades is often available as a nest of saws, one of which can be used to saw metal.

Backsaws have teeth like a crosscut saw and a rectangular blade that is stiffened with a length of steel or brass along its top edge. A backsaw is for more precise work than can be accomplished with other saws, such as making plywood cutouts as fence decorations.

Hand drills look and work like eggbeaters. With a set of bits or "points," they can be used to drill pilot holes for screws or other uses.

Brace and bits are for making holes larger than those possible with a hand drill. The brace is essentially U-shaped, with a chuck at one end and a flat, knob-type handle at the other. Bits range in size from 1/4 to 1 inch, but there are adjustable expansive bits that can be used to form holes as large as 3 inches. Bits used in a brace have screw points so they draw themselves into the wood as they turn.

Slip-joint pliers are made of drop-forged steel and are 8 inches long. They are called slip-joint because the jaws can be adjusted to grip objects of various sizes. They're excellent for general-purpose gripping, bending, and even occasional nail pulling. Good ones have a nice pivot action and include a short, sharp section in each jaw so the tool can be used to cut wire.

Clamshell diggers are two-handled shovels used for digging postholes. With this tool the fence builder plunges the blades into the soil and chews his way out by working the handles back and forth. It's difficult to use for digging holes deeper than 2 feet because the sidewalls interfere with the spreading of the handles.

Augers dig holes with a circular motion. There are two types of augers. One uses a screw blade and operates as a twist drill. The other has cutting blades combined with a scoop arrangement that holds the loose soil as it is bored out. Either type is best used in rock-free ground.

Circular saws are often called "cutoff" saws, and are used for crosscutting, ripping, beveling, mitering, and other routine operations that are performed much faster with circular saws than handsaws. Capacity is often judged in terms of blade diameter. Generally, the larger the blade, the heavier and more expensive the tool will be. Replacement blades will also cost more. Common blades are: combination blade, good for both crosscutting and ripping lumber; plywood blade for cutting plywood; hollow ground blade, which leaves a smooth edge on both lumber and plywood; and crosscutting and rip blades.

A fence stretcher, also called a come-along, is a block-and-tackle arrangement that pulls the wire or chain-link fabric tight between posts so that it can be secured (FIG. 3-2).

Cutting pliers are used to cut wire both off the roll and once it is stretched. Heavy-duty cutting pliers are safest.

When building masonry walls and fences, a concrete mixer is used for larger jobs to mix concrete for walls, footings, or other structures. Mixers come in all sizes. Most can be rented.

Concrete shovels are used to mix the ingredients. You can buy or rent a concrete shovel, or you can make one by straightening out a garden hoe or spade.

Wheelbarrows are useful. Rubber-tired metal wheelbarrows used for concrete work have a high body in the front to prevent spills when the handles are lifted. Wheelbarrows used in the garden can be sufficient.

Concrete working tools include tampers, floats, groovers, edgers, trowels, pails, and hoses.

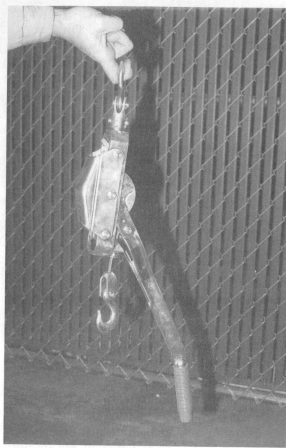

Fig. 3-2 Chain-link fence fabric stretcher. Val Ramos

Selecting materials

Most fences are all or at least partially of wood. Knowing something about wood and related materials can save you time and money and make your fence more attractive.

Wood is either hard or soft, a designation that has nothing to do with the actual density of the wood itself. These are botanical terms indicating that the wood has come from either a broad-leafed deciduous tree (hardwood) or a cone-bearing or evergreen tree (softwood). Some popular hardwoods are birch, maple, walnut, mahogany, and oak. Common softwoods include pine, fir, redwood, and cedar.

Nearly all wood fences are made of softwoods (TABLE 3-2).

Basic fences can be built from logs and saplings cut on the site, but most fence builders rely on the dressed lumber and prefabricated fencing sold in many lumberyards. Fence kits usually include all the materials you need for complete installation, down to the nails. The kit includes fence posts that have been treated, cut to the proper length, and notched or mortised as necessary to accommodate rails; the rails themselves; shaped pickets; and woven wire, or other fence siding. A fence kit saves you from estimating, ordering, and cutting the lumber to fit your plans. The cost of a fence kit might be higher or lower than the individual materials, depending on labor involved and local competition for business.

Table 3-2. Common Woods and Their Uses

Species	Properties	Outdoor uses
Cedar	natural resistance to decay not resistant to insects resists shrinking, swelling, warping easy to work with	decks walks fencing
Cypress	natural resistance to decay natural resistance to insects strong; finishes well easy to work with	decks
Fir Pine Spruce	not resistant to insects low resistance to decay strong; finishes well easy to work with does not weather well without a sealer	decks fencing
Hemlock	low resistance to decay not resistant to insects lightweight; uniform grain easy to work with	decks
Redwood	natural resistance to decay natural resistance to insects easy to work with; finishes well weathers well	decks fencing furniture

Sizing lumber

Familiar terms, like 2×4 and 1×8, are used to designate different sizes of lumber as nominal sizing rather than actual sizing (TABLE 3-3). A 2×4 is actually $1^{1}/_{2}×3^{1}/_{2}$ inches. All western woods and other softwood lumber that move from mills to building sites are ordered by these nominal sizes. Widths and thicknesses are slimmer than nominal. Most slimming occurs in the drying out process and in planing or finishing. These sizes for seasoned lumber are uniform throughout the country.

Table 3-3. Nominal and Dry Sizes for Seasoned Lumber

Nominal size (inches)	Actual dry size (inches)
1×2	$^{3}/_{4}×$ $1^{1}/_{2}$
1×4	$^{3}/_{4}×$ $3^{1}/_{2}$
1×6	$^{3}/_{4}×$ $5^{1}/_{2}$
1×10	$^{3}/_{4}×$ $9^{1}/_{4}$
1×12	$^{3}/_{4}×11^{1}/_{4}$
2×4	$1^{1}/_{2}×$ $3^{1}/_{2}$
2×6	$1^{1}/_{2}×$ $5^{1}/_{2}$
2×10	$1^{1}/_{2}×$ $9^{1}/_{4}$
2×12	$1^{1}/_{2}×11^{1}/_{4}$
3×6	$2^{1}/_{2}×$ $5^{1}/_{2}$
4×4	$3^{1}/_{2}×$ $3^{1}/_{2}$
4×6	$3^{1}/_{2}×$ $5^{1}/_{2}$

Grading lumber

Whether you purchase lumber in a fence kit or directly from the lumber dealer, it should conform to certain standards.

Construction lumber is sold in a variety of grades. The best quality is smoothly finished and generally free of knots and blemishes. Unless the appearance of the wood itself is vital to the fence design, there is nothing to be gained by buying the topmost grades at what might be three times the price you would pay for lesser grades that are satisfactory for fence construction. Knots and other defects that make lumber unsuitable for finishing work do not interfere with the usefulness of a fence, especially if the surface is painted or otherwise covered.

The function of lumber grading is to provide identification so the user can purchase wood suitable for the use intended. The official grading agency mark on a piece of lumber is assurance of its assigned grade. The grading practices of these agencies' member mills are supervised to assure uniformity. Figure 3-3 is a typical grade stamp. It's read as follows:

- A indicates the mark for the Western Wood Products Association (WWPA), the grading agency whose standards are used on this lumber.
- B indicates the mill number; each mill is assigned a permanent number for grade stamp purposes.
- C indicates an example of an official grade name abbreviation. The official grade name, as defined by the association, gives positive identification to the grade of lumber.
- D identifies the wood species.
- E denotes the moisture content of lumber when it's unseasoned, or "green," lumber.

Fig. 3-3   Grade stamp. Western Wood Products Association

You'll find other grading and wood association marks on wood. Figure 3-4 is a grade stamp for the American Wood Preservers Bureau. "LP-22" means the wood is treated to a minimum retention of .40 pounds per cubic foot and can be used in ground contact. LP-22 is recommended for all outdoor home projects.

Selecting materials   **35**

Fig. 3-4 *Grade stamp for pressure-treated wood.*
Western Wood Products Association

Figure 3-5 illustrates the redwood grade marks of the California Redwood Association. "Clear All Heart" is the finest grade of redwood and is used for siding, paneling, and cabinets. "Clear" is nearly as good, but it includes some cream-colored sapwood. "Construction Heart" is general-purpose redwood, for use where clearness (freedom from knot) is not a prime factor. "Construction Common" is similar to Construction Heart except that it contains sapwood. "Merchantable" has loose knots. Other redwood grades include "Select Heart" and "Select."

Fig. 3-5 *Redwood grade stamp.* California Redwood Association

Buying lumber

Some hints about measuring and buying lumber for your fence will help you purchase enough materials (TABLE 3-4).

Posts should be 2 to 2¹/₂ feet longer than the height of the fence. A 6-foot fence will require 8- to 8¹/₂-foot posts (FIG. 3-6). High, solid board fences need extra-long posts to permit a deeper foundation. You can figure the length as 40 percent longer than the height of the fence in these instances, using 25 to 30 percent for normal applications.

Round posts made from peeled logs should be slightly larger than squared posts. Use a peeled 6-inch-diameter post in place of a 4×4.

Stringers should be attached to a post every 8 to 10 feet, depending on the weight it will carry. You can use 2×4s as standard rails for board fences.

Pickets come in many sizes and styles. Standard thickness is 1-inch nominal (³/₄-inch actual), and width ranges from 2 to 6 inches nominal.

Boards are typically 1 inch (nominal) thick and 6 to 12 inches (nominal) wide.

Table 3-4. Lumber Scale or Board Feet per Timber

Length of timber	8	10	12	14	16	18	20	22	24
1×4	2²/₃	3¹/₃	4	4²/₃	5¹/₃	—	—	—	—
1×6	4	5	6	7	8	—	—	—	—
1×8	5¹/₃	6²/₃	8	9¹/₃	10²/₃	—	—	—	—
2×4	5¹/₃	6²/₃	8	9¹/₃	10²/₃	12	13¹/₃	—	—
2×6	8	10	12	14	16	18	20	—	—
2×8	10²/₃	13¹/₃	16	18²/₃	21¹/₃	24	26²/₃	—	—
2×10	13¹/₃	16²/₃	20	23¹/₃	26²/₃	30	33¹/₃	—	—
2×12	16	20	24	28	32	36	40	—	—
4×4	10²/₃	13¹/₃	16	18²/₃	21¹/₃	24	26²/₃	—	—
4×6	16	20	24	28	32	36	40	—	—
6×6	24	30	36	42	48	54	60	66	72

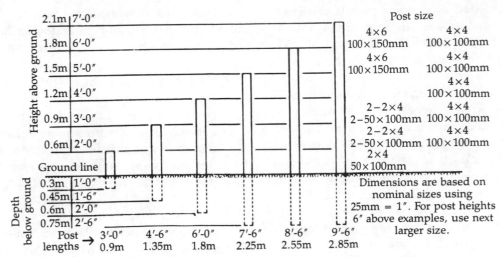

Fig. 3-6 Typical post size and embedment.

Information about choosing plywood and hardboard for fencing material is in chapter 10.

The success of your fence continues when you use a grade of lumber suitable for studs in walls ("Stud"), and using "Select" and "Struc-tural" grades if for fences with uses where more strength is needed (TABLE 3-5).

Some varieties of wood are better suited to fence building because they are naturally decay-resistant. Lumber cut from the heart of

Table 3-5. Dimensional Lumber Grades

Material	Grades	Comments
Boards (commons) Siding, paneling, shelving, sheathing, and form lumber	No. 1 Common No. 2 Common No. 3 Common	No. 1 Common boards are the ultimate in small-knot material for appearance uses, but less expensive. No. 2 and No. 3 Commons are most often used in housing for paneling, siding and shelving. Boards are generally available at building material dealers in 1×2 through 1×12.
Light framing	Construction Standard Utility	This category is for use where high strength values are not required such as studs, plates, sills, cripples, blocking, etc.
Studs	Stud	A popular grade for load and non-load-bearing walls. Limited to 10 ft. and shorter.
Structural light framing joists and planks	Select Structural No. 1 No. 2 No. 3	These grades fit engineering applications where higher strength is needed, for uses such as trusses, joists, rafters and general framing.

redwood, cedar, or cypress trees is extremely rot-resistant. Lumber cut from areas close to the bark of these trees will rot almost as quickly as lumber from more decay-susceptible woods like pine and fir.

Although entire fences are commonly built of decay-resistant wood, this immunity is mainly needed in the posts, which are vulnerable to attack by fungi and wood-destroying insects. Other parts of the fence are exposed to sunlight and air, and will not succumb as easily to decay. Many fence builders use heartwood for the posts and sapwood for the rest of the fence. Redwood or cedar posts and pine and fir stringers and boards are also used.

It's not always possible to find enough redwood, cedar, or cypress for your fence at a reasonable cost. The alternative is to treat wood with a preservative before installation, or purchase pressure-treated wood that can last up to 20 years.

Wood preservatives

Most wood, when exposed to continual soaking by water or when in contact with soil, is subject to deterioration by decay fungi and insects. The heartwood of some species is resistant to decay because of natural chemicals called extractives in the wood. Common species that have resistant or very resistant heartwood include black cherry, black locust, black walnut, cedars, osage orange, red mulberry, redwood, and white oak. Only the cedars and redwood are commonly available in all-heartwood grades in construction lumber, and may be used where modest decay hazards exist.

When high durability under severe exposure conditions is required, only wood that is pressure-treated with an approved wood preservative should be used. The term "wood preservative" denotes the treatment of wood with chemicals to impart resistance to degradation by living organisms.

Commercial preservatives may be classified into two groups: oil-type and water-borne. Each group has advantages and disadvantages.

- Oil-type preservatives fall into two main classes: coal-tar creosote and solutions of creosote in coal tar or petroleum oils; and solutions of a preservative chemical dissolved in a suitable non-aqueous carrier. In many solutions, pentachlorophenol is the preservative chemical. The carrier is often, although not always, an oil derived from processing of crude petroleum. Such carriers vary greatly in volatility, and which you choose will depend upon your need for cleanliness in the treated product.

The performance of the treated wood and the cleanliness of its surface are influenced by the carrier. In uses where the wood must be painted the carrier must consist of a volatile solvent.

Creosote is permanent, toxic to wood-destroying organisms, easy to apply, and has a long record of satisfactory use.

Although creosote is well-qualified for general outdoor use, it is not suitable for indoor use or uses that bring people in contact with the treated wood. Creosote-treated wood usually can't be painted over. Also, creosote vapors are harmful to growing plants, and food should not be stored where creosote odors are present.

Pentachlorophenol (penta) solutions also have a long record of satisfactory service in outdoor use. It is not suitable for interior use because the chemical may slowly volatize into the surrounding atmosphere. Penta-treated wood should not be used where contact with people is likely, or around plants.

The heavy oils in pentachlorophenol remain in the wood a long time and do not usually provide a clean or paintable surface. Volatile solvents, such as liquified pentachlorophenol, are used when the wood must look natural, or be painted or otherwise finished.

- Water-repellent preservative solutions combine water-repellent chemicals with a preservative in a light petroleum solvent that leaves the treated wood paintable. The preservative is usually pentachlorophenol, copper naphthenate, tributylitin oxide, or copper-8-quinolinolate. Water-based, water-repellent preservatives are available and preliminary testing indicates good performance.

In treatments using waterborne preservatives, the chemicals are dissolved in water alone or in water containing either ammonia or acidic compounds that hold the preservative chemicals in solution. Some chemical changes may take place within the wood, and if they result in compounds that are very low in water solubility, the preservative is called "leach-resistant." Waterborne preservatives that do not form insoluble compounds are assumed to be leachable.

The five leach-resistant waterborne preservatives are: acid copper chromate (ACC), ammoniacal copper arsenate (ACA), and three different formulations of chromated copper arsenate (CCA). Common trade names for these are: ACC—Celcure; ACA—Chemonite; CCA Type A—Greensalt; CCA Type B—Boliden CCA or Osmose K-33; CCA Type C—Wolman CCA. Although all these preservatives form relatively insoluble compounds during treatment, ACC is recommended for somewhat less rigorous exposure conditions than ACA and CCA.

Two leachable waterborne preservatives used to treat wood are chromated zinc chloride (CZC) and fluorchrome arsenate phenol (FCAP). These should only be used where leaching conditions are not severe.

The advantages of waterborne preservatives stem mainly from their cleanliness, paintability, and freedom from odor. Because water is added during treatment, the wood must be dried after treatment to the moisture content required for use.

Wood-preserving chemicals are applied to wood in several ways. In pressure methods chemicals are injected into the wood in a pressure retort or cylinder. About 90 percent of commercially treated wood is pressure impregnated. Non-pressure methods include soaking, dipping, brushing, and spraying. There are also specialized thermal and non-pressure diffusion processes.

Pressure treatment offers several advantages over non-pressure methods. In most cases, the chemicals penetrate deeper and more uniformly. Inspection and identification of pressure-treated wood products is conducted through the American Wood Preservers Bureau, an independent organization formed through an association of wood preservers.

Regardless of the method of treatment used, results can vary greatly within and between species. When pressure methods are used, the outer ring of sapwood of most species is impregnated much more readily than the heartwood. The widest difference between species is found in the treatability of the heartwood (TABLE 3-6). In a few species, even the heartwood takes treatment readily. In other species, even the sapwood is difficult to penetrate. Look for species identification on lumber as well as treatment certification.

Wood treated with a preservative should only be used when untreated material will not perform satisfactorily. If ordinary dry lumber

Table 3-6. Level of Treatment Difficulty of Heartwood

Least	Moderate	Difficult	Very difficult
basswood	cottonwood	eastern hemlock	alpine fir
green ash	Douglas fir (Coast)	grand fir	black locust
red oaks	E. white pine	hackberry	Douglas fir (Rocky Mt.)
redwood	Ponderosa pine	lodgepole pine	tamarack
river birch	red pine	noble fir	western red cedar
slippery elm	southern pines	spruces	white oaks
white ash	sugar maple	sycamore	
	western hemlock	western larch	
	yellow birch	white fir	

or other products will provide the required durability, the extra expense of using treated wood is not recommended.

Selecting the right preservative treatment and product depends upon the severity of the possible decay or insect hazard and upon the requirements of specific use. Figure 3-7 shows examples of the three levels of treatment (based on retention of chemical) for waterborne salt treatments. Wood products labeled for above-ground applications should not be used in continuous contact with soil or water. Material that has been treated for ground contact is suitable for use in contact with ground or water. Foundation material has even higher retention of the waterborne salt, and is approved for use in building foundations. For mild exposure and hazard conditions, wood treated with one of the non-pressure methods, using a water-repellent preservative, may be suitable.

Use only material treated with a waterborne preservative for indoor use or in applications where people come in contact with the product. The preservative most commonly used in buildings is CCA. For specialized applications that come close to or are in contact with foodstuffs, copper-8-quinolinolate is the only preservative recognized as suitable and safe.

When you use treated wood, you must also consider its ability to be painted or glued, and the corrosiveness of the preservatives to metal

Fig. 3-7 Typical stampings on pressure-treated wood.

fastenings. Generally, waterborne preservative treatments are most easily painted. The material must be dry and might require a light sanding or brushing to provide a paintable surface.

Wood treated with creosote or pentachlorophenol dissolved in a heavy petroleum solvent generally cannot be painted. You may also have difficulty painting wood that is pressure-treated with penta in a light petroleum solvent. Water-repellent preservative solutions applied with a brush, spray, or dip treatment generally can be painted readily.

Deposits on the surface of treated wood present problems in gluing. Oil-type preservatives typically present more problems than waterborne preservatives. Wood treated with very high retentions of creosote or pentachlorophenol in heavy solvents is practically nongluable. Low retentions of penta in a light petroleum solvent might be somewhat more adaptable to gluing than creosoted wood. Wood treated with waterborne chemicals can be glued, if properly dried. Always plane or sand the surface before gluing and select the adhesive most compatible with the preservative and the exposure conditions. Refer to the manufacturer's label on the glue container.

Metal fasteners used on treated wood don't corrode under dry conditions. Even under wet conditions, oil-type preservatives don't have a history of causing corrosion. But corrosion can occur when waterborne salt-treated wood is used under moist conditions. When wood is pressure-treated with non-leaching waterborne preservatives and is exposed to moist conditions, use stainless steel, silicon bronze, or copper fastenings to eliminate corrosion.

If wood cannot be kept dry and protected from deterioration by decay fungi and insects, preservative treatment can ensure long-term durability. Select the right preservative and the right treatment method for the application involved. Properly labeled pressure-treated wood products generally provide the maximum protection.

Nails

Nails are graded by size, type, and surface. Sizes are referred to in terms of "penny" (written "d" such as in "8d" or "8 penny"). The 2d nail is 1 inch long, and each succeeding two "ds" adds $1/2$ inch to the length. An 8d nail is $2^1/2$ inches long (FIG. 3-8). The nail type means its purpose and design: "common" for most applications, "concrete," "shingle," etc., for special nailing jobs. The surface is the finish on the nail. Bright nails are cleaned and uncoated. Galvanized are zinc-coated. Cement-coated nails have an adhesive for increased holding power, and blued nails are sterilized by heating them until an oxidation layer, blue in color, is formed. Most wood fence nails are 6d or 8d galvanized common or box.

Information about selecting wire, chain link, brick, and concrete for your fence is in the related chapters.

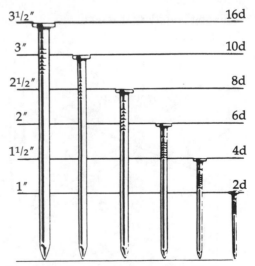

Fig. 3-8 Comparing common nail sizes. Georgia-Pacific Corp.

Basic fence construction

There are five basic steps involved in building fences of any kind of material:

1. Locate the fence.
2. Dig holes and set posts.
3. Add rails or stringers.
4. Install fence siding, if appropriate.
5. Coat and protect the fence.

Some fences will be built using a modified version of one or more of these steps, but they are built around this system.

Locating the fence

The first thing you need to know is, "Where is this fence going to go?" You should mark the fence line on the ground in some fashion, to ensure that the fence will be both legal and straight. This is a simple task if you are building within your property, but you should be more precise if you're building a boundary fence, because you might be building it for someone else.

If the original survey stakes are still in place, you can probably use them as boundary markers (FIG. 3-9). If you can't find them you might want to invest in a survey, or at least come to an agreement with adjoining neighbors as to where your common boundary lines run.

To lay out the line you'll need a 50- to 100-foot tape, a carpenter's square, a ball of mason's twine or good string, a few stakes, a hatchet, and a piece of chalk for markings.

Mark the corner or end points with a stake. Then run the string or mason's twine between the stakes, drawing it tight and tying it firmly to the stakes. Trim or go over any bushes or other obstructions.

Measure off the width of each section of fencing and place a stake. You can do this either with a measuring tape or by laying a stringer on the ground under the fence line, placing a stake, then advancing the stringer again to mark the next stake (future post) position.

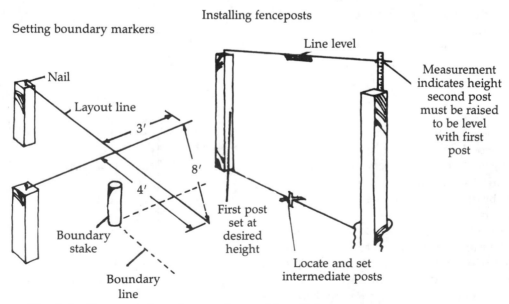

Setting boundary markers

Installing fenceposts

Line level

Measurement indicates height second post must be raised to be level with first post

Nail

Layout line

3'

8'

4'

First post set at desired height

Boundary stake

Boundary line

Locate and set intermediate posts

Fig. 3-9 *How to set boundary markers and install fence posts.* Wolmanized pressure-treated lumber

If you're building a long livestock fence, you can use a transit—bought, rented, or borrowed—to sight down your proposed fence line.

Holes and posts

Once your fence line is strung and the posthole sites are staked out, you're ready to start digging. The best size hole to dig depends on the kind of soil on which your fence is being built. The hole should be of a size that will give firm support to the post, while permitting water to drain away from around it. In open, sandy soils, make the hole only slightly bigger than the post. In heavy clay or adobe make the hole much larger and pack it with gravel. The gravel packing encourages water to drain away instead of remaining trapped around the post and allowing dry rot to begin (FIG. 3-10). If posts are to be set in concrete, dig the hole $2^{1}/2$ to 3 times the diameter of the post—about 10×10 inches for a 4×4 post.

Dig your holes with a posthole auger or clamshell digger. An auger won't be much good in rocky soil; a clamshell digger will work better. A digging bar and a spoon-bladed shovel might be necessary in very rocky soil. If necessary, you can drill into rock (use a star drill) and set a pin in the rock that will then be inserted into a drill shaft in the post. If the rock is shale, you can break it up with a sledge and pick.

The easiest way to make sure your fence will follow a straight line is to set opposite corner posts first. Set them permanently, then stretch a string or line between them and set intermediate posts. Shovel 3 or 4 inches of gravel into the bottom of the posthole, tamp it down, then place the post on top of it. Fill in about a third of the hole with gravel, soil, or concrete. Tamp it down to hold the post upright, then true up the post with a carpenter's level or plumb bob before filling and packing the rest of the hole (FIG. 3-11).

Rails or stringers

Rails are the horizontal members of the fence running from post to post. There may be one, two, three, or more rails per section—two are usual. Figures 3-12 – 3-16 illustrate how they are installed.

Fig. 3-10 *Capping and angling posts will reduce rot due to water standing on the top of the post.*

Fig. 3-11 *Where posts must be attached to cement foundations, use steel plates.* Val Ramos

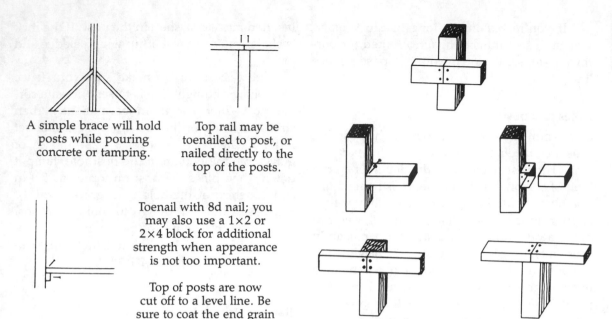

A simple brace will hold posts while pouring concrete or tamping.

Top rail may be toenailed to post, or nailed directly to the top of the posts.

Toenail with 8d nail; you may also use a 1×2 or 2×4 block for additional strength when appearance is not too important.

Top of posts are now cut off to a level line. Be sure to coat the end grain of the wood with a preservative after cutting.

Fig. 3-12 *Steps to installing the posts and rails.*

Western Wood Products Association

Fig. 3-13 *Rails can be either lap-joined on outside of the post or toenailed or set in fence brackets. The top rail can be lap-joined on the side or butted on top of the post.* Weyerhaeuser Co.

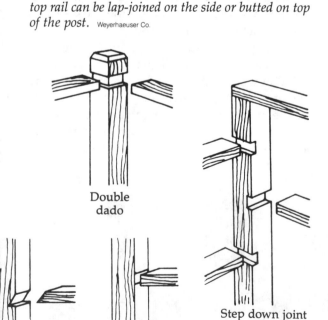

Overlapping joint

Bias miter joint

Double dado

Step down joint

Dado joint

Double dado

Angle grove joint

Simple butt joint

Fig. 3-14 *Rails can be set using various kinds of joints.*

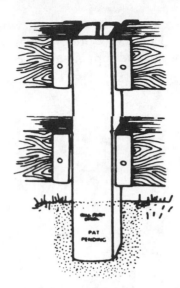

Fig. 3-15 Attaching rails to posts with a rail bracket. Val Ramos

Fig. 3-16 Attaching rails square steel posts with built-in brackets. Rollform, Inc.

Set the top rail into position inside, outside, or within the frame. If you're setting it within the frame, it's better to use a metal hanger for the stringer than to toenail it.

Set the middle and bottom stringers in the same way. Use a spirit level to keep the rails level. If the fence is descending a slope, the top rail can be level or descending, but the lower rail should generally follow the contour of the ground.

Post and rail fences may use larger-dimension lumber or split wood as rails—installed through the post or between a double post.

Siding

Siding is anything that's attached to the fence rails to cover the fence, such as pickets, boards, laths, grape stakes, plywood or other materials. Attaching siding is the easiest, yet most tedious, job.

If pickets, slats, or boards are to be attached with an opening between each, cut a slat to the exact width of the opening as a spacer. Nail a cleat to one end so it can hang on

the rail and butt the previous piece of siding. Then nail the next piece in place, shift the cleated spacer over, and start again.

A technique I've used to install siding is to nail a rail to the top of the posts so the boards butt up to it and against the previous board. Then the new board is nailed into place over the rails. To make this system go faster, have a helper place the boards. Drive a set nail, then finish nailing while the next board is placed into position. A section of fence goes up quickly this way.

Coating

There are many ways to coat your fence. The reasons for doing so are to beautify and to protect it.

Paints serve both purposes. Tell your paint dealer what you're planning to do, and he can recommend the right paint for the job. White is the traditional color for fences because it looks neat and clean—for awhile. Many fences are treated with stains for protection and color. Some folks prefer preservatives that allow the natural discoloration of the wood while protecting it. Common preservatives include penta, creosote, and copper sulfate. Fence coatings are applied by brush, roller, spray, or dripping. Information on coatings and application is given in chapters 1 and 12.

4

Rail fences

Rail fences are about the easiest to build. Most are built with lower grade materials. They require only basic tools and serve for many years

Rail fences can be seen everywhere: around residences, parks, playgrounds, and businesses, as corrals, and as other farm animal fencing. Some clearly define property lines and keep larger animals in or out. Others are simply decorative. If a rail fence is properly built, of good material, on a clear, solid bed, and kept free from bushes and other growth, the rail fence is as cheap as any fence and often just as effective.

The rail fence is often called a "pioneer fence." The fence is simple and inexpensive to build in areas where wood is plentiful. Some versions can be moved as new pasture fencing is needed.

The first rail fence was the picturesque zig-zag, named for its shape (FIG. 4-1). It was a by-product of the forest-clearing days when wood was plentiful and boundary lines were flexible enough to take a broad-gauge fence. As timber

and land became more valuable, the kinks began to disappear from the zigzag fence, and it straightened itself out. As the market for timber increased, the fence was made of fewer rails, eventually becoming the two- and three-rail fence of today.

The rails evolved from split wood to sawed lumber. Posts were added for a more efficient use of the wood.

The rail fence is most popular in rural settings. Its horizontal lines follow rolling or flat terrain gracefully. The fence is economical in lumber use, especially if it's built with wood on hand. It is also sturdy enough to hold larger animals.

There are some varieties of the rail fence that can easily be adapted to the suburban homesite. Light rail fences go best with ranch style homes, but they can improve the appearance of any yard. The low post and board or split-rail fence makes an excellent definition fence for the front yard. These fences discourage people from walking across the lawn or plants, but they don't block the view or shut

Fig. 4-1 *Zigzag fence.* Val Ramos

off sunlight to plants. Rail fences are decorative, versatile, and easy to build.

Zigzag fences

The zigzag rail fence is simplest to build, so let's start with it. If you have a surplus of timber on your property or would like to create a rustic effect in your garden, you can install a zigzag fence with little effort.

The most common zigzag rail lengths are 6, 7, and 8 feet and about 6 inches thick. Smaller rails are 4 inches thick.

Traditionally, the rails of a zigzag fence simply overlap each other on the end. A rock or concrete block can be used under the overlapping point to keep the bottom rail off the ground. You can strengthen your fence by toenailing spikes into the rails, driving dowels or steel pins down through rails, or by setting posts with the rails.

Zigzag fences are an excellent landscape addition to a large garden. They can provide support for climbing vegetables such as beans and tomatoes.

Post and rail fences

The next logical step in the evolution of the fence is the post and rail fence (FIGS. 4-2 and 4-3). Early posts and rails were made of small logs and split wood, but most of today's fences are built with dimensional lumber (FIG. 4-4). With such a variety of materials, the fence builder can create a barrier that is efficient, attractive, and easy to construct and maintain.

Posts are made of many styles and sizes of wood: rough-hewn, square dimensional, round peeled logs, and double posts. Their sizes range from 4 to 8 inches in diameter.

Posts can be set in dirt, gravel, concrete, or any combination of these materials. The depth is based on the height of the fence, the local frost line, and type of soil. The deeper the post, the more solid it generally is. Most rail fences have posts set 2 feet into the ground to provide support for the rails. Dig your hole deeper and set the post on gravel or a base stone to encourage drainage and prevent decay.

To align the posts, set the corner posts in

Fig. 4-2 Post and rail fence. Val Ramos

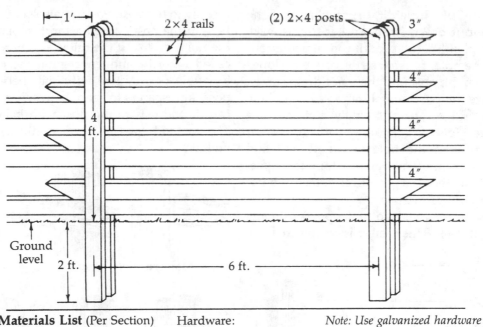

Materials List (Per Section)

Lumber:
4 pcs. 2×4×6′ posts
4 pcs. 2×4×12′ rails
4 pcs. 2×4×8′ rails
w/ shaped ends

Hardware:
Post to rails 80 – 10d
common nails
For section add:
2 pcs. 2×4×6′ posts
48 – 10d common nails

Note: Use galvanized hardware

Fig. 4-3 Detailed plans for an unusual post and rail fence. Wolmanized pressure-treated lumber

Fig. 4-4 *Dimensional rail fence.*

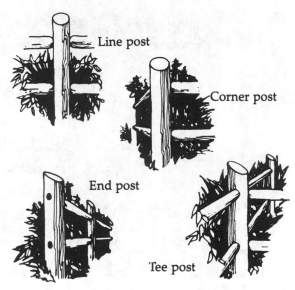

Fig. 4-6 *Attaching rails to posts.* _{Weyerhaeuser Co.}

place first. Put a little dirt or gravel around the post, tamp it down so that water drains away from the post, then repeat. If you're using concrete in the hole, finish it so the concrete slopes down from the post and the water drains away. Make sure the posts are plumb as you add hole material and compact it tightly. Let the concrete cure a few days before you attach rails, or, if you're filling the hole only with dirt and gravel, water and tamp the hole for a snug post (FIG. 4-5). If necessary, you can attach temporary supports to the posts.

Rails can be attached to the posts in many ways (FIG. 4-6). The easiest is to nail the rail directly to the post. You can also cut a notch or hole in the post—called a mortise—and insert the rail (FIG. 4-7). If the rail is also notched, it's called a mortise and tenon joint. You can build a double post system with rails between the posts and spacers to keep them separated. You can tie the rails to the post with baling wire. The methods possible are as diverse as the builders.

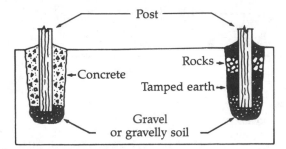

Fig. 4-5 *Two ways to fill rail fence postholes.* _{Weyerhaeuser Co.}

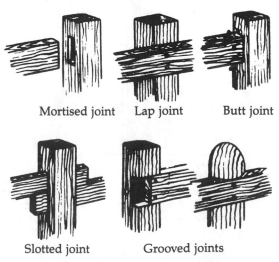

Mortised joint   Lap joint   Butt joint

Slotted joint   Grooved joints

Fig. 4-7 *Common post and rail joints.*

Post and board fences

The post and board fence is the next step in the evolution of the rail fence (FIGS. 4-8 and 4-9). It's similar in style and construction to the post and rail, but it uses the more efficient and more readily available dimensional lumber.

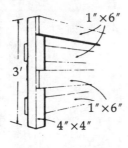

Fig. 4-8 Plans for a post and board fence. Georgia-Pacific Corp.

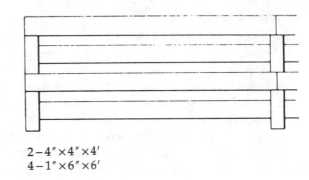

2−4″×4″×4′
4−1″×6″×6′

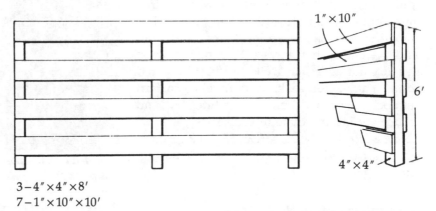

Fig. 4-9 Plans for a 6-foot post and board fence. Georgia-Pacific Corp.

3−4″×4″×8′
7−1″×10″×10′

generally used. When the posts are spaced the usual 8 feet, the use of 16-foot lengths will save labor and make a stronger fence.

Strong fences are required for corrals, feedlots, and similar areas where livestock are closely confined and may subject the fence to considerable pressure. For such areas, planks 2

Post and board fences are very popular on the farm and ranch where they commonly serve as corrals, and in the city where they are both functional and decorative. Figure 4-10 shows the two most common designs of post and board fences. These designs can be varied by increasing or decreasing the number of boards, their width, or the spacing between them.

For suburban fences, boards 1 inch thick (³/₄ inch dressed), 6 inches wide (5³/₄ inches dressed), and 6, 8, 10, 12, or 16 feet long are

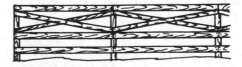

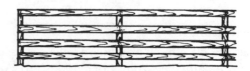

Fig. 4-10 Common post and board fences.

inches or more in thickness, 8 or more inches in width, and 10 to 16 feet in length are generally used. They should be spiked or bolted to substantial posts, spaced 5 or 6 feet apart.

Top and side fascia boards are used mainly for appearance. They add some protection and strength to the fence.

Lumber quality

Minimum requirements for lumber for fences and gates include moderate bending strength, medium decay and weather resistance, good nail-holding ability, and freedom from warp. Woods with these properties include cypress, Douglas fir, western larch, southern yellow pine, redwood, and white oak. The following woods weather well, but they have a small tendency to warp and are not strong and don't hold nails well: cedar, northern white pine, sugar pine, chestnut, and yellow poplar. The following woods are strong, hard, and hold nails well, but they have a tendency to warp and do not weather well: beech, birch, red gum, maple, red oak, and tupelo. Eastern hemlock, western hemlock, white fir, and spruce are intermediate in properties.

Use No. 1 or No. 2 softwood or No. 2 common hardwood grades of lumber for strong, durable gates and fences.

Preservative treatment

Fences and gates will last years longer if the wood is treated with a good preservative. If not treated, the wood might soon start to decay at joints or wherever moisture is held (FIG. 4-11).

Commercially treated lumber is available in most areas. Pressure-treated wood will last longer than that treated by other methods.

Construction

Construction of post and board fences is essentially the same regardless of the design. We'll consider the more important details of building

Fig. 4-11 *This post is rotting out because it was not pretreated.* Val Ramos

a four-rail fence, using 4-inch posts, 16-foot boards, and top and side fascia boards.

Slope (saw) the tops of the posts slightly toward the side to which the boards will be fastened, so the top fascia boards will slope toward that side.

At the start of the fence and at corners, set the first line post 7 feet 10 inches from the gate or corner post, center to center. Space the other line posts 8 feet apart, center to center. The first boards should extend across the face of the anchor post to the corner of the first or second line posts. Subsequent boards are nailed center to center on the posts.

You might have to shorten the spacing between posts near corners or the end of the fence to make it come out even. For the best appearance, however, make the last panel as nearly full length as possible.

In the first or first two panels, at the start of the fence and at corners, use 16-foot boards for the top and third rails and 8-foot boards for the second and fourth rails. Only two joints will fall on any one post with this arrangement, and you will have a stronger fence.

If you saw, trim, or bore preservative-treated boards, you might expose untreated or inadequately treated wood. Apply preservative to prevent decay.

For the best appearance, fasten the boards to the outside of the posts. If the fence will be subject to pressure—from livestock, for example—attach the boards to the inside of the posts.

Nail the boards to the posts with three ringshank or screwshank nails staggered to

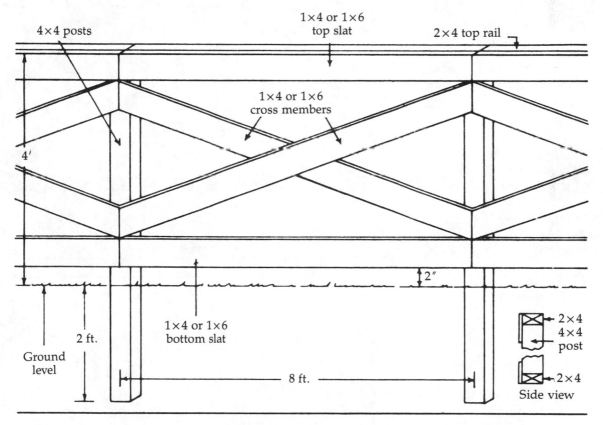

Materials list (Per Section)
Lumber:
1 pc. 4×4×4×6′ post
2 pcs. 2×4×8′ rails
2 pcs. 1×4×8′ rails
2 pcs. 1×4×10′ diagonals

Alternative:
2 pcs. 1×6×8′ rails
2 pcs. 1×6×10′ diagonals
Hardware:
2×4 framing 12–20d common nails
1×4 framing 28–6d common nails

Alternative:
1×6 framing 28–6d common nails
For end section add:
1 pc. 4×4×6′ post

Note: Use galvanized hardware

Fig. 4-12 *Detailed plans for a post and cross-rail fence.* Wolmanized pressure-treated lumber

avoid splitting the board. Hold the boards in place with cleats bolted to the posts for a stronger fence. This method makes it easier to remove the boards quickly if necessary.

In the first panel at the start of the fence and at the corners, use a 8-foot-long top fascia board. The top fascia board joints and the top fence board joints will fall on different posts. The top fascia should overlap both the top fence board and the vertical fascia board.

A variation of this construction is to use mortised rails. Posts are mortised to take rail tenons in one of two ways. A broad mortise lets the rails overlap side by side; a long narrow one lets them overlap one above the other. When rails overlap at the side, a very wide and heavy post is needed. This joint adjusts more easily to sharp changes in grade than a joint with one rail above the other.

Figure 4-12 includes plans for one kind of rail fence.

5

Picket fences

A "fence" means a picket fence to many people. The picket fence is traditional, decorative, and practical—especially for large, older homes on small lots. The picket fence has been modified to serve nearly every type of home imaginable. There is an inexhaustible variety of picket designs and combinations available (FIGS. 5-1 through 5-4). There are hundreds of patterns for picket tops, ranging from squared ends for a simple, straightforward fence to the intricate scroll-sawed patterns that are part of a formal design (FIGS. 5-5 and 5-6). Post caps range from plain, flat tops to fancy ornamental shapes such as the acorn, pineapple, turned goblet, and other designs (FIG. 5-7 on p. 58).

You will consider four factors when you select the overall design for your picket fence: fence height, picket width, ornamentation, and picket spacing. The typical picket fence is about 3 feet high. It has 3-inch pickets, pointed like the prow of a ship, spaced 3 inches apart. Variations are possible. Your fence might be 2 or 4 feet high. It could have narrow pickets widely spaced or broad pickets closely spaced.

The tops of the pickets could be rounded, square, or dart-shaped.

The effectiveness of the picket fence design is due to its repetitive quality, but in a long stretch of fence this becomes monotonous. There are various ways to introduce variety into the pattern:

- Alternate pickets of different heights.
- Mix different width pickets.
- Use tapered pickets.
- Alternate groups of pickets (three broad, three narrow, etc.)

Picket fences have some disadvantages. Some people feel that picket fences are too commonplace, and that there are fresher, more up-to-date fences from which to select. Picket fences give inadequate protection. A picket fence is an ineffective barrier to intruders, children can clamber over it, and an agile dog can leap it or tunnel under it. Because most picket fences are painted or whitewashed, they require periodic repainting because they lose

Fig. 5-1 *A well-built picket fence is a work of art.* California Redwood Association

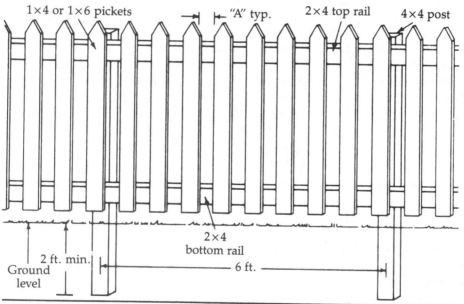

1×4 or 1×6 pickets   "A" typ.   2×4 top rail   4×4 post

2×4 bottom rail

2 ft. min.
Ground level

6 ft.

Materials List (Per section)
Lumber:
1 pc. 4×4×8' post
2 pcs. 2×4×6' rails
12 pcs. 1×4×5' pickets
Alternate:
8 pcs. 1×6×5' pickets

Note: 1×4 picket "A" = 2¹/2"
        1×6 picket "A" = 3¹/2"
Hardware:
Rails to posts 8 – 20d
    common nails
Picket to rails 96 – 6d
    common nails

Alternate:
1×6 picket to rails 64 – 6d
    common nails
For end section:
1 post, 1 picket
8 – 6d common nails

Fig. 5-2 *Detailed plans for a 5-foot-high picket fence.* Wolmanized pressure-treated lumber

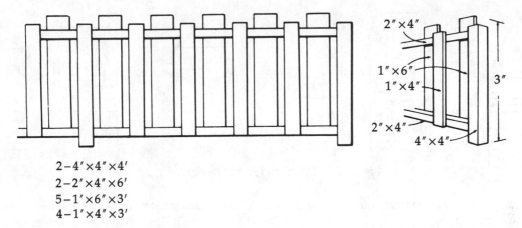

2−4″×4″×4′
2−2″×4″×6′
5−1″×6″×3′
4−1″×4″×3′

Fig. 5-3 *Alternate board picket fence.* Georgia-Pacific Corp.

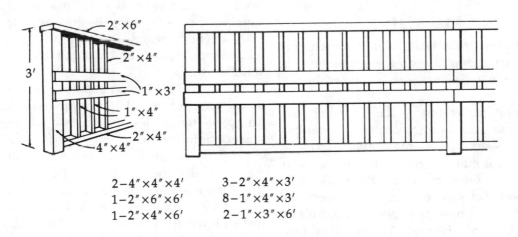

2−4″×4″×4′   3−2″×4″×3′
1−2″×6″×6′   8−1″×4″×3′
1−2″×4″×6′   2−1″×3″×6′

Fig. 5-4 *Unusual picket design for a 3-foot-high fence.* Georgia-Pacific Corp.

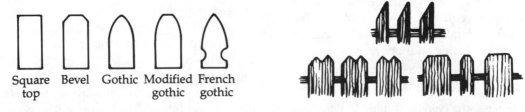

Square   Bevel   Gothic   Modified   French
  top   gothic   gothic

Fig. 5-5 *Typical picket cap designs.*

Fig. 5-6 *Various picket patterns.*

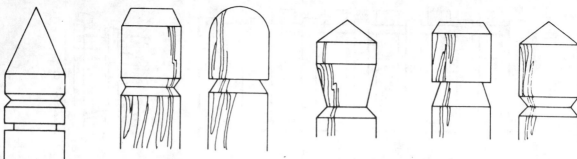

Fig. 5-7 *Typical picket post designs.*

their crisp, neat appearance quickly if allowed to weather too long.

Picket fences don't provide privacy and are thus inadequate for fencing an outdoor living area unless it's also shielded by shrubs. Homeowners with picket fences therefore often install two types of fences.

Materials

Picket fencing is available as fully constructed sections, components with shaped pickets, or individual materials that can be shaped by the builder.

Prebuilt picket fences can be purchased through many mail-order catalog companies, such as Sears or Montgomery Ward, or through local building material retailers. Wire picket fences often come in rolls of 25 or 50 feet. Wood picket fences are sold in sections complete with a post, two rails, and pickets to a width of 4, 6, or 8 feet. You can even buy them prepainted.

If you're buying a component fence, standard picket fence posts are 4×4. Common rails are made of 1×3 or 2×4 lumber depending on the size and required strength of the fence. Pickets are usually 1×3, 4, or 6 inches in lengths of 36, 42, or 48 inches.

Construction

Picket fences are easy to build. Unless you're handy with wood, it's better to buy precut

pickets rather than manufacture them yourself. You can do it, but a variety of power tools will be needed to help you cut and uniformly dress the vast number of pickets needed for the typical fence. If you decide to make your own, stay with standard-sized boards. For your picket tops copy a pattern you have noticed on a fence, or create your own. Make a cardboard template. Create the template the way children make valentine hearts. Draw half the pattern, fold the cardboard, and cut out both sides simultaneously.

If you're buying a prefabricated picket fence, make sure it will fit your property. Some cannot be used on a slope, because the panels will not fit the posts.

If dogs and other small animals persist in digging under your fence, install a baseboard that runs a few inches below the soil. Use a 1×6 or 1×8 and impregnate it with preservative, or it will rot away in a short time. You can also thwart animals by nailing chicken wire to the bottom rail on the inside, and burying the other end of the wire in the ground. Chicken wire will tend to be hidden by any plants you place along it.

A molding strip, nailed on the outside of the fence parallel to the top rail, will keep pickets from working loose and deter children from removing pickets.

If you select a picket with an unusual top design, you should order or make more than you need. Store them as replacements.

Chapter 3 gives step-by-step instructions about how to dig postholes, set posts, attach rails, and install siding on wood fences (FIGS. 5-8 and 5-9).

Fig. 5-9 *Corner posts need extra bracing to withstand elements and pressure.*

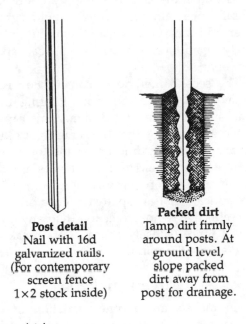

Post detail
Nail with 16d galvanized nails. (For contemporary screen fence 1×2 stock inside)

Packed dirt
Tamp dirt firmly around posts. At ground level, slope packed dirt away from post for drainage.

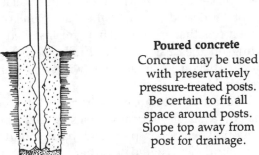

Poured concrete
Concrete may be used with preservatively pressure-treated posts. Be certain to fit all space around posts. Slope top away from post for drainage.

Fig. 5-8 *Setting posts in dirt and concrete.* Western Wood Products Association

Grape stake fences

The rustic cousin of the picket fence is the grape stake fence. A grape stake is simply a hand-split redwood stake about 2 inches square and anywhere from 3 to 6 feet in length. Grape stakes were first designed to support grape vines, but many years ago an enterprising fence builder began using them in fences. The grape stake fence can be seen today along rural and suburban roads.

Grape stakes are usually split from redwood heartwood, although sapwood varieties are sometimes used. If they are straight-grained and free of knots, they can be resplit to make 1×2s. A better method is to saw them in half lengthwise on a bench saw. This produces a 1×2 with one rustic side for display and one smooth side for nailing.

Grape stake fences are decay-resistant and require no maintenance, except to drive home a loose nail now and then. The stakes are light, easy to handle, and simple to install. The natural reddish tone weathers to a soft gray that blends smoothly with plantings and matches the warm tones of brick and stonework in the garden. Perhaps more than any other type of screen fence, grape stakes provide warmth to the barren lot when it's first fenced. Many types of fence merely accentuate the bleakness of an unplanted backyard.

Grape stakes are adaptable to many styles of construction. They may be driven into the soil or nailed like pickets to a fence frame, pointed tip up for rustic effect, or with the squared tip on top for a clean fence line. They may be fitted inside the frame to provide a two-sided fence. Also, grape stakes can be attached either vertically or horizontally, or in alternating panels of both to produce a different fence design.

Grape stake fencing is not right for everyone. Many people feel that it's overused as a fencing material in some areas of the country, especially on the West Coast. Also, many installations have been made indiscriminately, without regard for the suitability of the fence to the house, garden, and neighborhood. Some people object to its splintery qualities—a hazard to pets and children. Others don't like the weathered gray look of aged grape stake.

Building a grape stake fence is much like building any other wood frame fence. Posts and rails are installed. The siding (the grape stakes) is nailed into place. You can split the stakes and nail them short distances apart on the rail to save money.

Wear heavy gloves when handling grape stakes. Grape stakes splinter easily.

Slat pickets

Somewhere between the picket fence and its rustic cousin, the grape stake, is a type of fence put together with long, narrow slats. Like the picket it uses milled lumber, and like the grape stake it is a screen fence.

Slat fence materials include rough-finished redwood sawed into 1×1 or 1×2-inch strips. Because the redwood is cut from standard lumber, it's not limited to the 6-foot height of the grape stake. It can be built from 2 to 8 feet tall.

Even though the strips have to be cut as ordered at the lumberyard, they cost about the same as grape stakes. You might have the power tools to do the cutting yourself using larger, less expensive dimensional lumber.

Slat fences are more formal than grape stakes, but they often look more truly at home in a city environment than their splintery relative. Their clean lines give a stronger vertical

pattern than grape stakes with their irregular edges.

There are two basic ways to install the slat picket fence. The first and probably most popular is to nail the slats over the standard post and rail fence frame, just as you would a grape stake. You can either nail them into place snugly against each other, or you can space them apart.

The second method of construction is to overlay the slats on a solid fence to bring interest to an otherwise dull design. Slats can be stained effectively, either the same color as the primary fence or a different shade, or even a different color for accent. Slat fences are efficient in areas where wind is a problem. Wind tests indicate that an open slat fence provides more effective wind protection than any other type of fence. Closely spaced slats break up and disperse the wind.

Woven pickets

Woven pickets are another variation of the basic picket fence. Woven pickets are available in prefabricated form, either as panels or woven together in rolls. They are installed as siding on the basic post and rail wood fence frame. They make an effective windscreen and are durable.

Woven pickets are usually made of cedar and are available in many styles: peeled, machine-finished or complete with bark, round or half-round, and wired together or strung on steel rods. Check local building material stores and lumber yards for the cost, and further instructions on woven picket installation.

Picket fence ideas

A few ideas for designing your own picket fence follow:

Lath and picket By spacing your pickets about 5 inches apart and installing narrow wood lath in-between, you can give your fence strength and security at a lower cost.

Southern picket Common in the South, the southern picket fence has pickets with one side slanted at the top and the other side straight. These can easily be modified from 1×2 dimensional lumber by most homeowners with a jig on a sawhorse.

Split pickets Where wood is plentiful, rural fences can be sided with small timbers split lengthwise using a shake splitter and mallet or a bench saw.

Ornamental pickets By driving through the older parts of your town and neighboring communities, you can often find homes decorated with ornate pickets. Ask for permission to copy the design by tracing it on paper, or you might be able to purchase a broken picket that has the design intact. You could offer to replace the broken pickets in exchange for a few.

Sapling pickets A short rustic fence can be built with sapling pickets gathered from near river and creek banks. As a variation, the saplings can be woven together as rails and siding to form an unusual fence or barrier.

Wire and pickets You can weave your own fence with pickets and wire and a few simple tools. Wrap your first picket a few turns with wire, then twist it a few times before wrapping the next picket. This wire picket fence can then be stretched between posts to make an inexpensive, yet practical and decorative fence.

6

Board fences

As the size of the homestead has shrunk from sections to acres to feet, the fence has reflected the change. The short, open fence of the range has evolved into the tall, solid fence of the subdivision. There are two reasons for popularity of the high wood fence: security and privacy.

The typical board fence adds security to the property it surrounds because it is a solid barrier between the homeowner's world and the outside world (FIGS. 6-1 through 6-4). The board fence is designed to keep the inside world—children and pets—from getting out and the outside world—often children and pets—from getting in.

The high board fence adds privacy by blocking the view of passersby (FIG. 6-4). The homeowner can effectively enlarge his home by extending its walls to his property lines. The high board fence can also block undesired sights from view. The board fence is one of the most popular built today.

There are dozens of styles and designs of board fences being built throughout the country. Basic board fencing is often a series of 1×6 or 1×8-inch boards nailed side by side over a common post and rail fence frame. Height is usually 5 or 6 feet. Top designs can be flat, pointed, round, or framed.

Alternate board fences are "good neighbor" fences that are equally decorative on both sides. The first board is placed on one side of the rail, and the next is staggered and nailed to the opposite side (FIG. 6-5).

Alternate panel fencing places every other fence section facing your property (FIG. 6-6). Alternate panel is both neighborly and more solid than alternate board.

Channeled fences are constructed by cutting a channel for fence boards on the top of the bottom rail and the bottom of the top rail. Boards are then equally exposed to both sides (FIGS. 6-7 through 6-9).

Siding fences use siding identical to that on the home to cover the fence. Six-inch beveled siding is a common house siding that can be used to cover your fence (FIG. 6-10).

Fig. 6-1 *Common board fence designs.*

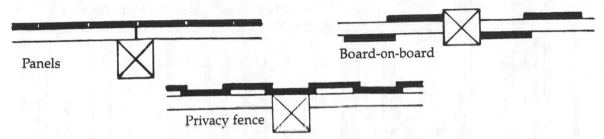

Fig. 6-2 *Top view of common board fence designs.*

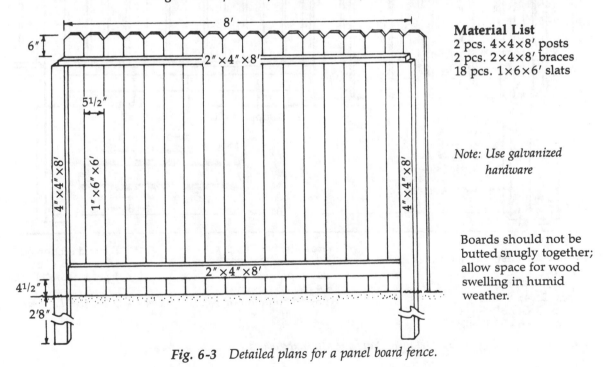

Material List
2 pcs. 4×4×8' posts
2 pcs. 2×4×8' braces
18 pcs. 1×6×6' slats

Note: Use galvanized hardware

Boards should not be butted snugly together; allow space for wood swelling in humid weather.

Fig. 6-3 *Detailed plans for a panel board fence.*

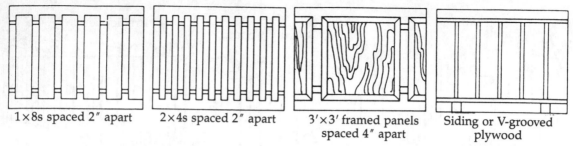

1×8s spaced 2″ apart   2×4s spaced 2″ apart   3′×3′ framed panels   Siding or V-grooved
                                                        spaced 4″ apart   plywood

Fig. 6-4 Common board fence designs used as screening. Wolmanized pressure-treated lumber

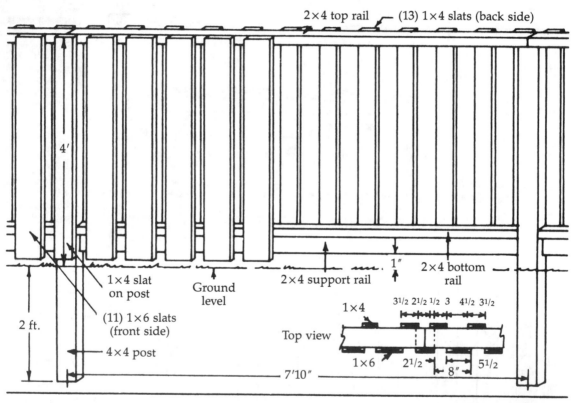

Fig. 6-5 Detailed plans for alternate board fence. Wolmanized pressure-treated lumber

Materials List (Per section)
Lumber:
1 pc. 4×4×6′ post
3 pcs. 2×4×8′ rails
13 pcs. 1×4×3′11″ slats
11 pcs. 1×6×3′11″ slats

Hardware:
2×4 framing 24–20d
   common nails
1×4 & 1×6 framing
   96–6d common nails

For end section add:
1 pc. 4×4×6′ post
1 pc. 1×4×3′11″ slat

Note: Use galvanized hardware

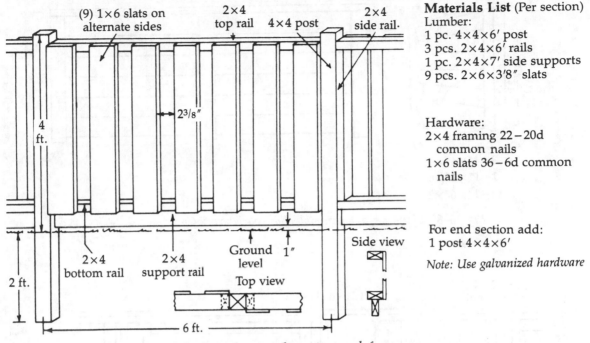

(9) 1×6 slats on alternate sides

2×4 top rail

4×4 post

2×4 side rail.

2³/₈″

4 ft.

2×4 bottom rail

2×4 support rail

Ground level 1″

Top view

Side view

2 ft.

6 ft.

Materials List (Per section)
Lumber:
1 pc. 4×4×6′ post
3 pcs. 2×4×6′ rails
1 pc. 2×4×7′ side supports
9 pcs. 2×6×3′8″ slats

Hardware:
2×4 framing 22–20d common nails
1×6 slats 36–6d common nails

For end section add:
1 post 4×4×6′

Note: Use galvanized hardware

Fig. 6-6 Detailed plans for an alternate panel fence. Wolmanized pressure-treated lumber

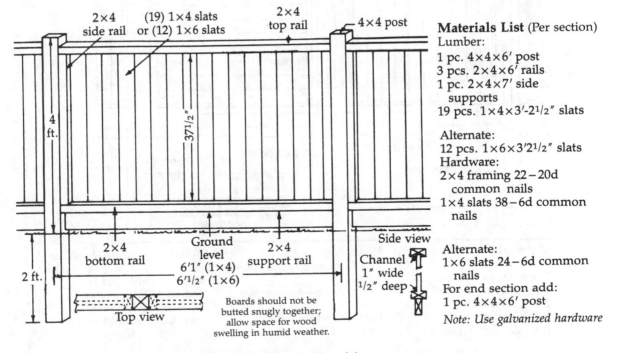

2×4 side rail

(19) 1×4 slats or (12) 1×6 slats

2×4 top rail

4×4 post

4 ft.

37¹/₂″

2×4 bottom rail

Ground level
6′1″ (1×4)
6′1/2″ (1×6)

2×4 support rail

Side view

Channel
1″ wide
¹/₂″ deep

2 ft.

Top view

Boards should not be butted snugly together; allow space for wood swelling in humid weather.

Materials List (Per section)
Lumber:
1 pc. 4×4×6′ post
3 pcs. 2×4×6′ rails
1 pc. 2×4×7′ side supports
19 pcs. 1×4×3′-2¹/₂″ slats

Alternate:
12 pcs. 1×6×3′2¹/₂″ slats
Hardware:
2×4 framing 22–20d common nails
1×4 slats 38–6d common nails

Alternate:
1×6 slats 24–6d common nails
For end section add:
1 pc. 4×4×6′ post

Note: Use galvanized hardware

Fig. 6-7 Detailed plans for a channeled board fence. Wolmanized pressure-treated lumber

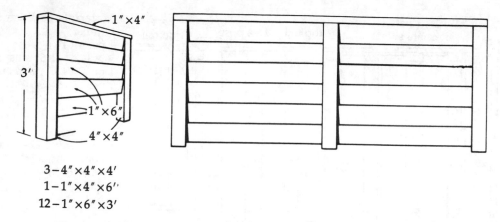

3 – 4″×4″×4′
1 – 1″×4″×6′′
12 – 1″×6″×3′

Fig. 6-8 *Plans for a horizontal channeled board fence.*

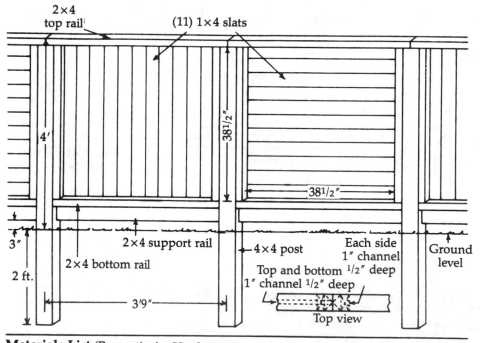

Materials List (Per section)
Lumber:
2 pcs. 4×4×6′ posts
1 pc. 2×4×8′ top rail
2 pcs. 2×4×14′ framing
7¹/₃ pcs. 1×4×10′
(Cut 22 – 3′3¹/₂″) slats

Hardware:
2×4 framing 30 – 20d common
    nails
1×4 slats 88 – 6d common
    nails
For end section add:
1 pc. 4×4×6′ post

Note: Use galvanized hardware

Boards should not be
butted snugly together;
allow space for wood
swelling in humid weather.

Fig. 6-9 *Detailed plans for an alternate panel channeled fence.*

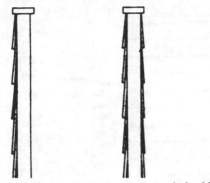

Fig. 6-10 *Side view of single-siding and double-siding fence.* Western Wood Products Association

Horizontal boards can be installed to make an unusual and decorative board fence, especially in an area where everyone else has vertical board siding—but make sure your fence doesn't become a ladder for intruders.

Diagonal boards make an interesting design (FIG. 6-11). Louver board fences have boards installed at an angle to direct wind and the view. Boards may be stationary or movable (FIG. 6-12).

Basket weave fences are easy to construct and decorative. They are increasingly popular with do-it-yourself fence builders (6-13).

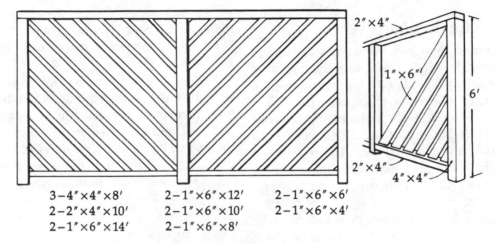

3–4″×4″×8′	2–1″×6″×12′	2–1″×6″×6′
2–2″×4″×10′	2–1″×6″×10′	2–1″×6″×4′
2–1″×6″×14′	2–1″×6″×8′	

Fig. 6-11 *Typical diagonal board fence plans.* Georgia-Pacific Corp.

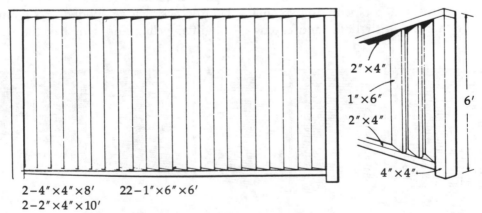

2–4″×4″×8′	22–1″×6″×6′
2–2″×4″×10′	

Fig. 6-12 *Plans for a louver board fence.* Georgia-Pacific Corp.

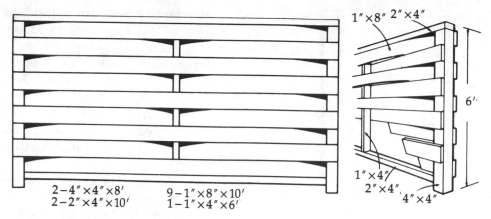

Fig. 6-13 *Plans for a basket weave fence.* Georgia-Pacific Corp.

2–4″×4″×8′
2–2″×4″×10′

9–1″×8″×10′
1–1″×4″×6′

1″×8″ 2″×4″

6′

1″×4″
2″×4″
4″×4″

Basic board fences

The common high board fence is a useful and easy-to-build fence. Unfortunately, many of these fences give a cheerless, boxed-in feeling to the yard and become monotonous.

Try to imagine a decorative design for your board fence. Review ideas in this book, and study designs in your area (FIG. 6-14). You might find one that will complement your property as well as fill its primary purpose.

Solid board fences are expensive because they require lots of lumber, consequently, the fence should justify the cost. The solid fence gives absolute privacy, but often at the expense of making a person feel imprisoned behind it. Its blank surfaces are cool and impersonal, especially in a yard with little landscaping.

Many solid board fences have an obvious "backside" that can make neighbors feel you're inhospitable.

These might seem like unsolvable problems for the do-it-yourself fence builder. Many homeowners have been discouraged and settled for fences that seem friendlier and are cheaper to build. Others have approached the problem head-on and have designed solid board fences that are decorative *and* functional.

Designing tips

Board fences can be made interesting by using a pattern. At the sacrifice of some privacy, a tall board fence may be opened up slightly to give a lighter feeling and a hint of the world out-

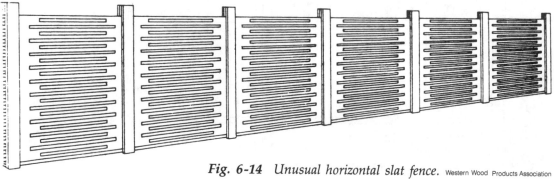

Fig. 6-14 *Unusual horizontal slat fence.* Western Wood Products Association

side. Boards may be set slightly separated, like pickets, or be placed slantwise within the frame to form a louvered fence. The upper quarter of the fence may be left open, or fitted with an inset of lattice or open-spaced slats.

The blank surface area can be broken up by using materials that give pattern or texture to the structure, such as board and batten, siding, or tongue and groove; by alternating panels with vertical and horizontal boards; or by varying the direction of the fence, using a zigzag or serrated fence line. Horizontal siding will give the fence a strong horizontal feeling and appear to stretch a small garden. Vertical siding will seem to compress a long fence.

The right-side, wrong-side problem can be solved by designing the frame side so that it has strong interest in itself, or by fitting the boards wholly within the frame so the fence appears the same from both sides. The frame side can also be improved with a simple trellis that will fill in with colorful vines.

A solid fence can be treated as an integral part of the house plan. Designed as an extension of the house wall to enclose the outdoor living area, it gives a feeling of continuity to outdoor-indoor living within its enclosure. Viewed through a glass wall, it becomes an outer wall of the house itself. The inner surface should therefore be finished in materials that harmonize with the interior wall materials and color schemes. The public side of the fence is surfaced with the same materials as the house—siding, shakes, or board and batten. Your home is economically enlarged.

Construction

Basic board fences are simple to construct. Tools you'll need include a hammer, shovel, tape measure, string, and posthole digger. Materials include posts, rails, boards, gates, nails, galvanized hangers, gate hardware, stakes, gravel, and concrete.

When you locate your fence line, the fence should be built entirely on your property unless a common ownership agreement between you and your neighbor has been arranged. Go over the property lines carefully. If you have any doubts about their location, have your property surveyed.

The location and setting of the posts is the most important factor determining how attractive and long-lasting your fence will be. Here are the steps:

1. Stake out the property lines and stretch a string between the stakes.
2. Locate the corner posts and gates.
3. Mark off the post spacings, not to exceed 8 feet on center.
4. For pedestrian gates, locate the posts a minimum of 3 feet apart.
5. Start construction by setting corner and gateposts first.

When backfilling postholes compact gravel in the bottom of the hole for drainage, followed by about 8 inches of concrete for stability. The remainder of the hole should be filled with more compacted gravel topped off with dirt. This allows maximum drainage, resulting in a longer post life and fewer costly repairs.

To assemble the fence, first locate the 2×4 rails about 12 inches from the top and bottom of the posts (FIG. 6-15). The location of the rails

Fig. 6-15 *Three ways to attach rails to posts on board fences.*

on the posts depends on the style of fence you're building. Always use galvanized nails or hangers when constructing a fence.

Locate the fence boards up to 1 inch off the ground. Plumb with a level as your assembly progresses.

If your materials are unseasoned, expect shrinkage as your fence dries out: 1×4 boards will shrink about 1/8 inch, and 1×6 boards about 3/16 inch in width. Shrinkage of posts and rails is proportionate if unseasoned.

Dimensions are fairly standardized. Favored heights are 5, 5 1/2, and 6 feet. Posts are usually 4×4 or 6×6 inches set 6 to 8 feet apart. Standard 2×4s serve as rails. A third rail is often recommended for fences taller than 5 feet.

Basic board fences call for substantial foundations because they are heavy and subject to wind damage. The boards you use should be of good quality. For a knotless surface, it's necessary to buy select grades of lumber. For crackless joints, use boards with interlocking edges, such as shiplap or tongue and groove, or cover the joints between boards with battens.

Alternate board fence

This type of fence goes by many names including board-and-board, alternate board, and shadow fence. It has the advantages of the basic board fence, but it is a "good neighbor" fence. It also has many of the louver fence's advantages without having the high installation cost.

The frame is simple to build. Boards are nailed to the frame with an open space left between them slightly narrower than the board. Another set of boards is then nailed to the other side of the frame, with the open spaces opposite the boards on the first side. The fence looks the same on both sides.

The bafflelike arrangement of the board breaks up strong wind currents but allows air

to circulate freely. Like louvers, when the boards are placed vertically, they filter light and provide limited privacy. When the boards are set horizontally, they create absolute privacy, but completely obstruct direct sunlight. This fence creates interesting shadow patterns as the sun advances, unlike the basic board fence—hence the name shadow fence.

The alternate board fence can be assembled with mediocre lumber because minimal warping is not noticeable in this design. One disadvantage is that the fence is limited in value as a security fence. Small animals can wiggle their way through vertical or horizontal panels, and the horizontal variety offers an attractive climbing surface for children and intruders.

Building an alternate board fence is quite similar to constructing the basic board fence. The primary difference is that a spacer is needed so that placement of boards is uniform. The common board used is a 1×6. A spacer is made out of a 1×4 with a cleat nailed to one end so that it can rest on the rail. The first side is sided in the following order:

1. Nail the fence board in place, checking plumb with a carpenter's level.
2. Set the spacer on the rail against the previous board.
3. Butt the next board up against the spacer and nail it into place.
4. Lift the spacer from between the two boards and lay it up against the second board. Repeat.
5. When you're done with one side of your alternate board fence, simply start the second side with the spacer rather than the board. Make sure the alternate board is evenly spaced over the gap on the opposite side of the fence.

Although this is an exceptionally strong fence, it usually calls for extra bracing to prevent the boards from sagging. An extra rail, halfway between top and bottom, will keep the vertical boards from warping. An extra post or 2×4 halfway between standard posts will keep horizontal boards from sagging.

Louver fences

The louver fence is handsome, useful, and quite expensive to build (FIG. 6-16). Louvers give privacy without cutting off light and air or destroying the view. By adjusting the angle of the louvers, you can use the fence for several purposes. By orienting the louvers to the path of the sun, they can furnish maximum light and shade for plants. If you set them with their "blind" side toward the public, you can use them to screen a service area or a drying yard without shutting off the flow of air needed to disperse rubbish odors or speed drying of clothes.

Narrow panels placed near entryways or front windows permit the householder to view the street or entry walk, while a passerby will not be able to look into the home.

Vertically placed louvers provide only "progressive privacy." Some part of the area behind the louvers will be fully visible through the fence as a person moves along it. Horizontal louvers are needed to secure absolute pri-

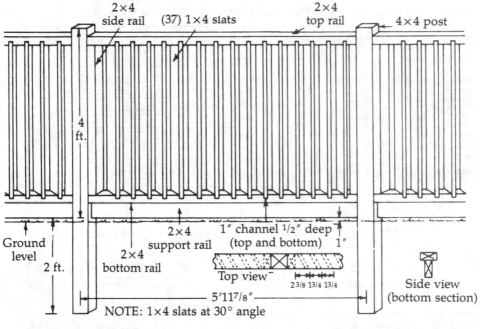

Materials List (Per section)
Lumber:
1 pc. 4×4×6′ post
3 pcs. 2×4×6′ rails
1 pc. 2×4×8′ (cut 2–4′) side supports
37 pcs. 1×4×3′5½″ slats

Alternate:
1 pc. 1×4×10′ (cut 2–5′) spacers
Hardware:
2×4 framing 22–20d common nails
1×4 slats 148–6d common nails

Alternate:
1×4 spacers 152–6d common nails
For end section add:
1 pc. 4×4×6′ post

Note: Use galvanized hardware

Fig. 6-16 *Detailed plans for a louvered board fence.* Wolmanized pressure-treated lumber

vacy. While these louvers provide a more effective screen, they are subject to structural weaknesses that discourage many builders.

Louver fences are strong in design (FIG. 6-17). The pattern of alternating strips of shadow and highlight, which varies through the day as the sun's angle changes, provides an interesting feature. Louver fences are meant to be seen and consequently should be carefully worked into the landscape plan. They should not be concealed under vines or hidden behind shrubs. Overplanting along the fence line will close off the view and interfere with the free flow of air through the louvers.

Because of its architectural quality, lou-vered fencing should be matched to the design of the house. It's often treated as a part of the house, or as a means of tying the house to something such as a carport or an outdoor room. If the fence is painted or stained the same color as the house, the relationship can be further strengthened. Although louvered fencing can be used with most styles of architecture, it looks best with modern structures that use simple planes, angles, and shadows to achieve their exterior lines and design.

The principal faults of the louver fence are its high cost and certain inborn weaknesses. Much of the expense involved in erecting a louver fence is due to the extra cost in premium

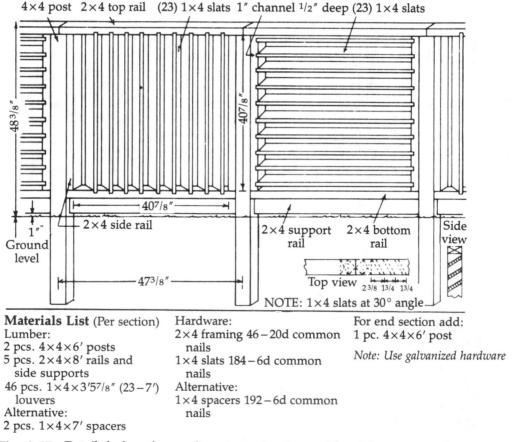

Materials List (Per section)
Lumber:
2 pcs. 4×4×6' posts
5 pcs. 2×4×8' rails and
  side supports
46 pcs. 1×4×3'5⁷/₈" (23−7')
  louvers
Alternative:
2 pcs. 1×4×7' spacers

Hardware:
2×4 framing 46−20d common
  nails
1×4 slats 184−6d common
  nails
Alternative:
1×4 spacers 192−6d common
  nails

For end section add:
1 pc. 4×4×6' post

Note: Use galvanized hardware

Fig. 6-17 Detailed plans for an alternate section louvered board fence. Wolmanized pressure-treated lumber

lumber and careful workmanship needed to prevent the fence from deteriorating.

Louver fencing requires more material than any other board fence. More vertical boards are required per running foot than for a solid board fence of comparable height. The louvers are supported only at the ends without center bracing, and tend to warp and twist after several months' exposure to sun and rain. To prevent this, many fence builders use top grade (and top price) kiln-dried lumber and apply some type of moisture seal. If the louvers are installed horizontally, they will develop a sag unless the span between the posts is fairly short or the boards are supported in the middle.

Another complication is due to the heavy weight of the fence structure. Much of the weight of the louvers is borne by the bottom rail, which might sag and throw the framing out of alignment. The whole structure requires staunch posts and substantial foundations.

Louver fences consume a surprising quantity of paint because of the unusually large surface area that must be covered. You rarely see louver fencing used for long, meandering boundary lines. It's usually found in fairly short installations and placed expertly where the fullest advantage can be obtained from its features.

There are basically two ways to build a louver fence. The first is to set the posts, attach the top and bottom rails, and nail the louvers in place. Toenail them to the bottom rail and drive through the top rail, most easily done by two workers. One works at the top rail, and the other works the lower one.

The other system is to construct the fence in sections on the ground, then lift the completed panels into place and nail them to the posts. If you have a flat surface on which to work, such as a driveway or garage floor, you might find this method easier.

Louvers can be set at almost any angle (FIG. 6-18). Some are installed at right angles to the fence line, but the accepted angle is 45 degrees. Use a template to make sure the louvers are spaced properly for nailing. You won't have to measure each board's gap.

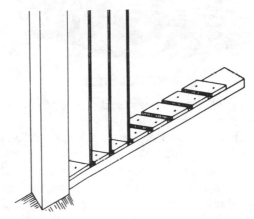

Fig. 6-18 *Installation of louvers or baffles and spacers.* Western Wood Products Association

Use boards heavy enough to resist warping. Many builders user 1×4s or 1×6s.

Attach a beveled or slanted cap along the top to shed rainwater and keep it from seeping into the exposed grain of the wood.

You can sometimes reduce construction costs by eliminating posts and constructing the fence on concrete foundation pylons with nailing surfaces. Horizontal louver fencing can be effectively built in 4-foot-wide sections using spacers cut at a 45-degree angle and installed between each board along the posts.

Basket weave fences

Basket weave fences use a minimum of material to get a solid screen, are attractive from both sides, and surprisingly strong for their weight (FIG. 6-19). It's a favorite with contractors because they can use inexpensive 1/2-inch stock for construction. Some people, however, prefer the material in shorter fences because it

Fig. 6-19 *Common basket weave fence.*

is difficult to look at for very long—and even more difficult to paint.

The basket weave fence is built around the basic board fence frame: 4×4 posts and 2×4 rails. Many basket weave fences, however, are built with 4 feet between posts rather than 8 feet.

The strips can be any standard width between 4 and 12 inches; 8 and 10 inches are the most popular. The thickness should be 1/2 to 1 inch so the stock can bend for the weave. Rough finish lumber is usually preferred, and redwood or cedar strips are the most common.

Start your fence at the bottom and nail the end of one strip horizontally to the post. Weave it across the fence around 1×2 stock that isn't nailed into place. Begin the next strip on the opposite side of the post, or at least alternate the direction of the strip around the 1×2 stock for a woven effect. Nails are only needed for attaching the strips to the posts.

Baskets weave fences are the most difficult to paint, even with a spray gun. Plan to paint, stain, or preserve the fence before construction. For a true basket weave effect, use the strips as both horizontal and vertical boards.

Accent screen

A fence within a fence doesn't need to be opaque. It can be a simple accent screen (FIG. 6-20). This grill, or eggcrate, accent screen is designed to highlight a planter box or separate garden areas without totally blocking them out (FIG. 6-21).

Materials for Accent Screen

Framing 2×4 construction heart redwood
Grille member 2×4 construction common or construction heart
Posts 4×4 construction heart
Post sheathing 2×4 and 2×6 construction heart
Cap and bottom rail 2×6 or 2×8 construction heart (depending on the amount of overhang desired)

The accent screen can also be built of cedar or pressure-treated lumber.

Prefabrication is the key to building this screen. Once you've set the posts at desired intervals (up to 8 feet), position and nail post sheathing. Take careful measurements between the sheathed posts to ensure a snug grille panel fit. The panels can be constructed flat in a large, level area and carried to the site for erection.

After determining panel width, cut and lay out the horizontal 2×4 framing members and place the 2×4 vertical framing members on top (FIG. 6-22). Make sure the edges are square, and nail. Prior to nailing, predrill frame and grille members to prevent splitting.

Next, lay out the vertical 2×2 grille members. Use two 2×2s for spacers. Adjust if necessary to even out spacing. Nail first grille member at both ends, space, nail second, and so on. Then turn the panel over and repeat the process with horizontal grille members. When finished, nail horizontal grille members to vertical members. Then nail horizontal grille members to vertical members at every second bearing.

Fig. 6-20 Accent screen. Georgia-Pacific Corp.

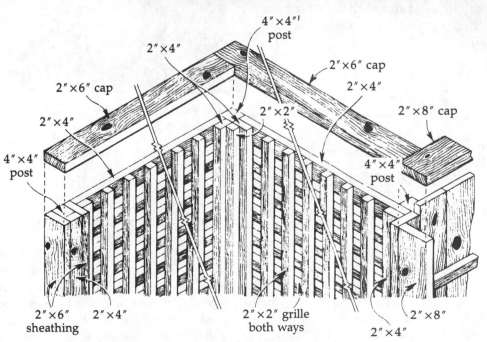

Fig. 6-21 Details of an accent screen. California Redwood Association

Labels on diagram: 4"×4" post, 2"×4", 2"×6" cap, 2"×4", 2"×8" cap, 2"×6" cap, 2"×4", 2"×2", 4"×4" post, 4"×4" post, 2"×6" sheathing, 2"×4", 2"×2" grille both ways, 2"×4", 2"×8"

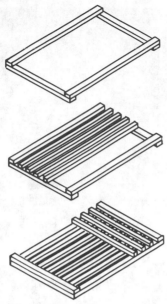

Fig. 6-22 *Three stages of accent screen construction.* California Redwood Association

If a bottom rail is desired, nail it to the posts before positioning panels. The rail should be the same size as the cap. Nail panels to post sheathing and rail. Then add the cap (FIG. 6-23).

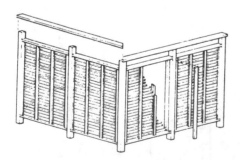

Fig. 6-23 *Capping an accent screen.* Georgia-Pacific Corp.

Remember, nails and fasteners should be stainless steel, aluminum alloy, or top quality, hot-dipped galvanized to prevent stain streaks (FIG. 6-24). Use 12d nails to attach grille members to frame and 8d nails to attach members to one another. Use 16d nails to join 2×4 frame members and to attach panels to posts.

Fig. 6-24 *Comparison of weathered aluminum and steel nails on a fence.* Aluminum Association

View divider

Sometimes you want a hole in your fence. The view divider's framed openings can be left open, or filled with hanging plant baskets, climbing vines, or decorative inserts. Figures 6-25 through 6-27 illustrate how the grille divider is constructed. Use construction heart redwood for posts and the bottom stringer and construction common for other components. You can also use cedar or a pressure-treated wood.

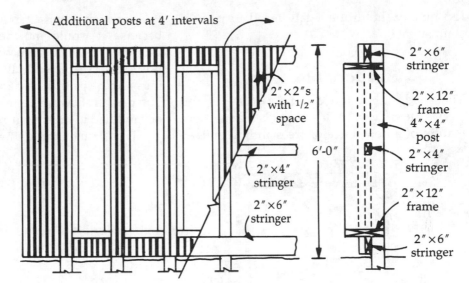

Additional posts at 4' intervals

2"×2"s with 1/2" space

6'-0"

2"×4" stringer

2"×6" stringer

2"×6" stringer

2"×12" frame

4"×4" post

2"×4" stringer

2"×12" frame

2"×6" stringer

Fig. 6-25 *Cross section of view divider.* California Redwood Association

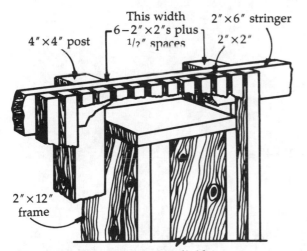

This width
6 − 2"×2"s plus
1/2" spaces

4"×4" post

2"×6" stringer

2"×2"

2"×12" frame

Fig. 6-26 *Capping the view divider.* California Redwood Association

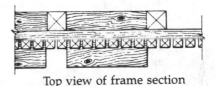

Top view of frame section

Fig. 6-27 *Top view of view divider.* California Redwood Association

Posts are 4×4s set at 4-foot intervals. Posts also flank each "window." The width of the window framing is 15½ inches, so set the four flanking posts 15½ inches apart, or 19½ inches on center. Set posts at least 2 feet in the ground and align carefully. Anchor posts in concrete. Tamp some earth or gravel around the bottom of the post before pouring to keep the concrete from sealing off the post and preventing drainage.

Nail the top and bottom 2×6 stringers to the posts. Measure the height between stringers and the space between flanking posts (slight variations in post settings are almost inevitable), and construct the 2×12 frames to fit. Then nail them up between posts.

Now nail the 2×4 stringer midway between top and bottom stringers, cutting short lengths to fit between the frames. Predrill nail holes in the 2×2 vertical members to prevent splitting, then nail these to the stringers, using one nail at each stringer. Cut 6-inch lengths of 2×2 to fit above and below the windows.

Nail all members with 16d nails. Nails should be stainless steel, aluminum alloy, or top quality, hotdipped galvanized to prevent stain streaks.

Shadow box fence

The shadow box fence detail (FIGS. 6-28 and 6-29) is most easily built when it is planned as a feature of a new fence or freestanding divider.

It is rarely appropriate in a property line fence because it would intrude into a neighbor's property. Its main attraction is that the inset portion serves splendidly to showcase plantings and helps break up long fence selections. The design shown here may be copied directly or modified to meet your needs.

The "frame" through which the plants are

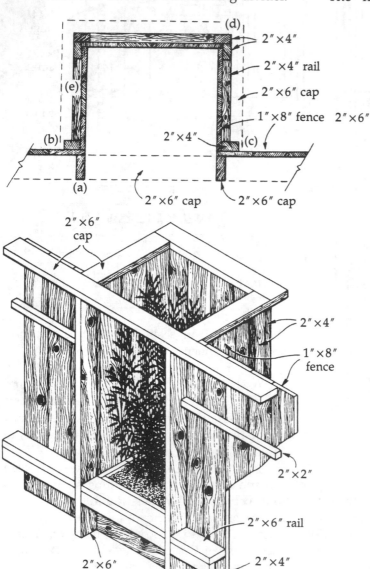

Fig. 6-28 *Shadow box fence dimensions.* California Redwood Association

Fig. 6-29 *Shadow box fence installation.* California Redwood Association

seen is formed from 2×6 pieces. This also helps support the cap. The shadow box is supported by vertical 2×4s and connected to the fence with horizontal 2×4 rails into which fence boards and caps are nailed.

Install the 2×6 vertical "frame" members first to determine the width of the shadow box. Position and nail the regular fence boards before doing any further work. Next, position and nail vertical 2×4s, prenailing two corner 2×4s at 90-degree angles, and attach with horizontal 2×4 rails top and bottom. The perimeter of the shadow box should rest on the ground.

Once vertical and horizontal 2×4s are in place, attach fence boards as shown. The 2×6 caps may then be added. Plants in containers can be placed in the completed shadow box, or the lower area can be filled with garden soil and planted.

For a special effect, outdoor lighting can be installed to accent the planting and the shadow box.

7

Chain-link fences

Chain link is one of the most efficient fencing materials for many homes and commercial applications. It offers maximum visibility, adapts to irregular ground, keeps out most intruders, allows complete air passage, and needs little maintenance to ensure a long life.

The biggest objection many people have to chain-link fences is that it adds no privacy. This objection can be overcome through landscaping; by wood, metal, or plastic inserts; and with panels.

Chain-link fences are often less expensive to install and maintain than traditional wood fences. You don't need a contractor to install it; many fence supply companies will rent or loan you the special tools you need to install a chain-link fence.

Installing a chain-link fence

Figures 7-1 and 7-2 illustrate the various components of a chain-link fence, and provide instructions for determining the quantity to buy of each component. Once you have your mate-

rials, there are eight simple steps to installing a chain-link fence:

1. Survey property lines.
2. Locate and set terminal posts.
3. Locate and set line posts.
4. Apply fittings to terminal posts.
5. Apply top rail.
6. Hang fabric.
7. Stretch fabric.
8. Hang gates.

You need a posthole digger, fence stretcher, wire grip and stretch bar, cutting pliers, an adjustable end wrench, tape measure, and a carpenter's level.

Survey property lines   Before you start, be sure your boundaries and property lines are legally established, and your proposed fence lines do not stray over them. Place your fence line 2 to 4 inches inside your property line to avoid encroaching on adjoining property with the concrete foundation.

Locate and set terminal posts   Determine

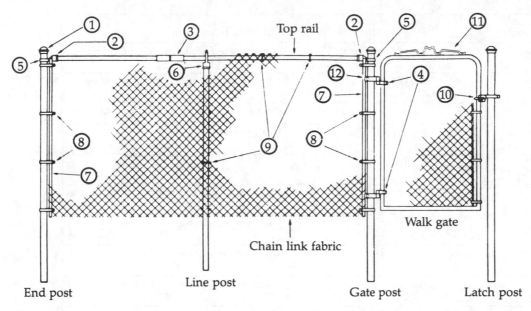

Fig. 7-1 *Chain-link fence components. Numbers refer to parts on the materials list in* FIG. 7-2.

the location of end, corner, and gate posts (referred to as terminal posts). The distance between gateposts is determined by adding the actual width of the gate to an allowance for hinges and latches. Single walk gates require 3³/₄ inches for hinges and latches. Double drive gates require 5¹/₂ inches. A 3-foot walk gate should measure 32¹/₄ inches wide. Adding 3³/₄ inches to the width means that the distance between posts (inside face to inside face) should be 36 inches.

When digging postholes, avoid underground cables and pipelines: contact your local utilities for locations. Figure 7-3 illustrates the right and wrong way to dig terminal and line postholes. Terminal postholes should be 10 inches wide at the top and 12 inches wide at the bottom. Line postholes should be 8 inches wide at the top and 10 inches at the bottom. If you're using a clamshell posthole digger, widen the bottom of the hole by simply angling the digger and scraping the sides, or use a small shovel to finish out the hole.

Mark all posts with crayon or chalk for the

correct height of the fence you are installing. Terminal posts should be set 2 inches higher than the fabric width. Measurement C in FIG. 7-4 dictates the hole depth.

Set the terminal posts in concrete using a 1-2-4 concrete mix: 1 part cement, 2 parts sand, and 4 parts gravel. Mix a fairly heavy solution: too much water weakens concrete and can cause cracking. Use a carpenter's level to set posts plumb. Crown all post footings for water drainage by sloping concrete away from the post.

Because no two pieces of ground are alike or completely level, you must plan the contour of your installation in advance (FIG. 7-5). To make the top of your fence straight, compensate for ground level variations by adjusting the amount of post above the ground to a level line of sight. In some cases it's necessary to trench the ground if the ground level is high, or, if the ground level is low, fill it with dirt. You can make a ground contour installation.

Locate and set line posts Mark the grade line on all line posts measuring from the top

Pieces	Item—description	Quantity to use
(1)	 Fabric (50 feet per roll)	Divide total footage by 50 and round up
(2)	Top rail 21′ × 1-3/8″ O.D. swaged	Divide total footage by 21 and round up
(3)	Line post 1-5/8″ O.D.	Divide total footage by 10 and round up
(4)	 Loop caps 1-5/8″ × 1-3/8″	Use 1 per line post
(5)	Terminal post 2-1/2″ O.D.	—
(6)	 Tension bar	Use 1 per end or gate post, 2 per corner post
(7)	 Brace band	Use 1 per tension bar
(8)	Rail ends 1-3/8″	Use 1 per tension bar
(9)	 Tension band	Use 4 per tension bar or 1′ per foot of fence height
(10)	5/16″ × 1-1/4″ carriage bolts	Use 1 per tension or brace band
(11)	 Post caps (acorn style) 2-1/2″	Use 1 per terminal post
(12)	 Alum cut ties	Use 1 per foot of fence—packaged 100 per bag
(13)	Walk gate (3′ or 3-1/2′ wide)	—
(14)	 Double drive gate (10′ or 12′ wide)	—
(15) 	Male hinge 2-1/2″	Use 2 per walk gate and 4 per double drive gate
(16)	3/8 × 3 carriage bolts	Used with the male hinge, 1 per hinge
(17)	 Female hinge 1-3/8″	Use 2 per walk gate and 4 per double drive gate
(18)	3/8 × 1-3/4 carriage bolts	Used with female hinge, 1 per hinge
(19)	 Fork latch	Needed on walk gates only—1 per gate

Tools

1. Post hole digger
2. Wheelbarrow, shovel and hoe to mix and transport concrete
3. Tape measure
4. Level
5. String and stakes or Mason's line
6. Pliers
7. Fence stretcher (block and tackle, ratchet-type power pull, etc.)
8. 1/2″ × 9/16″ wrench or crescent wrench
9. Hacksaw or pipe cutter

Fig. 7-2 Materials list for chain-link fencing.

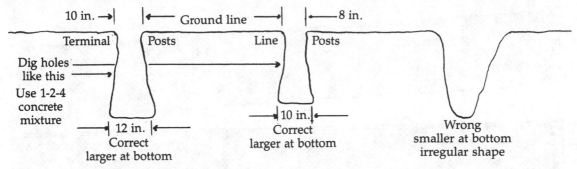

10 in. →| |← Ground line →| |←—8 in.

Terminal   Posts   Line   Posts

Dig holes
like this

Use 1-2-4
concrete
mixture

12 in. |← |10 in.| Wrong
Correct   Correct   smaller at bottom
larger at bottom   larger at bottom   irregular shape

Fig. 7-3 *The right and wrong way to dig fence posts.* Builders Fence Co., Inc.

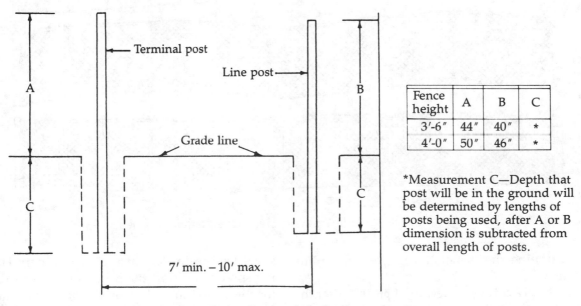

Fence height	A	B	C
3'-6"	44"	40"	*
4'-0"	50"	46"	*

*Measurement C—Depth that post will be in the ground will be determined by lengths of posts being used, after A or B dimension is subtracted from overall length of posts.

Terminal post

Line post

Grade line

7' min. – 10' max.

Fig. 7-4 *Estimating posthole depth.* Builders Fence Co., Inc.

down. Then measure the distance between terminal posts and check the line post spacing chart (TABLE 7-1) for the exact distance to allow between the posts.

Stretch a mason's line from outside to outside of terminal posts once you're sure the concrete has set up sufficiently. The line postholes should be lined up so that when they are set in the center of their holes, their centers will line up with the terminal post centers. This means the outside faces of the line posts will be about

1/4 inch inside the line stretched between the outside of the terminal posts. Dig the line postholes and set the line posts.

Stretch your mason's line taut 4 inches below terminal post tops and use it as a guide to align the height of line posts (FIG. 7-6). If it's necessary to adjust the height of any post, simply raise or lower the post before the concrete sets up. Use your level to keep the post plumb while adjusting the height. It's best to let the concrete set up for about a day before

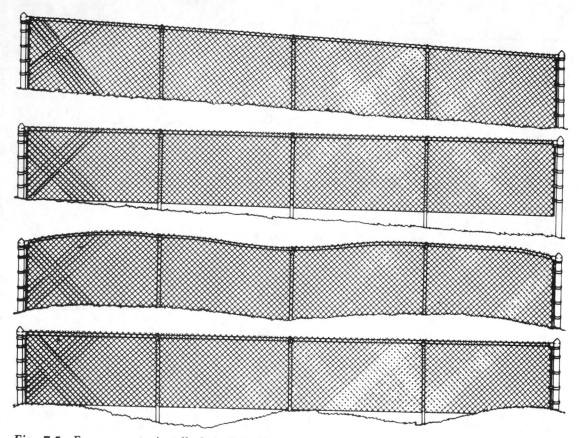

Fig. 7-5 *Four ways to install chain-link fencing over uneven terrain.* Builders Fence Co., Inc.

continuing the installation of your chain-link fence.

Apply fittings to terminal posts After the posts are installed and the concrete has set, slip the tension and brace bands onto the terminal posts (FIG. 7-7). The tension bands should be spaced approximately 10 to 12 inches apart. Do not spread or distort the bands. All bolt heads for the bands should be on the outside of the fence, and the threaded ends should be on the inside. Apply all the terminal post caps.

Apply top rail The loop caps are now

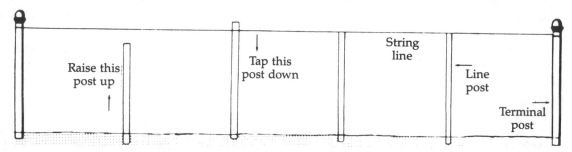

Fig. 7-6 *Adjusting line posts to proper height.*

Table 7-1. Line Post Spacing

Space	Set post apart	Space	Set post apart	Space	Set post apart	Space	Set post apart	Space	Set post apart
30 ft.	10 ft.	51 ft.	8 ft. 6 in.	71 ft.	8 ft. 9 in.	92 ft.	9 ft. 2 in.	112 ft.	9 ft. 4 in.
31 ft.	7 ft. 9 in.	52 ft.	8 ft. 8 in.	72 ft.	9 ft.	93 ft.	9 ft. 3 in.	113 ft.	9 ft. 5 in.
32 ft.	8 ft.	53 ft.	8 ft. 10 in.	73 ft.	9 ft. 2 in.	94 ft.	9 ft. 5 in.	114 ft.	9 ft. 6 in.
33 ft.	8 ft. 3 in.	54 ft.	9 ft.	74 ft.	9 ft. 3 in.	95 ft.	9 ft. 6 in.	115 ft.	9 ft. 7 in.
34 ft.	8 ft. 6 in.	55 ft.	9 ft. 2 in.	75 ft.	9 ft. 4 in.	96 ft.	9 ft. 7 in.	116 ft.	9 ft. 8 in.
35 ft.	8 ft. 9 in.	56 ft.	9 ft. 4 in.	76 ft.	9 ft. 6 in.	97 ft.	9 ft. 7 in.	117 ft.	9 ft. 9 in.
36 ft.	9 ft.	57 ft.	9 ft. 6 in.	77 ft.	9 ft. 7 in.	98 ft.	9 ft. 8 in.	118 ft.	9 ft. 10 in.
37 ft.	9 ft. 3 in.	58 ft.	9 ft. 8 in.	78 ft.	9 ft. 9 in.	99 ft.	9 ft. 9 in.	119 ft.	9 ft. 10 in.
38 ft.	9 ft. 6 in.	59 ft.	9 ft. 10 in.	79 ft.	9 ft. 10 in.	100 ft.	10 ft.	120 ft.	10 ft.
39 ft.	9 ft. 9 in.	60 ft.	10 ft.	80 ft.	10 ft.	101 ft.	9 ft. 2 in.	121 ft.	9 ft. 3 in.
40 ft.	10 ft.	61 ft.	8 ft. 8 in.	81 ft.	9 ft.	102 ft.	9 ft. 3 in.	122 ft.	9 ft. 4 in.
41 ft.	8 ft. 2 in.	62 ft.	8 ft. 10 in.	82 ft.	9 ft. 1 in.	103 ft.	9 ft. 4 in.	123 ft.	9 ft. 5 in.
42 ft.	8 ft. 5 in.	63 ft.	9 ft.	83 ft.	9 ft. 3 in.	104 ft.	9 ft. 5 in.	124 ft.	9 ft. 7 in.
43 ft.	8 ft. 6 in.	64 ft.	9 ft.	84 ft.	9 ft. 4 in.	105 ft.	8 ft. 6 in.	125 ft.	9 ft. 7 in.
44 ft.	8 ft. 9 in.	65 ft.	9 ft. 3 in.	85 ft.	9 ft. 6 in.	106 ft.	9 ft. 7 in.	126 ft.	9 ft. 8 in.
45 ft.	9 ft.	66 ft.	9 ft. 5 in.	86 ft.	9 ft. 7 in.	107 ft.	9 ft. 8 in.	127 ft.	9 ft. 9 in.
46 ft.	9 ft. 2 in.	67 ft.	9 ft. 7 in.	87 ft.	9 ft. 8 in.	108 ft.	9 ft. 9 in.	128 ft.	9 ft. 10 in.
47 ft.	9 ft. 5 in.	68 ft.	9 ft. 8 in.	88 ft.	9 ft. 9 in.	109 ft.	9 ft. 10 in.	129 ft.	9 ft. 10 in.
48 ft.	9 ft. 7 in.	69 ft.	9 ft. 10 in.	89 ft.	9 ft. 10 in.	110 ft.	10 ft.		
49 ft.	9 ft. 9 in.	70 ft.	10 ft.	90 ft.	10 ft.	111 ft.	9 ft. 3 in.		
50 ft.	10 ft.			91 ft.	9 ft. 2 in.				

Fig. 7-7 *Tension and brace bands on terminal post.*
Val Ramos

attached. They are set with the top rail hole off-set toward the outside of the fence, making flush the outside face of the top rail through the loop caps.

Join the top rail with swaged end where required. The end of the top rail fits into the rail end fittings on the terminal post (FIG. 7-8).

Hang fabric After assembling the frame-work, unroll the fabric on the ground along the fence line, starting at a terminal post. Slide the tension bar through the last link in your fabric. Attach this combination to the terminal post using the tension band and bolts provided (FIG. 7-9).

If more or less fabric is needed to span the opening, connect or remove it as shown in FIG. 7-10. The fabric should be on the outside face of all posts, with either the knuckled or twisted edge at the top, as desired. It should be loosely attached to the top rail by a tie wire (FIG. 7-11).

Stretch fabric Fabric should be stretched from the terminal post already attached to the opposite terminal post. Insert the tension bar in the end of the fabric and attach the fence stretcher to the bar (FIG. 7-12). Ratchet-type power pull, large carpenter's clamps, block and tackle, or a similar device may be used. Most

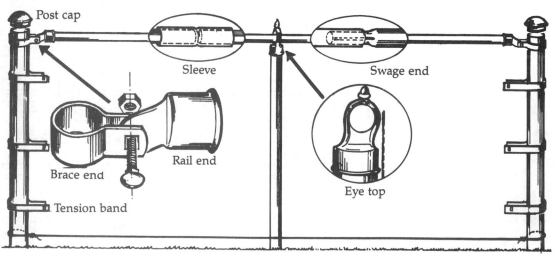

Fig. 7-8 *Chain-link fence posts, rails, and fittings.* Builders Fence Co., Inc.

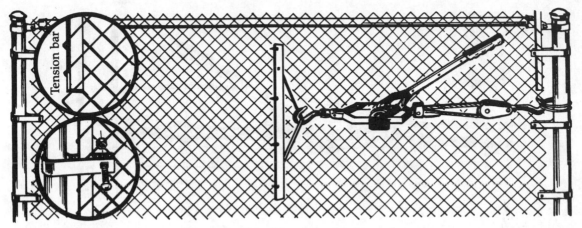

Fig. 7-9 *Stretching fence fabric.*

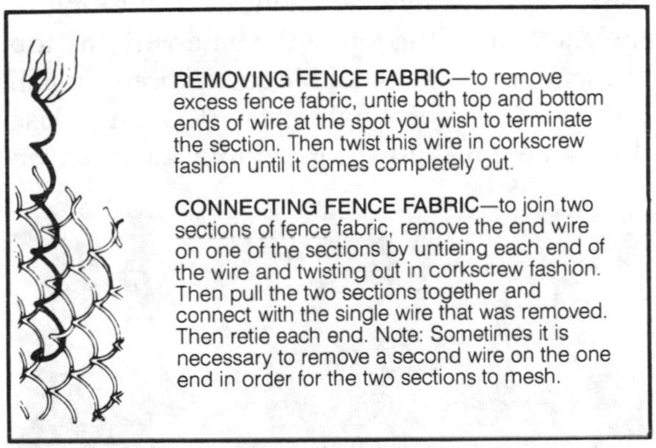

REMOVING FENCE FABRIC—to remove excess fence fabric, untie both top and bottom ends of wire at the spot you wish to terminate the section. Then twist this wire in corkscrew fashion until it comes completely out.

CONNECTING FENCE FABRIC—to join two sections of fence fabric, remove the end wire on one of the sections by untieing each end of the wire and twisting out in corkscrew fashion. Then pull the two sections together and connect with the single wire that was removed. Then retie each end. Note: Sometimes it is necessary to remove a second wire on the one end in order for the two sections to mesh.

Fig. 7-10 *How to remove or connect fence fabric.*

wire stretching tools of this type can be rented or borrowed locally.

As you stretch the fabric, test it for tension. It's stretched enough when it gives slightly. The top of the fabric should be located approximately 1/2 inch above the top rail to ensure proper height. After the fence fabric is sufficiently tight, remove the excess fabric as shown in FIG. 7-10 and connect the tension bar to the post with tension bands. Fasten the fabric to the top rail and line posts with tie wires spaced approximately 18 inches apart.

For most residential installations, the fabric

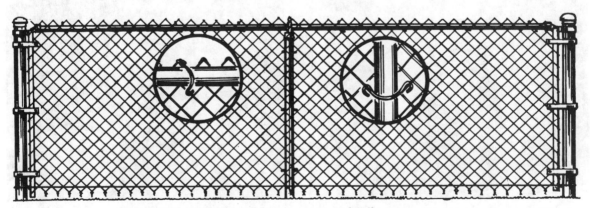

Fig. 7-11 *Attaching fabric to posts and rails.* Builders Fence Co., Inc.

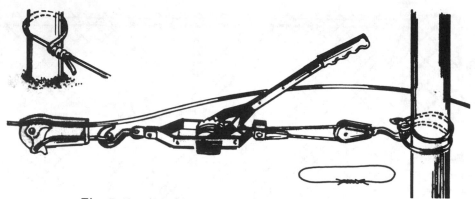

Fig. 7-12 *Attaching the fabric stretcher.* Builders Fence Co., Inc.

should be installed with the smooth edge up. If added security is necessary, you can install the fabric with barbs up.

Hang gates After the entire fence has been completed, apply male hinges to one of the gateposts, hanging the top hinge upside down to prevent the gate from being lifted off (FIG. 7-13). Loosely apply the female hinges on

the gate frame and slip them onto the male hinges that have been installed on the gatepost. Set the hinges to allow for full swing of the gate. Align the top of the gate with the top of the fence. Tighten all hinges securely. Install the gate latch for single gates (FIG. 7-14). Use the same procedure for double gates as on

Fig. 7-13 *Male and female hinge.* Val Ramos

Fig. 7-14 *Gate latch.* Val Ramos

88 *Chain-link fences*

walk gates, but install a center latching device, called a fork latch.

Shopping for a chain-link fence

Now that you see how simple installing a chain-link fence can be, here's a closer look at the basic components of a chain-link fence.

Wire size The wire size is traditionally measured by gauge. Gauge designations can be and often are confusing for the consumer. Remember that the smaller the gauge number, the bigger (thus stronger) the wire.

Mesh size The size of the wire mesh is also important in determining the type of fence you ultimately have installed (TABLE 7-2). These two items—wire and mesh size—affect both price and durability.

The size of the mesh is determined by measuring the distance between the parallel sides of the mesh. Common sizes are 2$^1/_8$ inches and 2 inches (mesh size for tennis court fencing is

Table 7-2. Standard Diamond Count for Various Heights of Chain-link Fabric: 2-inch Mesh

Fabric height	Diamond count	
	11 gauge	9 gauge
36"	10$^1/_2$	10$^1/_2$
42"	12$^1/_2$	12$^1/_2$
48"	14$^1/_2$	13$^1/_2$
60"	17$^1/_2$	17$^1/_2$
72"	20$^1/_2$	20$^1/_2$
84"	24$^1/_2$	24$^1/_2$
96"	27$^1/_2$	27$^1/_2$
108"	31$^1/_2$	31$^1/_2$
120"	34$^1/_2$	34$^1/_2$
132"	37$^1/_2$	37$^1/_2$
144"	41$^1/_2$	41$^1/_2$

usually 1$^3/_4$ inches in diameter). Larger mesh takes less steel and is less costly.

Framework The chain-link fabric is supported by a framework consisting of line posts, terminal and corner posts, and top rail. They

Single walk gate

Fig. 7-15 Single walk and double drive gates.

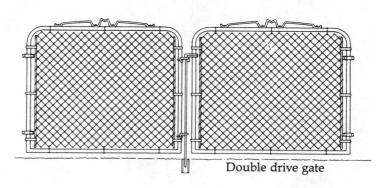

Double drive gate

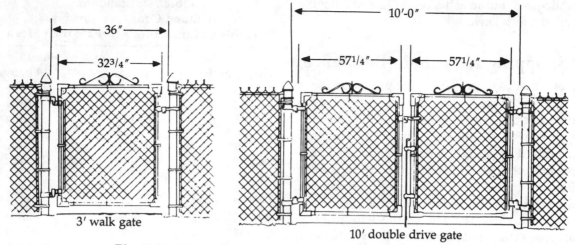

Fig. 7-16 Dimensions for single walk and double drive gates.

are held together by a set of specialized fence fittings. This entire framework will be coated with either zinc or vinyl for long life and protection against the elements.

In residential fences the line posts are normally 1⅝ inches O.D. (outside diameter), with varying wall thicknesses depending on your individual desire for strength and rigidity. Terminal and corner posts may be 1⅞ or 2⅜ inches O.D.

The top rail is normally 1⅜ inch O.D. It comes in 21-foot lengths joined by sleeves or swaged ends that slide together.

Gates A gate is the only moving part of a fence and should be constructed sturdily with strong hinges, latches, and gateposts for long, trouble-free service. Make certain that the gate you order provides a large enough opening to accommodate easily any items that you will be moving in or out of the enclosed area—such as garden equipment, lawn furniture, a recreational vehicle, etc. (FIGS. 7-15 and 7-16). You might want automatic closing and latching devices. These items and rolling gates are readily available. More detailed specifications for galvanized steel and aluminum chain-link fences are included in appendix C.

8

Livestock fences

Fences should be planned carefully whatever their purpose. This is especially important on farms where fences represent a large investment, and their location and arrangement could affect production, efficiency, and livelihood.

Permanent fences should be constructed well and made of good materials. Temporary fences need not be so sturdily constructed and may be made of less expensive materials. The kinds of fences commonly used on farms include board, woven wire, barbed wire, combination woven wire and barbed wire, cable and electric.

Preparatory work

Before erecting a fence, lay out the fence line and clear it.

Figure 8-1 illustrates how to lay out a fence line on level ground. Set a stake at each end of the proposed fence line and station another person at one of the ends. Starting from that end, set a stake every 100 feet, with the other person verifying the alignment of the stake being set with the two end stakes.

Figure 8-2 shows how to lay out a fence line over hills where you can't see the other end stake. Set two stakes on top of the hill where both can be seen from both end stakes. Line up the two stakes, first with one end stake, then with the other. You might have to move one or both stakes several times to obtain satisfactory alignment.

Fence lines should be cleared of trees, brush, stumps, rocks, old fences, and other obstructions that might interfere with construction of the fence or detract from its appearance. The easiest and quickest way to clear a fence line is to use a bulldozer or a bulldozer blade mounted on a tractor. You can knock down small trees and old fencing, clear brush, level high spots, and fill in low spots with this equipment.

Large trees can be cut or pulled down with a tractor. If you pull them down, use a heavy rope, cable, or log chain long enough to keep you safe from the falling tree. Be careful of the

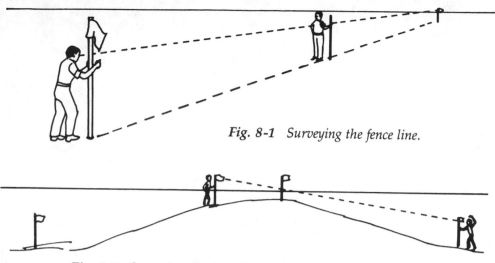

Fig. 8-1 *Surveying the fence line.*

Fig. 8-2 *Surveying the fence line over rough terrain.*

dangerous recoil if the rope, cable, or chain should break. When trees, large brush, and old fencing have been removed, you can plow down or turn under small brush and grass with a disk harrow or field cultivator.

If you clear a strip through woods or thicket, make it wide enough so you can easily distribute the posts and unroll the fence. A wide strip can later serve as a roadway or fire lane.

When you are replacing old fencing, you might want to use some of the old, sound posts. The easiest way to remove them from the ground is to use the hydraulic lift on a tractor or an A-frame.

Old wire usually is not worth saving. Never leave it in fence corners or other places where it might become a hazard to livestock. You can stake it in ditches to help prevent soil erosion.

Fence posts

Fence posts may be made of wood, steel, or concrete. Concrete posts are used mainly in farm fencing. You will determine the kind,

size, and number of posts to use by considering the availability and cost of the different kinds of posts, the kind of fence you plan to erect, how strong it needs to be, and how long you want it to last.

Wood

Wood posts can be purchased in most areas and are comparatively low in cost. The farm woodland might be a good source of wood posts.

You should use the most durable wood posts available for permanent fencing or, better still, use pressure-preservative treated posts. The durability of untreated wood posts, even of the more decay-resistant kinds, depends largely on the heartwood. Untreated sapwood of any species will usually rot in one to three years.

The probable life expectancy of untreated wood posts made mostly of heartwood is: Osage orange, 25–30 years; red cedar and black locust, 15–25 years; sassafras, 10–15 years; white oak, blackjack oak, and cypress, 5–10 years; southern pine, sweet gum, hick-

Table 8-1. Life Expectancy, in Years, of Treated and Untreated Fence Posts

Kind of wood	Untreated	Treated		
		Pressure	Hot and cold bath	Cold soak
Osage orange	25-30			
Western red cedar	12-15	20-25	20-25	
Lodgepole pine	2-4	20-25	15-20	10-20
Ponderosa pine	2-4	20-25	15-20	10-20
Aspen, cottonwood	1-3	15-20	10-15	5-10
Juniper, western*	20			
Locust, black*	20			
Douglas fir	3-6	20-35	15-25	10-20
Western hemlock	3-6	20-35	15-25	10-20

*heartwood

ory, red oak, sycamore, yellow poplar, cotton-wood, and willow, 2–7 years (TABLE 8-1).

Osage orange, red cedar, and black locust posts might no longer be available in some areas. If less durable posts are used, they should be treated with a good wood preservative to protect them against decay and insect damage. Depending on the kind of preservative used and the method by which it was applied, treated posts can have their life extended 10–30 years.

Pressure-treated posts—those treated with preservative by commercial processes—are usually more durable and more environmentally safe than home-treated posts.

Wood posts can usually be bought in lengths of 5 1/2 to 8 feet and in diameters of 2 1/2 to 6 inches or larger. Posts 5 inches or larger in diameter are generally used for anchor posts: gate, corner, end, and braced line posts. Line posts for straight, open field woven wire fences are sometimes as small as 2 1/2 inches in diameter, but a minimum diameter of 3 1/2 inches is recommended (FIG. 8-3). Four- or 5-inch posts should be used for barn lots, corrals, and in sandy and wet soils.

The height of the fence and the depth you set posts determine the required length of the posts. Anchor posts are usually set 3 to 3 1/2

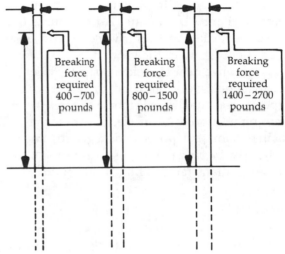

Fig. 8-3 *Approximate strength of wooden posts.*

feet in the ground, and line posts are usually set 2 to 2 1/2 feet.

Steel

Steel posts offer a number of advantages. They are lightweight, fireproof, extremely durable, and easily driven into most soils. Also, they will ground the fence against lightning when in contact with wet or moist soil.

Figure 8-4 shows the more common kinds of steel posts. The U-bar, studded Y, and

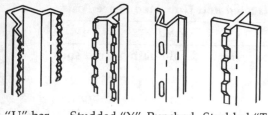

"U" bar   Studded "Y"   Punched   Studded "T"
channel

Fig. 8-4   Common steel posts.

punched channel posts are line posts, and the studded T post is a corner post. Steel posts are usually sold in lengths of 5, 5$^{1}/_{2}$, 6, 6$^{1}/_{2}$, 7, 7$^{1}/_{2}$, and 8 feet.

Animals crowding against fences tend to force steel posts out of line. Anchor plates that are bolted, clamped, or riveted to the posts keep them firmly in the ground.

If you live near oil fields, boiler factories, or repair shops, you might be able to buy used pipe, at reasonable cost, to use as fence posts. The pipe should be at least 1$^{3}/_{4}$ inches in diameter for line posts and larger for anchor posts. For heavy anchor posts, use pipe 6 to 8 inches in diameter and fill it with concrete.

Concrete

Concrete posts are used mostly as anchor posts (gate, corner, and end posts) in farm fences. Where a fence angles slightly, a concrete post will prevent the wire from pulling line posts out of line. Concrete posts can be extremely durable, lasting 30 years or longer, if they are well made. Otherwise, they will start to crumble in a few years.

Concrete line posts are usually 4 inches square and are cast several at a time in forms of the desired length. Anchor posts are usually larger and are cast in place.

Woven wire fences

Woven wire fencing is made in different designs with different horizontal spacing (FIG. 8-5). Those for farm and general use include field or stock fencing, poultry yard fencing, chicken fencing, and wire netting. Chain-link fence, a more stylized form, is designed mainly for use on home lots (see chapter 7). In most kinds of woven wire fencing you have a choice of fencing weight, protective coating on the wire, and style or design.

(Furnished in 20-rod rolls)

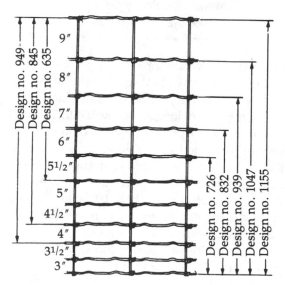

Fig. 8-5   Horizontal wire spacing for different designs of woven wire field fence.

Weight

The weight of woven wire fencing is determined by the gauge or size of the line, or horizontal, wires. The lower the gauge number, the larger the wire. The larger the wire, the stronger and more durable the fencing. Field or stock fencing, for example, comes in four weights (TABLE 8-2).

The stay (vertical) wires in the fencing are usually of the same gauge as the filler (intermediate) wires. They may be spaced 6 or 12 inches apart.

Table 8-2. Weights & Gauges of Stock Fencing

	Gauge of top and bottom line wires	Gauge of filler line (intermediate) wires
Light weight	11	14½
Medium weight	10	12½
Heavy weight	9	11
Extra heavy weight	9	9

Protective coatings

Most woven wire fencing is either zinc-coated (galvanized) or aluminum-coated. Chain-link fences also come with a vinyl resin coating, which makes a more attractive fence.

The coating on zinc-coated fencing may be class 1, 2, or 3. The class number indicates that the fencing has at least the minimum amount of galvanizing per square foot of wire surface. Class 3 generally has at least twice as much zinc as class 1. The thicker the zinc coating, the more corrosion-resistant the fencing is. The class number will be indicated on the fencing roll tag.

The coating on aluminum-coated fencing is usually about 0.25 ounce per square foot of wire surface. This usually isn't indicated on the tag.

Under the same climatic conditions, aluminum-coated fencing could be expected to resist corrosion three to five times longer than zinc-coated fencing with the same thickness of coating. If the coating is broken so that the wire is exposed to the air, the zinc would give better protection. While both metals act as "sacrificial agents"—they corrode instead of the wire—in rural atmospheres an oxide film tends to form on the aluminum coating and limits its ability to protect the wire. Any wire fencing will resist corrosion longer in a dry climate than in a humid area or in an industrial atmosphere.

Styles or designs

The styles or designs of woven wire fencing are designated by a three- or four-digit number—for example, 932 or 1155. The first or first two digits indicate the number of line wires in the fencing, and the last two indicate fence height in inches. Style 1155, for example, has 11 line wires and is 55 inches high.

Figure 8-6 shows the five most commonly used styles or designs of field or stock fencing: 1155, 1047, 939, 832, and 726. Barbed wire is also shown.

The suggested fencing for livestock applications follows:

Cattle and horses Use fence A or B, as shown in FIG. 8-6. The single barbed wire at the top prevents the animals from mashing down the fence.

Hogs Use fence C, D, or E shown in FIG. 8-6 without the barbed wires above the woven wire. The barbed wire below the woven wire discourages the animals from crawling or rooting under the fence. Styles 939 and 832 are available with a barbed bottom wire. Style 726 (fence E without barbed wire) is convenient for temporarily confining hogs while they eat corn.

Sheep Use style 832 or 726—fence D or E shown in FIG. 8-6, without barbed wire. Barbs could tear the sheep's fleece.

Figure 8-7 shows a fence for protecting sheep from dogs and coyotes. The extended barbed wire at the top discourages predators from jumping the fence. Adding an apron of woven wire 18 inches wide along the ground will prevent predatory animals from burrowing beneath the fence.

Cattle, horses, hogs, and sheep in the same field Use fence A, B, D, or E shown in FIG. 8-6.

Poultry garden and chick fencing Poultry garden fencing comes in two standard styles—2158 and 1948. Chick fencing comes in three styles—2672, 2360, and 2048.

Wire netting of 1- or 2-inch mesh is made

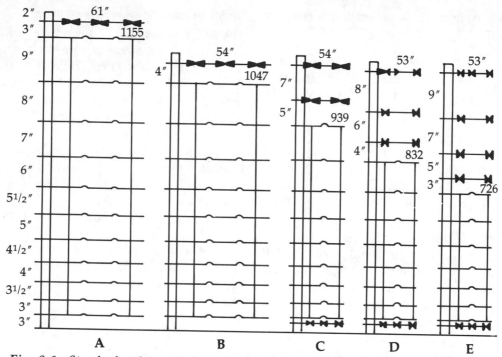

Fig. 8-6 Standard styles or designs of woven wire fencing combined with barbed wire. Stay (vertical) wires are spaced 12 inches in fences A and B and 6 inches in C, D, and E.

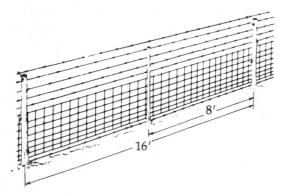

Fig. 8-7 Typical sheep fence.

is recommended for confining baby chicks, turkey poults, and goslings.

Setting posts

Setting untreated wood posts in concrete is not recommended. The post could shrink away from the concrete, leaving a crack by which moisture can enter. With durable or treated posts, though, the stability provided by concrete might justify its use. Setting treated posts in concrete is recommended when the fences might be subjected to heavy strain from animals or wind.

Dirt-set wood posts may be set in predug holes or driven into the ground. Power posthole diggers or post drivers can save much time and labor. Post drivers are available that can drive posts up to 8 inches in diameter.

in nine lengths, ranging from 12 to 72 inches. The netting is commonly used for fencing small poultry yards, cages, poultry house windows, and tree guards. The 1-inch mesh wire

For a stronger fence, set steel anchor posts (gate, corner, end, and braced line posts) in concrete. Steel posts meant to be dirt-set are available, but they will not provide as strong an assembly. Steel line posts should be driven directly into the ground and not set in concrete.

Corner- and end-post assemblies

Corner- and end-post assemblies are the foundation of a fence. If one fails, the whole fence or a section of it could fail.

Figure 8-8 shows different types of wood assemblies. The double-span assemblies have more than twice the strength of the single-span assemblies and only half the horizontal and vertical movement under heavy loads. Type C is superior to A and B, and B is superior to A.

Single-span assemblies may be used for fence lengths up to 10 rods. Use double-span construction for fence lengths of 10 to 40 rods. Minimum sizes recommended for the components of the assemblies are given in TABLE 8-3.

Table 8-3. Minimum Sizes Recommended for Components of Single-span and Double-span Assemblies

Single spans:

Corner post	6-inch diameter
Brace post	5-inch diameter
Brace	4-inch diameter
Tie	two double strands of No. 9 gauge wire

Double spans:

Corner post	5-inch diameter
Each brace post	4-inch diameter
Each brace	4-inch diameter
Each tie	two double strands of No. 9 gauge wire

The height of the fence and the depth posts are set determine the length of posts needed. The posts should be set at least 3½ feet in the ground.

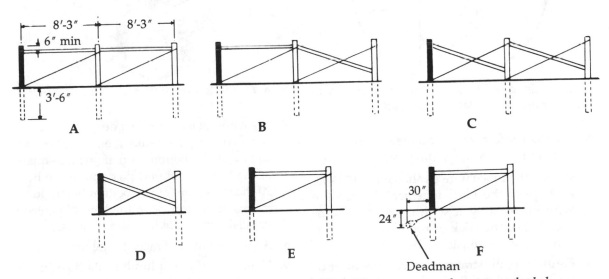

Fig. 8-8 Wood corner- and end-post assemblies. The corner or end posts are shaded.

Constructing Single-span Assemblies

(Repeat for double-span assemblies)

1. Dig the holes for the anchor and brace posts. Space them 8 feet apart.

2. Set the anchor post but not the brace post. Tamp the soil firmly as you replace it around the post. Lean the top of the post 1 inch away from the direction of the fence pull, so it will straighten to a plumb position when the fence is stretched.

3. Stand the brace post in its hole and fasten the wood brace to both posts. Use dowel pin construction for a strong assembly (FIG. 8-9).

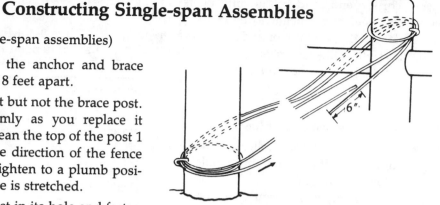

Fig. 8-10 *Fastening wire brace or tie in wood corner- or end-post assembly.*

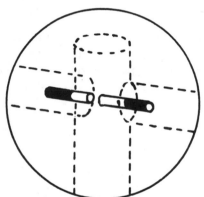

Fig. 8-9 *Use dowel pins to connect a wood brace to a wood corner or end post or brace post.*

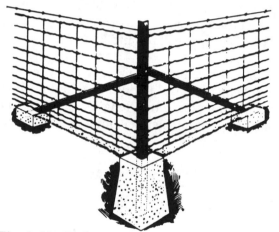

Fig. 8-11 *Steel corner and braces set in concrete.*

4. Set the brace post. Tamp the soil firmly as you replace it around the post.

5. Attach the brace wire as shown in FIG. 8-10, and splice the ends together. Tighten the wire by twisting it with a strong stick or rod. Leave the stick or rod in place so you can adjust the tension when necessary.

6. Figure 8-11 illustrates steel corner- or end-post assembly. Both the post and the braces should be set in concrete (FIG. 8-12).

7. Dig a hole at least 3½ feet deep for the post. For a corner post, make the hole 20 inches square at the bottom and 18 inches square at the top. For an end post, make the hole 20 inches square at the bottom but 18 to 20 inches at the top, with the long dimension parallel with these hole dimensions.

8. Attach the metal braces to the post.

9. Holding the post plumb in its hole, mark the holes for the braces on the ground. The braces should enter the concrete pier 6

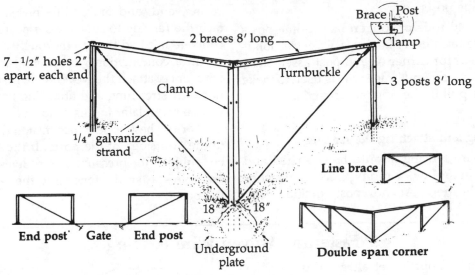

Labels in figure:
Brace Post
7–1/2" holes 2" apart, each end
2 braces 8' long
Clamp
Turnbuckle
Clamp
3 posts 8' long
1/4" galvanized strand
Line brace
End post Gate End post
18" 18"
Underground plate
Double span corner

Fig. 8-12   Attaching brace wire to corner brace.

inches below the ground surface and extend 6 inches into the concrete. The center of the holes will be closer to the post than where the braces touch the ground.

10. Dig the holes for the braces, making them at least 18 inches deep and 20 inches square at the top and bottom. At least 8

inches of the concrete pier should be below the frost line.

11. Holding the post plumb in its hole, place the concrete around it and the braces. Tamp the concrete as you pour it. Slope it slightly away from the post and braces to drain water.

Line posts

Line posts are usually spaced 14, 16, or 20 feet apart for field fencing and 10 to 16 feet apart for home lot fencing. Closer spacing might be necessary if the ground is uneven or if you need a stronger fence. You may have to shorten the spacing between the posts to equalize it near the corner or end of the fence. Set wood line posts 2 to 2 1/2 feet in the ground, and steel line posts 1 1/2 to 2 feet deep. Stretch a cord, rope, or wire between the two anchor posts to serve as a guide in aligning the posts.

When set in low places, line posts should be weighted down, set in concrete, or provided with subsoil cleats to help hold them in the ground. Don't set line posts in a gully or stream where they could be washed out by a heavy flow of water. If the fence line crosses a narrow gully or stream, stretch the fence straight across from a well-secured post on each bank. Barbed wire can be stretched below the fence to prevent stock from crawling under it.

If the gully or stream is wide, terminate the fence section on the one bank with an end-post assembly and start a new section on the other bank. Install a floodgate across the gully or stream to restrain livestock.

Braced-line posts

In fences 40 rods or longer, braced-line posts should be used every 20 yards. Construction is the same as for corner or end-post assemblies, except that a second brace wire is used to make the fence pull in the opposite direction.

Stretching and attaching the fencing

Woven wire fencing should be stretched and attached in sections running from one anchor post to the next. Anchor posts include gate, corner, end, and braced-line posts. Don't attach the fencing to concrete-set posts until the concrete has had time to thoroughly harden.

In a combination woven wire and barbed wire fence, attach the woven wire first. Instructions for stretching and attaching barbed wire will be given later in this chapter.

For the best appearance, fasten the fencing to the "outside" of the posts. If the fence will be subject to pressure—from livestock, for example—fasten the fencing to the "inside" of the posts.

Fastening Woven Wire Fencing

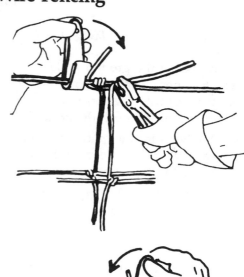

1. Starting about 2 feet ahead of the anchor post, unroll the fencing to the second line post and stand the fence roll on end.

2. Remove one or two stay wires from the end of the fencing to free enough length of each line wire to wrap around the post and splice on itself.

3. With the next stay wire against the post, staple the fence to the post at the desired height.

4. Starting with the middle wire, wrap each line wire around the post and back on itself. Make five wraps around the wire, using a splicing tool (FIGS. 8-13 and 8-14).

5. Unroll the fencing to the next anchor post.

6. Four to 8 feet beyond the second anchor post, set a dummy post for attaching the stretcher unit. Brace the post as shown in FIG. 8-15.

7. Prop the fencing against the line posts with stakes. Support it at the top, about a foot from every third or fourth post, and on the opposite side from the stretcher unit.

8. Attach the stretcher unit to the fencing and to the dummy post. Use a single-jack unit for fencing up to 32 inches in height and a double-jack unit for higher fencing (FIG.

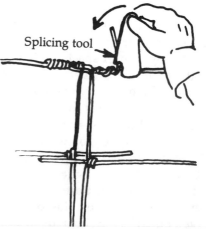

Splicing tool

Fig. 8-13 Splicing woven wire.

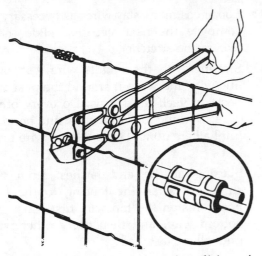

Fig. 8-14 *Compression sleeve for splicing wire.*

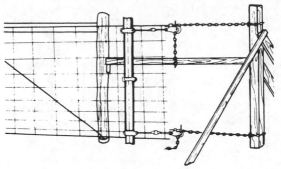

Fig. 8-15 *Fence stretcher in position, with braced "dummy" post at right.*

8-16). Attach the jack of a single-jack unit to the center of the bar, and attach the jacks of a double-jack unit so the wires are divided equally between the jacks.

9. Stretch the fence slowly so that the tension will be evenly distributed over the entire

length. Check the fencing during the stretching operation to make sure it is riding free at all points. Continue the stretching until the tension curves in the wire are straightened out about one-third. Don't overstretch the fence. If the tension curves are straightened out too much, the fence will lose some of its springiness.

10. Staple the line wires to the anchor posts (FIG. 8-17).

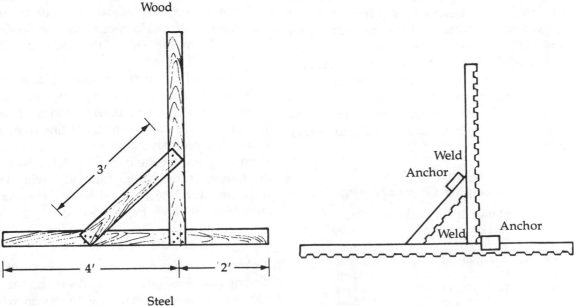

Wood

Steel

Fig. 8-16 *Ways to construct fence jacks.*

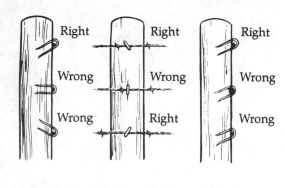

Drive staples
at angle

Do not drive
staples parallel
to side of post

Leave wire
loose
in staple

Fig. 8-17 Stapling wire to wooden posts.

11. Loosen as many stay wires as necessary to complete the next step and slide them toward the stretcher.

12. Starting with the middle wire, cut each line wire and wrap it around the post and back on itself four turns. Do every other wire, working toward the top and bottom, until all are done. Leave the top wire until last.

13. Starting at the end farthest from the stretcher, fasten the fencing to the line posts. Fasten the top wire first, then the bottom wire, and then every other wire until all are fastened.

Contour fencing

Contour fencing might be required on terraced land or in strip-cropping. It calls for slightly different construction.

Post spacing Post spacing must be reduced whenever there is much curve in the fence line to keep the posts from overturning. To determine the proper spacing, stake out a smooth curve along the terrace or contour strip. Space the stakes about 14 feet apart.

At any one point of curvature, select three consecutive stakes and stretch a string between the first and third stakes. Measure the distance from the center stake to the string and space the posts as outlined in TABLE 8-4.

Repeat the above procedure whenever the curvature of the fence line appears to change noticeably.

Table 8-4. Post Spacing for Contour Fencing

Distance from center stake to string	Post spacing
4 inches or less	14 feet
5 to 6 inches	12 feet
7 to 8 inches	10 feet
9 to 14 inches	8 feet
15 to 20 inches	7 feet

Check that no post is out of line of a smooth curve. With a smooth curve, the fencing will pull equally against each post.

Setting posts Lean the top of the post about 2 inches toward the side to which the fencing will be attached. When the fence is stretched, the post will straighten to a plumb position.

Installation On curves, attach the fencing to the outside of the posts so it will pull against the posts. This might mean that the fencing will first be on one side of the posts, then on the other.

Contour fencing can usually be stretched in 20- to 40-rod sections. It might be necessary to stretch it in 10-rod sections on sharp curves. Where the curvature of the fence line changes materially, you can start a new section at the sharpest point on the curve. Stretch a section of contour fencing from the end having the least curvature, so the end having the most curvature will have the least tension.

Barbed wire fences

Barbed wire is used in conjunction with other fencing and alone (FIGS. 8-18 and 8-19 and TABLE 8-5). Its use in combination with woven wire fences and for electric fences is covered in the

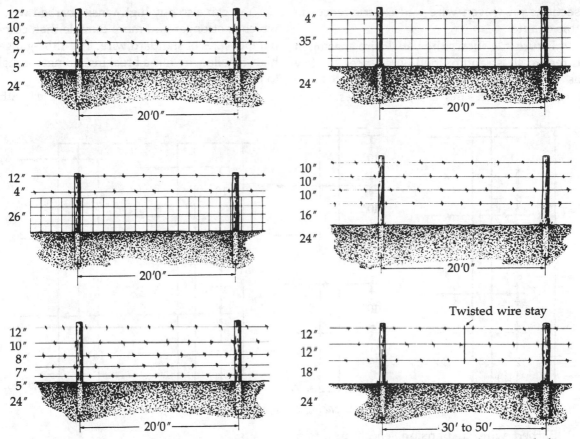

Fig. 8-18 *Three common barbed wire sheep fences.*　　**Fig. 8-19** *Three common barbed wire cattle fences.*

Table 8-5. Barbed Wire Specifications

Line wire gauge	Shape	Points	Barbs Wire gauge	Spacing (inches)	Wraps on line wire	Approx. wt./80 rd.
12¹/₂	half round	2	14	4	1	76
12¹/₂	round	2	14	4	2	80
13¹/₂ H.T.*	round	2	14	4	2	64
14	round	2	16	4	2	52
12¹/₂	flat	2	12¹/₂	4	1	77
12¹/₂	round	4	14	5	2**	88
12¹/₂	half round	4	14	5	1	83
13¹/₂ H.T.*	round	4	14	5	2**	71
15¹/₂ H.T.*	round	4	16	5	2**	41

*High tensile strength wire.
**Wrapped around both strands; interlocked with one barb projecting between the strands.

sections on woven wire and electric fences in this chapter.

Figure 8-20 shows the usual wire spacing in three- to six-strand barbed wire fences. As few as two strands are sometimes used to fence large cattle ranges in the western states.

You can also buy high-tensile barbed wire, which is stronger and more durable than comparable sizes of standard wire. The 13½-gauge high-tensile wire has a breaking strength equal to that of the 12½-gauge standard wire.

Barbed wire, like woven wire, comes with

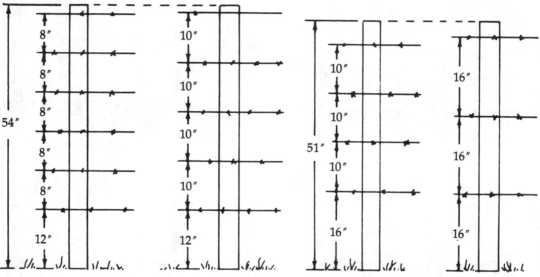

Fig. 8-20 Typical spacing of wires in barbed wire fences.

Barbed wire suspension fences are often used as cross fencing and boundary fencing on large cattle ranges. They consist of four to six strands of wire supported by posts spaced 8 to 12 feet apart. Twisted wire stays, spaced about 16 feet apart, hold the wire apart.

When cattle come in contact with a suspension fence, it sways back and forth. The fence beats against the cattle and discourages them from trying to go through it.

Figure 8-21 shows the kinds of standard barbed wire commonly available. The 12½-gauge wire (TABLE 8-6) with two-point barbs is the most widely used for cattle ranges. For smaller fields where cattle might subject the fence to considerable pressure, four-point barbs might be more effective. The lighter 14-gauge wire is commonly used for temporary fencing.

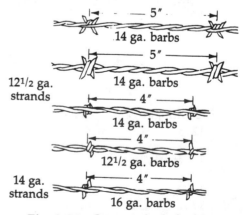

Fig. 8-21 Common barbed wire.

a protective coating of zinc or aluminum. The thickness of the coating is the same as on comparable sizes of woven wire. Under the same

Table 8-6. Decimal Equivalents of Steel Wire Gauge

Gauge number	Wire diameter (in.)
9	0.1483
10	0.1350
11	0.1205
12¹/₂	0.0990
13	0.0915
14	0.0800
14¹/₂	0.0760
15¹/₂	0.0670
16	0.0625

climatic conditions, aluminum-coated wire is more durable than zinc-coated wire.

Barbed wire is especially dangerous to work with because of the barbs. Precautions are necessary:

- Wear heavy leather gloves, boots or high shoes, and tough, close-fitting clothing.
- Never use a tractor to stretch woven wire or barbed wire fencing. While on the tractor, you might not be able to tell when the fencing has been stretched to the breaking point. If the wire should break, you could be injured seriously by the recoil of the clamp bar, chain, or fencing.
- Carry staples, nails, or other fasteners in a metal container or in an apron—not on your person. Never carry them in your mouth.
- When stretching barbed wire or woven wire, stand on the opposite side of the post from the wire and stretcher unit.
- If you handle preservative-treated posts, don't rub your hands or gloves on your face or other parts of your body. Some people are allergic to the chemical.

Strong anchor post assemblies are essential if the barbed wire does not have tension curves. Any pressure on the fence will be transferred directly to the posts.

Installation is the same whether the wire is used in combination with another fencing or alone as fencing.

Installing Barbed Wire Fencing

1. Unroll, stretch, and fasten one line at a time. In a combination fence, attach the barbed wire below the woven wire first. Then attach the wires above the woven wire, starting with the lowest one and working upward.

2. Fasten one end of the wire roll to the anchor post leaving enough wire free to wrap around the post and splice. If the anchor post is a gatepost, remove the barbs from the wire to be tightly wrapped around the post to prevent injury to people, or animals using the gate.

3. Wrap the wire around the post and splice it onto itself, 3¹/₂ to 4 turns (FIG. 8-22).

4. Unroll the wire along the ground to the next anchor post. Unroll it straight off the roll—not off the side.

5. Set up a dummy post about 8 feet beyond the second anchor post and brace it. If you're erecting a combination woven wire

continued

Fig. 8-22 *Wrap splice for splicing barbed wire.*

and barbed wire fence, you can use the dummy post set-up to stretch the woven wire fencing. Attach a fence stretcher or a block and tackle unit to the dummy post. Attach the wire to the stretcher unit.

6. Stretch the wire until it's fairly tight. Be careful not to stretch it so tightly that it breaks. You could be injured by the recoil.

7. Fasten the wire to the anchor post (FIG. 8-23).

8. Remove the barbs from a sufficient length of wire to wrap around the anchor post and splice on itself.

9. Cut and untwist one of the two strands of wire; the other strand will maintain the tension. Wrap the cut strand around the post and back on the wire $3^1/_2$ to 4 turns. Leave enough space between each turn to interwrap the second strand. Cut the second strand, wrap it around the post, and splice it on the wire.

10. Fasten the wire to the line posts (FIG. 8-24).

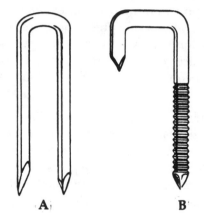

Fig. 8-23 *(A) U-shaped staple. (B) L-shaped deformed shank staple.*

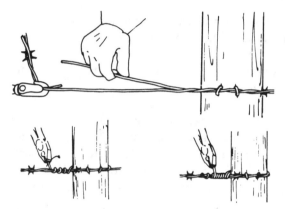

Fig. 8-24 *Connecting barbed wire to a fence post.*

Cable fences

Cable fences consist of heavy galvanized cables attached to metal or wood posts. Cable makes strong, durable fencing when constructed of good materials.

The cable fence is an excellent choice for feedlots and similar areas where the cattle are closely confined. It allows unrestricted air circulation, resulting in maximum cooling of the animals in warm weather. Combined with woven wire fencing or barbed wire, the fencing can be used to confine hogs, sheep, cattle. Detailed instructions for constructing the fencing should be obtained from fence manufacturers or dealers.

Figure 8-25 shows construction where the cables run through holes drilled through wood posts. Each cable is attached to the anchor post by a spring assembly. The cable is stretched with a block and tackle until the spring begins to open and is then clamped around the next anchor post. When necessary, the tension of the cable is adjusted by tightening or loosening the spring.

Electric fences

An electric fence consists of one or more electrically charged wires supported by, but insulated from, wood or metal posts. Either smooth wire or barbed wire may be used. A controller,

Fig. 8-25 Typical installation of cable fencing.

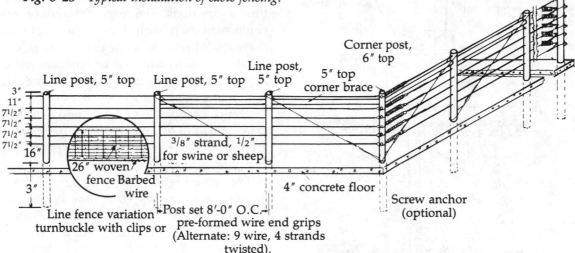

Line post, 5" top   Line post, 5" top   Line post, 5" top   Corner post, 6" top

5" top corner brace

3"
11"
7½"
7½"
7½"
7½"
16"

3/8" strand, 1/2" for swine or sheep

26" woven fence Barbed wire

3"

4" concrete floor

Screw anchor (optional)

Line fence variation turnbuckle with clips or   Post set 8'-0" O.C. pre-formed wire end grips (Alternate: 9 wire, 4 strands twisted).

commonly called a fence charger, is required to regulate the amount and timing of the current through the wire (FIG. 8-26).

Electric fencing is commonly used to confine cattle and horses, but it also can be used to control hogs and sheep. A single charged wire along the top or side of a wood fence or other kind will deter stock from crowding the fence and breaking it down. By electrifying it, it may be possible to use an old, permanent fence in poor condition.

Electric fencing is low in cost, economical to operate, and easy to erect and move around. The fence must be kept in continuous operation, so the livestock are trained to respect it, in order to be completely effective.

The fencing should be installed and operated according to the National Electrical Code,

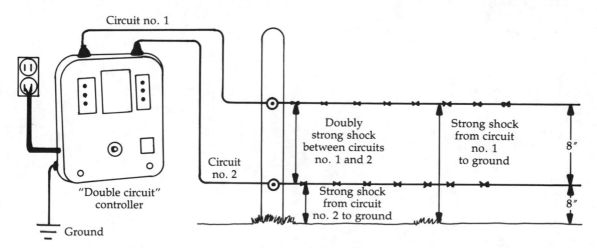

Circuit no. 1

"Double circuit" controller

Ground

Circuit no. 2

Doubly strong shock between circuits no. 1 and 2

Strong shock from circuit no. 2 to ground

Strong shock from circuit no. 1 to ground

8"

8"

Fig. 8-26 Typical hook-up of a double circuit electric fence controller.

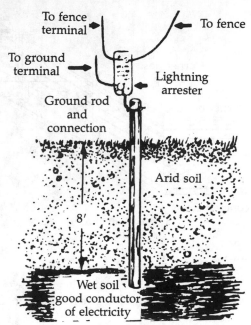

To fence terminal

To fence

To ground terminal

Lightning arrester

Ground rod and connection

Arid soil

8'

Wet soil good conductor of electricity

Fig. 8-27 Installation of lightning arrester.

state and local regulations, and the manufacturer's directions. The fence charger and other equipment used should carry the label of Underwriter's Laboratories or the Industrial Commission of Wisconsin. Fence chargers not carrying these labels could cause injury and death to humans and livestock.

Fence chargers are usually designed to operate on 110–120 volts. Battery-operated units are available for use where electric power is not available.

Approved fence chargers emit the current intermittently and not continuously. The "on" time is usually $1/10$ of a second 44 to 55 times a minute. The shock is strong, but it is short and harmless.

Locate your fence charger in a building—it must be protected from the weather. Figure 8-27 illustrates the installation of a lightning arrester on an electric fence.

9

Masonry fences and walls

Masonry fences and walls are excellent long-term investments. They can be both functional and decorative (FIGS. 9-1 and 9-2).

Brick, stone, and concrete walls can mark boundaries, keep people in or out, control privacy and the elements, retain soil, and improve the visual effect of your property. Masonry walls and fences can be constructed by most patient do-it-yourselfers, once they have the right tools and understand the basics of building with masonry (FIG. 9-3).

Masonry tools

Figure 9-4 illustrates the most common mason's tools. They can be purchased, rented, or borrowed at minimal cost.

Trowels The trowel is usually triangular. The largest size is from 9 to 11 inches long and from 4 to 8 inches wide. The length and weight of the trowel to use depends on you, the mason. You should select the one that you can handle best. Generally, the short wide trowels are best because the weight is nearer the wrist

and doesn't put as much strain on it. Trowels used for pointing and striking joints are smaller: 3 to 6 inches long and 2 to 3 inches wide. The trowel is used to mix and pick up mortar from the board, throw the mortar on the block, spread mortar, and tap the block down into its bed.

Chisel or bolster This tool is used to cut concrete block. It's $2^{1}/_{2}$ to $4^{1}/_{2}$ inches wide.

Hammer The mason's hammer has a square face on one end and a long chisel peen on the other. It weighs from $1^{1}/_{2}$ to $3^{1}/_{2}$ pounds and is used for splitting and rough-breaking blocks.

Jointer This tool is used for making various kinds of joints. There are several different types of jointers: rounded, flat, or pointed, depending on the shape of the mortar joint desired.

Figure 9-5 illustrates other mason's tools.

Square The square is used to measure right angles and lay out corners.

Mason's level The level enables the mason to plumb and level walls. It's from 36 to 48

Fig. 9-1 *Masonry walls and fences can be functional and decorative.* Brick Institute of America

Fig. 9-2 *This brick fence is purely decorative.* Brick Institute of America

Fig. 9-3 Concrete block fences can be built by nearly anyone. Val Ramos

Fig. 9-4 Common mason's tools.

inches long and is made of wood or metal. When the level is placed horizontally on the masonry and the bubble in the center tube is in the center of the tube, the masonry is level. When the level is placed vertically against the masonry and the bubble in the end tube is in the center of the tube, the masonry is plumb. An offset line from the face of the work should be established for long, high walls or tall columns. To assure straightness and plumbness, offset checks between this line and the face should be made often.

Straightedge The straightedge can be of any length, up to 16 feet, and should be $1^1/8$ inches thick and 6 to 10 inches wide. The top and bottom edges must be parallel. The straightedge can be used as an extension of the

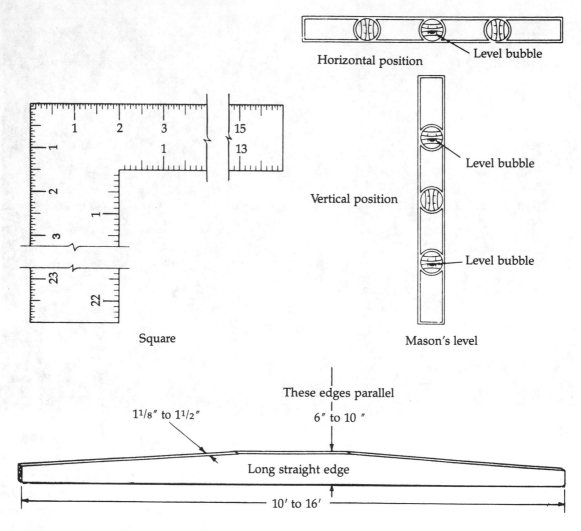

Fig. 9-5 Square, mason's level, and straightedge.

level to cover distances longer than the length of the level.

Miscellaneous tools Additional equipment required includes shovels, mortar hoes, wheelbarrows, chalk, plumb bobs, and a 220-foot ball of No. 18 to 21 hard-twisted cotton cord.

Mortar box and mortarboard These tools you can build yourself (FIG. 9-6). The mortar box is used to mix mortar by hand. It should be

as watertight as possible. The mortarboard is usually from 3 to 4 feet square. The board should be thoroughly wetted down before any mortar is placed on it to prevent the wood from absorbing moisture and causing the mortar to dry out. The mortar should be kept rounded up in the center of the board, and the outer edges should be kept clean. If spread in a thin layer, the mortar will dry out quickly, and lumps will often form.

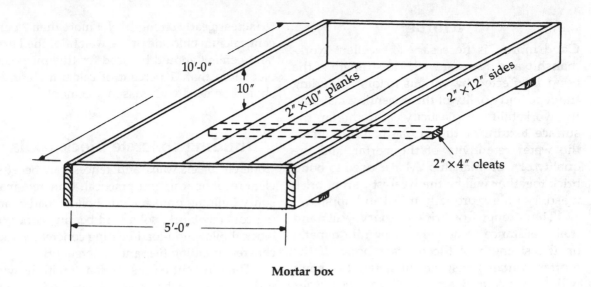

10'-0"

10"

2" × 10" planks

2" × 12" sides

2" × 4" cleats

5'-0"

Mortar box

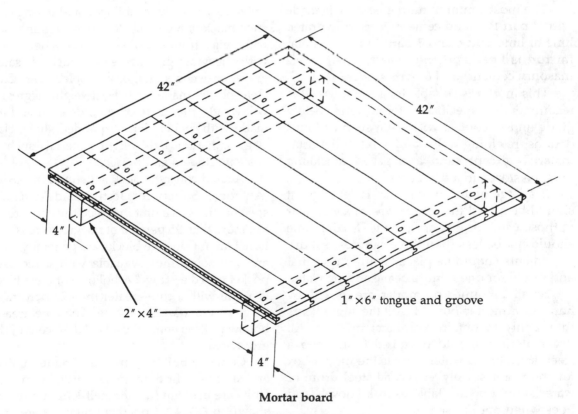

42"

42"

4"

2" × 4"

4"

1" × 6" tongue and groove

Mortar board

Fig. 9-6 Mortar board and mortar box.

Mortar

Good mortar is necessary to excellent workmanship and a strong wall. The strength of the bond is affected by various factors, including the type and quality of the cementing material, the workability or plasticity of the mortar, the surface texture of the mortar bedding areas, the water retentivity of the mortar, and the quality of workmanship. Mortar used to bond brick together will be the weakest part of brick masonry unless properly mixed and applied.

The strength of brick masonry walls and their resistance to penetration by rain depend on the strength of the mortar's bond. If the mortar contains insufficient water, the bond will be weak and spotty. When brick walls leak, it is usually through the mortar joints.

The most common mortar mixture is made with 1 part Portland cement, $1/4$ part hydrated lime or lime putty, and 3 parts sand. A similar mixture is 1 part Portland cement, 1 part type 2 masonry cement, and 6 parts sand.

This mortar is suitable for general use. It is recommended specifically for masonry below grade and in contact with earth such as foundations, retaining walls, and walks. All mortar materials except sand and slaked quicklime must be stored in a dry place.

If a large quantity of mortar is required, it should be mixed in a drum-type mixer similar to those used for mixing concrete. Mixing time should not be less than three minutes. All dry ingredients should be placed in the mixer first and mixed for one minute before adding water.

Small amounts of mortar are mixed by hand in a mortar box. Mix all the ingredients thoroughly to obtain a uniform mixture. All dry materials should be mixed first. Keep a steel drum full of water close to the mortar box for the water supply. A second steel drum of water should be available to soak shovels and hoes when not in use.

Calcium chloride is sometimes added to mortar to accelerate the rate of hardening and to increase early strength. Not more than 2 percent calcium chloride of the weight of the Portland cement should be used for this purpose. Not more than 1 percent of calcium chloride should be used with masonry cements.

Building concrete block walls

Concrete block walls and fences can be efficient, economical, and practical. Concrete masonry building units include hollow load-bearing concrete block, solid load-bearing concrete block, hollow non-load-bearing concrete block, concrete building tile, and concrete brick.

The different blocks are made with heavyweight or lightweight aggregates and are referred to as heavyweight and lightweight units, respectively. A hollow load-bearing concrete block of 8 by 8 by 16 inches nominal size will weigh from 40 to 50 pounds when made with heavyweight aggregate such a sand, gravel, crushed stone, or air-cooled slag. Concrete blocks made with lightweight aggregate will weigh from 25 to 35 pounds each and are made with coal cinders, expanded shale, clay, slag, or natural lightweight materials such as volcanic cinders and pumice.

A solid concrete block is defined by ASTM (American Society for Testing and Materials) specifications as a unit in which the core area is not more than 25 percent of the gross cross-sectional area. Concrete blocks are generally solid and are sometimes available with a recessed pocket called a "frog." A hollow concrete block is a unit with a core greater than 25 percent of its gross cross-sectional area. The core area of hollow units is generally 40 to 50 percent of the gross area.

Concrete building units are made in sizes and shapes to fit different construction needs. Units are made in full and half-length sizes, as shown in FIG. 9-7. Concrete unit sizes are usually referred to by their nominal dimensions. A unit measuring $7^5/8$ inches wide, $7^5/8$ inches

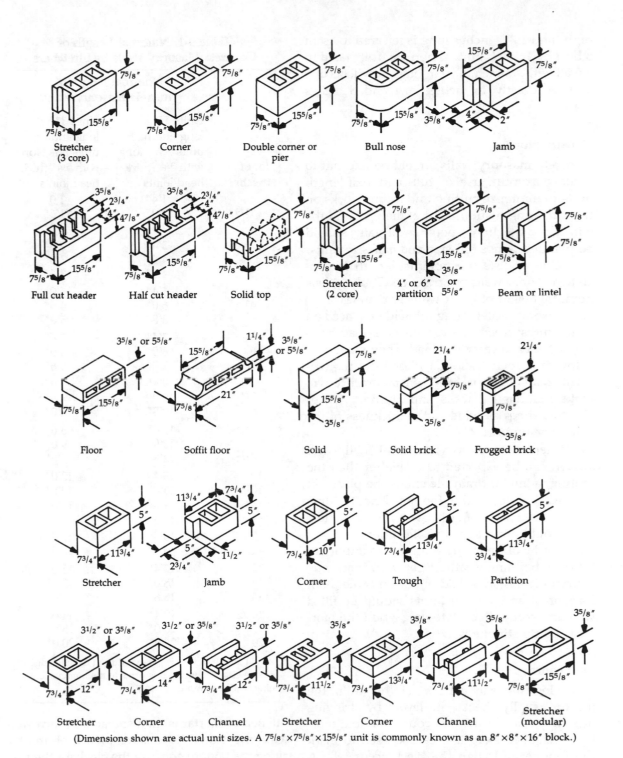

Stretcher (3 core) Corner Double corner or pier Bull nose Jamb

Full cut header Half cut header Solid top Stretcher (2 core) 4" or 6" partition Beam or lintel

Floor Soffit floor Solid Solid brick Frogged brick

Stretcher Jamb Corner Trough Partition

Stretcher Corner Channel Stretcher Corner Channel Stretcher (modular)

(Dimensions shown are actual unit sizes. A $7^5/8'' \times 7^5/8'' \times 15^5/8''$ unit is commonly known as an $8'' \times 8'' \times 16''$ block.)

Fig. 9-7 Typical sizes and shapes of concrete masonry units.

high, and 15⁵/8 inches long is referred to as an 8 by 8 by 16-inch unit. When the unit is laid in a wall with ³/8-inch mortar joints, it will occupy a space exactly 16 inches long and 8 inches high.

Construction

Concrete masonry walls should be laid out to make maximum use of full- and half-length units to minimize cutting and fitting blocks on the job. Length and height of the wall and the width and height of openings for gates should be planned to use full-size and half-size units.

Table 9-1 lists the nominal length of concrete masonry walls by stretchers. Table 9-2 lists nominal height of block walls by courses.

Masonry wall footings should be placed on firm, undisturbed soil of adequate load-bearing capacity to carry the load. They should be below frost penetration. Unless local requirements read otherwise, the general practice is to make footings for walls and masonry fences 1¹/2 to 2 times as wide as the thickness of the wall they support.

When the ground water level in the wet season can be expected to be higher than the footing, a line or drain tile should be placed in the outer side of the footing. The tile line should have a fall of at least ¹/2 inch in 12 feet and should drain to a suitable outlet.

Good workmanship is always an important factor in building weathertight walls. Each masonry unit should be laid plumb and true. Both horizontal and vertical joints should be filled well and compacted by tooling when the mortar is partly stiffened.

First course

After locating the corners of the wall, the mason usually checks the layout by stringing out the blocks for the first course without mortar. A chalked snap line can be used to mark the footing and align the block accurately. A

Table 9-1. Nominal Length of Concrete Masonry Walls by Stretchers

	Nominal length of concrete masonry walls	
No. of stretchers	Units 15⁵/8″ long and half units 7⁵/8″ long with ³/8″-thick head joints	Units 11⁵/8″ long and half units 5⁵/8″ long with ³/8″-thick head joints
1	1′4″	1′0″
1¹/2	2′0″	1′6″
2	2′8″	2′0″
2¹/2	3′4″	2′6″
3	4′0″	3′0″
3¹/2	4′8″	3′6″
4	5′4″	4′0″
4¹/2	6′0″	4′6″
5	6′8″	5′0″
5¹/2	7′4″	5′6″
6	8′0″	6′0″
6¹/2	8′8″	6′6″
7	9′4″	7′0″
7¹/2	10′0″	7′6″
8	10′8″	8′0″
8¹/2	11′4″	8′6″
9	12′0″	9′0″
9¹/2	12′8″	9′6″
10	13′4″	10′0″
10¹/2	14′0″	10′6″
11	14′8″	11′0″
11¹/2	15′4″	11′6″
12	16′0″	12′0″
12¹/2	16′8″	12′6″
13	17′4″	13′0″
13¹/2	18′0″	13′6″
14	18′8″	14′0″
14¹/2	19′4″	14′6″
15	20′0″	15′0″
20	26′8″	20′0″

(Actual length of wall is measured from outside edge to outside edge of units and is equal to the nominal length minus ³/8″ (one mortar joint).)

full bed of mortar is then spread and furrowed with the trowel to ensure plenty of mortar along the bottom edges of the block for the first

Table 9-2. Nominal Heights of Concrete Masonry Walls by Courses

No. of courses	Nominal height of concrete masonry walls	
	Units $7^5/_8$" high and $^3/_8$"-thick bed joint	Units $3^5/_8$" high and $^3/_8$"-thick bed joint
1	8"	4"
2	1'4"	8"
3	2'0"	1'0"
4	2'8"	1'4"
5	3'4"	1'8"
6	4'0"	2'0"
7	4'8"	2'4"
8	5'4"	2'8"
9	6'0"	3'0"
10	6'8"	3'4"
15	10'0"	5'0"
20	13'4"	6'8"
25	16'8"	8'4"
30	20'0"	10'0"
35	23'4"	11'8"
40	26'8"	13'4"
45	30'0"	15'0"
50	33'4"	16'8"

(For concrete masonry units $7^5/_8$" and $3^5/_8$" in height laid with $^3/_8$" mortar joints. Height is measured from center to center of mortar joints.)

course. The corner block should be laid first and carefully positioned. All blocks should be laid with the thicker end of the face up to provide a larger mortar-bedding area. Mortar is applied only to the ends of the faces for vertical joints. Several blocks can be placed on end. Each block is then brought over its final position and pushed downward into the mortar bed and against the previously laid block to obtain a well-filled vertical mortar joint.

After three or four blocks have been laid, the mason's level is used as a straightedge to assure correct alignment of the blocks. The blocks are carefully checked with the level, brought to proper grade, and made plumb by tapping with the trowel handle.

The first course of concrete masonry should be laid carefully so it's properly aligned, leveled, and plumbed, and so that succeeding courses will be straight and true.

Laying up the corners

After the first course is laid, mortar is applied only to the horizontal faces of the block. Mortar for the vertical joints may be applied to the vertical faces of the block to be placed, to the previously laid block, or to both to ensure well-filled joints.

The corners of the wall are built first, usually four or five courses higher than the wall's center. As each course is laid at the corner, it's checked with a level for alignment, for level, and for plumb. Each block is carefully checked with a level or straightedge so the faces of the block are all in the same plane to ensure true, straight walls.

A course pole is handy to have. It's simply a board with markings 8 inches apart, designed to provide an accurate method of determining the top level of the masonry for each course.

Laying blocks between corners

When filling in the wall between the corners, a mason's line is stretched from corner to corner for each course. The top outside edge of each block is laid to this line. Tip the block slightly toward you so you can see the edge of the course below.

To ensure a good bond, do not spread mortar too far ahead or it will stiffen and lose its plasticity. As each block is laid, cut off excess mortar extruding from the joints with the trowel and throw it back on the mortarboard to be reworked into the fresh mortar. Dead mortar that has been picked up from the scaffold or from the floor should not be used.

When installing the closure block, butter all edges of the opening and all four vertical edges with mortar. Carefully lower the block into place. If any of the mortar falls out, leaving an open joint, remove the block and repeat the procedure.

Tooling

Weathertight joints and the neat appearance of concrete block walls depend on proper tooling. The mortar joints should be tooled after a section of the wall has been laid and the mortar has become "thumbprint" hard. Tooling compacts the mortar and forces it tightly against the masonry on each side of the joint.

All joints should be tooled concave or V-shaped (FIG. 9-8). Horizontal joints should be tooled first, followed by striking the vertical joints with a small S-shaped jointer. Mortar burrs remaining after tooling is completed should be trimmed off with a trowel flush with the face of the wall or removed by rubbing with a burlap bag.

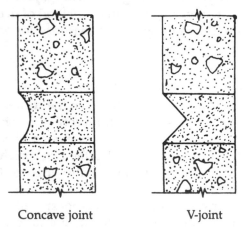

Concave joint   V-joint

Fig. 9-8 Tooled mortar joints.

Control joints

Control joints are continuous vertical joints built into concrete masonry walls and fences to control cracking resulting from unusual stress. The joints are intended to permit slight wall movement without cracking. Control joints

should be laid up in mortar just as any other joint. Full- and half-length blocks are used to form a continuous vertical joint.

Intersecting bearing walls

Intersecting concrete load-block bearing walls should not be tied together in a masonry bond except at the corners. Instead, one wall should terminate at the face of the other wall with a control joint at the point. Bearing walls are tied together with a metal tie bar $1/4 \times 1/4 \times 28$ inches, with 2-inch right-angle bends on each end. Tie bars are spaced not over 4 feet apart vertically. Bends at the ends of the tie bars are embedded in cores filled with mortar or concrete. Pieces of metal lathe placed under the cores support the concrete or mortar filling.

Building brick walls and fences

Brick masonry uses units small enough to be placed with one hand, which are laid in courses with mortar joints. Bricks are kiln-baked from various clay and shale mixtures. The chemical and physical characteristics of the ingredients vary considerably; these and the kiln temperatures combine to produce brick in many colors and hardnesses.

Bricks

Standard bricks manufactured in the United States are $2^{1}/4 \times 3^{3}/4 \times 8$ inches. English bricks are $3 \times 4^{1}/2 \times 9$ inches. Roman bricks are $1^{1}/2 \times 4 \times 12$ inches. Norman bricks are $2^{3}/4 \times 4 \times 12$ inches. The actual dimensions vary sightly.

The bricklayer frequently cuts the brick into various sizes, shown in FIG. 9-9. They are called half or bat, three-quarter closure, quarter closure, king closure, queen closure, and split. They are used to fill in the spaces at corners and such other places where a full brick will not fit. The six surfaces of a brick are called the face, side, cull, end, and the beds (FIG. 9-10).

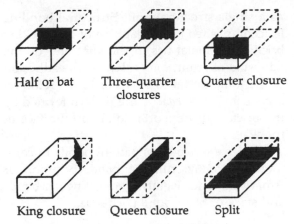

Half or bat   Three-quarter   Quarter closure
closures

King closure   Queen closure   Split

Fig. 9-9   *Ways to cut brick.*

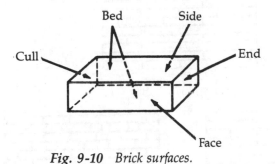

Fig. 9-10   *Brick surfaces.*

Good bricklaying depends on workmanship and efficiency. The work must be arranged in such a way that the bricklayer is continually supplied with brick and mortar. Mason's tools and equipment needed for bricklaying are the same as those for concrete block construction.

There are many types of brick. Some are different in formation and composition; others vary according to their use.

Building brick The term building brick, formerly called common brick, is applied to brick made of ordinary clays or shales and burned in kilns in the usual manner. These bricks do not have a special color or surface texture. Building brick is also known as hard and kiln-run brick. It is generally used for the backing courses in solid or cavity brick walls. The harder and more durable kinds are preferred for this purpose.

Face brick Face bricks are used in the exposed face of a wall. They are durable and look good. The most common colors of face brick are various shades of brown, red, gray, yellow, and white.

Clinker brick When bricks are over-burned in the kilns, they are called clinker brick. This type of brick is usually hard and durable and maybe irregular in shape.

Pressed brick The dry press process is used to make this brick. It has regular smooth faces, sharp edges, and perfectly square corners. Ordinarily, all press brick is used as face brick.

Glazed brick In this type of brick, one surface is glazed in white or another color. The ceramic glazing consists of mineral ingredients that fuse together in a glasslike coating during burning. It's particularly suited for walls or partitions in hospitals, dairies, laboratories, or other buildings where cleanliness and ease of cleaning is necessary. It is also sometimes used as a decorative brick for designs in outdoor walls and fences.

Firebrick This is made of a special clay that will withstand the high temperatures of fireplaces and boilers without cracking or decomposing.

Cored brick Cored bricks are made with two rows of five holes extending through their beds to reduce weight. There is no significant difference between the strength of walls constructed with cored brick and those constructed with solid brick. Resistance to moisture penetration is about the same for both types of walls. The most easily available brick that will meet your requirements should be used whether the brick is cored or solid.

European brick The strength and durability of most European clay brick, particularly English and Dutch, compares favorably with the clay brick made in the United States.

Building brick walls and fences   **119**

Sand-lime bricks Sand-lime bricks are made from a lean mixture under mechanical pressure and hardened under steam pressure. They are used extensively in Germany and are available in many parts of the United States.

Bonds

The term bond, when applied to masonry, has three different meanings: structural bond, mortar bond, and pattern bond. *Structural bond* is the method by which individual bricks are tied together to cause the entire assembly to act as a single structural unit. Structural bonding is accomplished by overlapping or interlocking bricks with metal ties in the joint and by the adhesion of grout. *Mortar bond* is the adhesion of the joint mortar to bricks or to the reinforcing steel. *Pattern bond* is the pattern formed by the brick and the mortar joints on the face of the wall.

There are five basic pattern bonds in common use today: running bond, common or American bond, Flemish bond, English bond, and stack or block bond (FIG. 9-11).

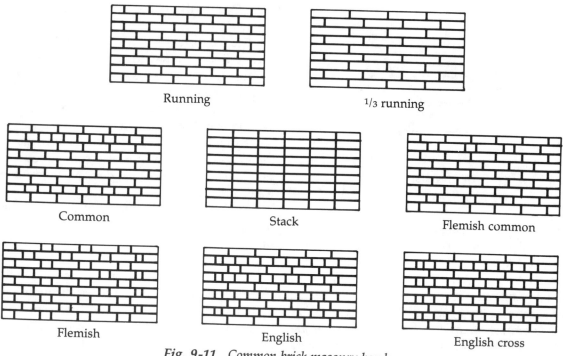

Running

⅓ running

Common

Stack

Flemish common

Flemish

English

English cross

Fig. 9-11   Common brick masonry bonds.

Brick Bonds

- **Running bond** This is the simplest of the basic pattern bonds. The running bond consists of all stretchers. Because there are no headers used in this bond, metal ties are usually used. Running bond is used largely in cavity wall construction and veneered brick walls.
- **Common or American bond** Common bond is a variation of running bond that has a course of full-length headers at regular in-

tervals. These headers provide structural bonding and pattern. Header courses usually appear at every fifth, sixth, or seventh course, depending on the structural bonding requirements.

- **Flemish bond**   Each course of brick is made up of alternate stretchers and headers. The headers in alternate courses are centered over the stretchers in the intervening courses. Where the headers are simply for visual detail, you may use half brick called blind headers.
- **English bond**   English bond is composed of alternate courses of headers and stretchers. The headers are centered on the stretchers, and the joints between stretchers in all courses line up vertically. Blind headers are used in courses that are not structural bonding courses.
- **Stack or block bond**   Stack bond is purely a pattern bond. The bricks don't overlap. All vertical joints are aligned. This pattern is usually bonded to the backing with rigid steel ties. In large wall areas and in load-bearing construction, it's best to reinforce the wall with steel pencil rods placed in the horizontal mortar joints. The vertical alignment requires dimensionally accurate units.
- **English cross or Dutch bond**   This bond is a variation of English bond, and differs only in that vertical joints between the stretchers in alternate courses do not line up vertically. These joints center on the stretchers themselves in the course above and below.

When laying bricks, a course is one of the continuous horizontal layers (or rows) of masonry that form the masonry structure when bonded together. A stretcher is a masonry unit laid flat with its longest dimension parallel to the face of the wall. A header is a masonry unit laid flat with its longest dimension perpendicular to the face of the wall. It is generally used to tie two wythes of masonry together (FIG. 9-12). A wythe is a continuous vertical 4-inch or larger section or thickness of masonry that separates flues in a chimney (FIG. 9-13).

A bull header is a rowlock brick laid with its longest dimension perpendicular to the face of the wall. A bull stretcher is a rowlock brick laid with its longest dimension parallel to the face of the wall. A soldier is a brick laid on its end so that its longest dimension is parallel to the vertical axis of the face of the wall.

Bricklaying

The trowel should be held firmly with the thumb resting on top of the handle and not encircling it (FIG. 9-14).

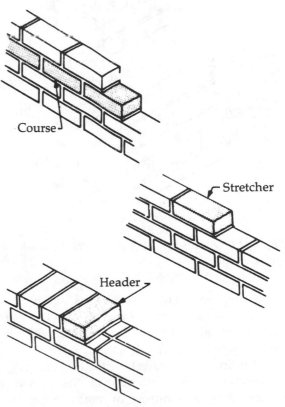

Fig. 9-12   A course, a stretcher, and a header.

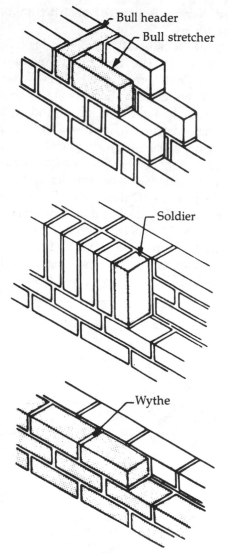

Fig. 9-14   *Correct way to hold a trowel.*

Fig. 9-13   *A bull header, a bull stretcher, a soldier, and a wythe.*

If you are right-handed, pick up mortar with the left edge of the trowel from the outside of the pile. Pick up the correct amount to spread over one to five bricks.

Holding the trowel with its left edge directly over the centerline of the previous course, drop a windrow of mortar along the wall until the trowel is empty. Return remain-

ing mortar to the board. Work from left to right along the wall if you are right-handed. Cut off excess mortar with the trowel edge and throw it back on the mortarboard.

With the mortar spread about 1 inch thick for the bed joint, make a shallow furrow down the center, then push the brick into the mortar. If the furrow is too deep, there will be a gap left between the mortar and the brick bedded in the mortar. This gap will reduce the resistance of the wall to water penetration.

The mortar for a bed joint should not be spread out too far in advance; a distance of four or five bricks is advisable. Mortar that has been spread out too far will dry out, resulting in a poor bond. The mortar must be soft and plastic so the brick can be easily bedded in it.

After the bed joint mortar has been spread, place as much mortar on the end of the brick as will stick. Then push the brick into place so excess mortar squeezes out at the head joint and at the sides of the wall (FIG. 9-15). The head joint must be completely filled with mortar, which must be done by placing plenty of mortar on the end of the brick. After the brick is bedded, excess mortar is cut off and used for the next end joint. Surplus mortar should be thrown to the back of the mortarboard for

Fig. 9-15   Laying a brick.

Step 1

retempering, if necessary. The proper position of the brick is determined by the use of a cord.

Bricks are inserted in a space left in a wall as shown in FIG. 9-16. A thick bed of mortar is spread (step 1). The brick is shoved into this deep bed of mortar (step 2) until it squeezes out at the top of the joint at the face tier and at the header joint (step 3), so that the joints are full of mortar at every point.

Cross joints in header courses must be completely filled with mortar. The mortar for the bed joint should be spread several brick widths in advance. Then mortar is spread over the entire side of the header brick before it is placed in the wall. The brick is then shoved into place so that mortar is forced out at the top of the joint, and the excess mortar is cut off.

Figure 9-17 shows the method of laying a closure brick in a header course. Before laying the closure brick, plenty of mortar should be placed on the sides of the brick already in place (step 1). Mortar should also be spread on both sides of the closure brick to a thickness of about 1 inch (step 2). The closure brick should then be laid in position without disturbing the brick already in place (step 3).

Before laying the closure brick in stretcher courses, the ends of the brick on each side of the opening to be filled should be covered well

Step 2

Step 3

Fig. 9-16   Laying inside brick.

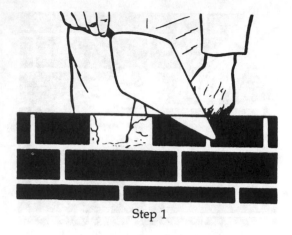

Step 1

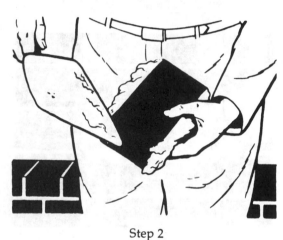

Step 2

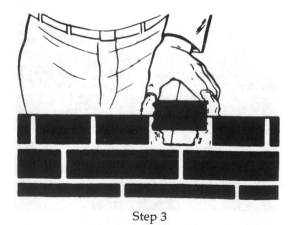

Step 3

Fig. 9-17 *Making closure joints in header courses.*

with mortar. Plenty of mortar should then be thrown on both ends of the closure brick.

There is no hard and fast rule regarding the thickness of the mortar joint. Brick that is irregular in shape might require mortar joints up to $1/2$ inch thick. All brick irregularities are taken up in the mortar joint. Mortar joints $1/4$ inch thick are the strongest. They should be used only with regularly shaped bricks.

Slushed joints are those made by depositing the mortar on the head joints so the mortar will run down between the bricks to form a solid joint. This isn't good practice. Even when the space between the brick is completely filled, there's no way to compact the mortar against the faces of the brick and poor bond results.

Cutting brick

If a brick is to be cut to an exact line, the bolster or brick side of the cutting edge should face the part of the brick to be saved and also face the bricklayer. One blow of the hammer on the brick set should be enough to break the brick. Extremely hard brick will need to be cut roughly with a hammer head so there is enough brick left to cut accurately with the brick set (FIG. 9-18).

For normal cutting work, such as for making closures and bats required around openings in walls and for the completion of corners, the brick hammer should be used. The first step is to cut a line all the way around the brick with light blows of the hammer head. When the line is complete, a sharp blow to one side of the cutting line will split the brick at the cutting line. Rough places are trimmed using the blade of the hammer (FIG. 9-19). The brick can be held in the hand while being cut.

Joint finishes

Exterior surfaces of mortar joints are finished to make the brickwork more waterproof and to

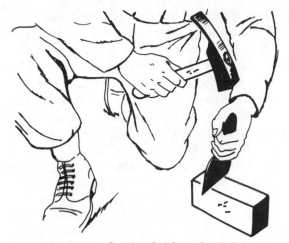

Fig. 9-18 Cutting brick with a bolster.

Striking brick to one
side of cutting line

Trimming rough spots

Fig. 9-19 Cutting brick with a hammer.

improve appearance. There are several kinds of joint finishes (FIG. 9-20). The more important types are discussed below. When joints are cut flush with the brick and not finished, cracks

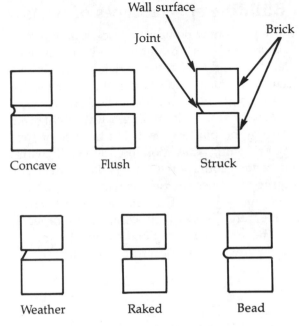

Fig. 9-20 Joint finishes.

are immediately apparent between the brick and the mortar. Although not deep, they are undesirable and can be eliminated by finishing or tooling the joint. In every case the mortar joint should be finished before the mortar is hardened to any appreciable extent. The jointing tool is shown in FIG. 9-4).

Concave joint The best weathertight joint is the concave joint. This joint is made with a special tool after the excess mortar has been removed with the trowel. The tool should be slightly larger than the joint. Use force to press the mortar right against the brick on both sides of the mortar joint.

Flush joint The flush joint is made by keeping the trowel almost parallel to the face of the wall while drawing the point of the trowel along the joint.

Weather joint A weather joint sheds water more easily from the surface of the wall. It is formed by pushing downward on the mortar with the top edge of the trowel.

Building special types of walls

Many walls may be built of brick. Solid 8- and 12-inch walls in common bond are usually used for solid wall construction in the United States. The most important of the hollow walls are the cavity wall and the rowlock wall.

Cavity walls Providing a watertight wall that may be plastered without the use of furring or lathing, they look like solid walls without header courses (FIG. 9-21). No headers are required because the two tiers of brick are held together by metal ties installed every sixth course, and on 24-inch centers. To prevent waterflow to the inside tier, ties must be angled in a downward direction from the inside tier to the outside tier.

bottom of the cavity is above ground level. It is drained by weep holes placed in the vertical joints between two bricks in the first course of the outer tier. These holes may be formed by leaving the mortar out of some vertical joints in the first course. The holes should be spaced at about 24-inch intervals. The air space also gives the wall better heat and sound insulation properties.

Rowlock-back walls One type of rowlock wall is shown in FIG.9-22. The face tier of this wall has the same appearance as a common bond wall with a full header course every seventh course. The backing tier is laid with the brick on edge. The face tier and backing tier are tied together by a header course as shown. A 2-inch space is provided between the two tiers of brick, as for a cavity wall.

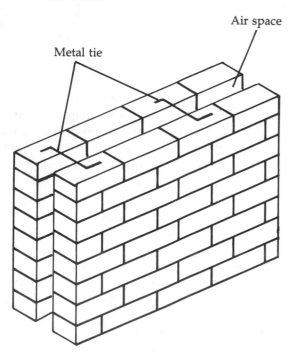

Fig. 9-21   Details for a cavity wall.

The 2-inch cavity between the two brick tiers provides a space down which water that penetrates the outside tier may flow without passing through to the inside of the wall. The

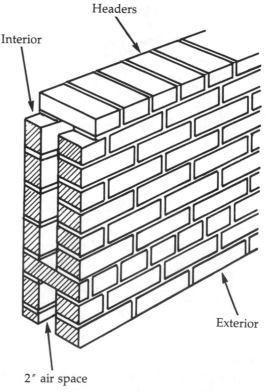

Fig. 9-22   Details of a rowlock-back wall.

An all-rowlock wall is constructed with brick in the face and backing tier, both laid on edge. The header course would be installed at every fourth course: three rowlock courses to every header course.

A rowlock wall is not as watertight as the cavity wall. Water is able to follow any crack present in the header course and pass through the wall to the outside surface.

Partition walls Partition walls that carry very little load can be made using one tier of brick only. This produces a wall 4 inches thick. A wall of this thickness is laid up without headers.

Bricks are laid in partition walls according to the procedure given earlier for making bed joints, head joints, cross joints, and closures. The line is used the same as for a common bond wall. Corner leads for these walls are erected first. The wall between is built up afterward.

Building brick arches

A brick arch can be an attractive addition to a garden gate opening. It can often be constructed by the patient novice bricklayer.

A brick arch can support a heavy load if properly constructed. The ability to support loads is derived primarily from its curved shape. Several arch shapes can be used; the circular and elliptical shapes are the most common (FIGS. 9-23 and 9-24). The width of the mor-

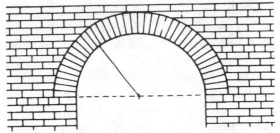
Fig. 9-24   Circular arch.

tar joint is less at the bottom of the brick than it is at the top, and it should not be thinner than 1/4 inch at any point. Arches made of brick must be constructed with full mortar joints. As laying progresses, make sure the arch doesn't bulge out of position.

A brick arch is constructed on a temporary support that is left in position until the mortar is set. The temporary support is made of wood (FIG. 9-25). For arches up to 6 feet in span, 3/4-inch plywood should be used for temporary supports. Two pieces cut to the proper curved shape are made and nailed to 2×4s placed between them. This will provide a wide enough surface to support the brick adequately. The temporary support should be held in position with wedges that can be driven out when the mortar is hardened enough for the arch to be self-supporting.

Fig. 9-25   Use a template in arch construction.

Construction of an arch is begun at its two ends or abutments. The brick is laid from each end toward the center or crown. The key or middle brick is the last to be placed. There

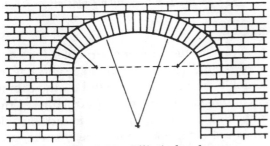
Fig. 9-23   Elliptical arch.

should be an odd number of bricks in order for the key or middle brick to come at the arch's center. The arch should be laid out in such a way that no brick need be cut.

The best way to determine the number of bricks required for an arch is to lay a temporary support on its side on level ground and set brick around it. Adjust the spacing until the key brick comes at the exact center of the arch. When this has been done, the position of the brick can be marked on the temporary support to be used as a guide when the arch is actually built.

Building stone walls

Stone walls and fences make a decorative addition to most yards. Many do-it-yourselfers shy away from stone masonry because it looks complicated. It isn't.

There are two basic types of stone walls you can build. Either can be laid up with or without mortar. If strength and stability are desired, mortar should be used.

Random rubble is the crudest of all types of stonework. One doesn't lay the stone in courses (FIG. 9-26). Each layer must contain bonding stones that extend through the wall (FIG. 9-27). This produces a wall that is well tied together. The bed joints should be horizontal for stability, but the "builds" or head joints may run in any direction.

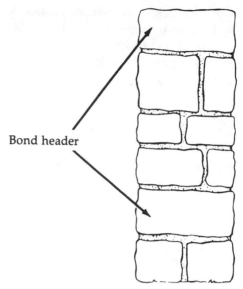

Bond header

Fig. 9-27 Rubble stone masonry wall showing bonding stone.

Coursed rubble is assembled of roughly squared stones in such a manner as to produce approximately continuous horizontal bed joints (FIG. 9-28).

Fig. 9-28 Coursed rubble masonry.

Stone

The stone for use in random rubble stone masonry should be strong, durable, and cheap. Durability and strength depend on the chemical composition and physical structure of the stone. Some more commonly found suitable stones are limestone, sandstone, granite, and slate. Unsquared stones obtained from nearby ledges or quarries and fieldstones may be

Fig. 9-26 Random rubble masonry.

used. The size of the stone should not be so large that two men cannot easily handle it. A variety of sizes is necessary to avoid using lots of mortar.

Mortar

The mortar for use in random rubble masonry may be composed of Portland cement and sand in the proportions of 1 part cement to 3 parts sand by volume. Such mortar shrinks excessively and does not work well with the trowel. A better mortar to use is Portland cement/lime mortar as suggested earlier in this chapter. Mortar made with ordinary Portland cement will stain most types of stone. If staining must be prevented, nonstaining white Portland cement should be used instead. Lime doesn't usually stain the stone.

Laying rubble stone masonry

Workmanship in laying stone masonry affects the economy, durability, and strength of the wall more than any other factor. Here are the basic rules for laying rubble stone masonry.

- Each stone should be laid on its broadest face.
- If appearance is to be considered, the larger stones should be placed in the lower courses. The size of the stones should gradually diminish toward the top of the wall.
- Porous stones should be moistened before being placed in mortar to prevent the stone from absorbing water from the mortar, thereby weakening the bond between the stone and the mortar.
- The spaces between adjoining stones should be as small as practical. These spaces should be completely filled with mortar and smaller stones.

- If you must remove a stone after it has been placed on the mortar bed, it should be lifted clear and reset.
- The footing is larger than the wall itself. The largest stones should be used in it to give the greatest strength and lessen the danger of unequal settlement. The footing stones should be as long as the footing is wide, if possible. The footing stones should be laid in a mortar bed about 2 inches deep. Fill all space between the stones with mortar and smaller stones.
- The thickness of the bed joint will vary depending on the stone used. When making the bed joint, spread enough mortar on the stone below the one being placed to fill the space between the two stones completely. Take care not to spread the mortar too far ahead of stone-laying.
- Bond stones should occur at least once in every 6 to 10 feet of wall. These stones pass all the way through the wall (FIG. 9-27). Each head joint should be offset from adjacent head joints above and below it as much as possible (FIG. 9-26) to bond the wall together and make it stronger.
- If the wall need not be exactly plumb and true to line, the level and line will not be used; the wall can be laid by eye. Frequent sighting is necessary. If the wall must be exactly plumb and erected to line, corner posts of wood should be erected to act as corner leads. The stone is laid with a line. No particular attention must be paid to laying the stone in level courses. Some parts of the stone will be farther away from the line than other parts.

10

Other fence materials

Fencing materials are only limited by the fence builder's imagination. Successful barriers have been built from lumber, logs, twigs, living plants, clay, adobe, stones, concrete, bricks, wire, glass, plastic, iron, steel, aluminum, tin cans, bottles, railroad ties, wagon wheels, canvas, and hundreds of other natural and man-made materials (FIGS. 10-1 and 10-2).

Solid panel fences

One of the simplest and least expensive fences or screens to erect is the solid panel fence. The solid panel fence goes up quickly, and there are many materials and textures from which to choose. The panels make a good display surface, and ensure complete privacy.

The solid panel fence or screen has a few drawbacks: The panels need strong structural support, especially in windy areas. A long panel fence seems confining. And some of the materials will need periodic painting or treatment to prevent weathering.

Plywood

Softwood plywood is one of the most versatile building materials available. Plywood is a flat panel made of a number of thin sheets of wood (veneer) glued under pressure. The grain of each sheet is perpendicular to the grain of the adjacent sheets. This cross bonding produces great strength in both directions, and the glue line forms a bond stronger than the wood itself.

Plywood comes in many species and thicknesses. The most common size is 4×8 feet and from 1/4 to 3/4 inch thick. Plywood comes in interior and exterior grades. More of the lower veneer grades are permitted in the interior type, and the interior glue does not have to be waterproof. Specify only exterior grade plywood for your fence.

Plywood is available in several appearance grades (A, B, C, and D). The veneer used for the face of each panel determines the grade of the product.

Plywood is also classified by group based

Fig. 10-1 Fences can be constructed of nearly any material, including plastic pipe and chain. Val Ramos

Fig. 10-2 Wood 4×4 posts make good fences and walls. Val Ramos

on the strength of the species used to make it. Group 1 is the strongest, made up largely of Douglas fir and southern pine plywood.

Hardboard

Hardboard is a smooth panel without knots or grain. It's almost entirely natural wood—cellulose for strength and lining for bonding power, as in the tree itself. The difference is that the fibers are rearranged to provide special properties. Hardboard is tough and dense. Under most conditions it won't crack, splinter, check, craze, or flake in outdoor environments. It's generally available in panel sizes up to 4×8 feet and in thicknesses from 1/8 to 1/4 inch.

There are three basic types of hardboard. Tempered hardboard is a manufacturing process that introduces oil into the board. The oil is permanently "set" with a heat process. This gives the board greater abrasion resistance, strength, and moisture resistance. It's used for exterior applications such as fencing. Other specially-treated hardboards are available in exterior siding patterns, both lap and panel.

Tempered hardboard comes in several textures: smooth, striated, corrugated, or perforated. Both plywood and hardboard need a solid frame of posts and rails to stand up to wind and weather. You will need to paint hardboard even more frequently than plywood. If possible, build your fence in 4×8-foot sections to get the greatest use of each sheet of hardboard.

Corrugated aluminum

Corrugated aluminum provides a bright surface that is useful for reflecting warmth into dark corners of the garden. It's also good in a patio around a barbecue. Corrugated aluminum comes in sheets 26 inches wide and 7, 8, 10, and 12 feet long. Corrugated aluminum doesn't rust, but it will corrode if allowed to touch the ground.

Fiberglass panels

Fiberglass panels are inexpensive, decorative fencing materials that are enjoying increased popularity—especially for enclosing pool areas. The panels stop foot traffic, but don't block sunlight. They are also easy to build with and maintain.

Fiberglass panels have a fiberglass core sealed between layers of polyester resin. The panels are available in many colors and designs. Because the panels are quite flexible, you'll need to build your frames—a basic wood fence frame of post and rails—smaller for extra support. Corrugated fiberglass panels can be overlapped and nailed into place with aluminum nails with neoprene washers.

Plastic screen

Plastic screen fencing consists of regular window screen sealed in translucent plastic. Plastic screen fencing diffuses images so that people within a few feet of the screen cannot see through it. Plastic screen fencing is inexpensive to install and maintain.

Install plastic screen the same as you would install porch screen. Attach it to your frame with battens or molding strips, so it can be removed easily when it's damaged or needs replacement.

Glass

There are many places in the United States where the difference between comfort and discomfort outdoors is determined by the wind, due to the windchill factor. One of the greatest windbreak fences is the glass fence, which offers a view while blocking the wind.

The way you build your glass fence will depend on the local velocity of the wind and the stability of the soil. Your frame must be substantial. Many glass windscreens are built on top of low masonry walls, or anchored to heavy concrete foundations.

Double-weight window glass or ¹/₈-inch plate glass is adequate for installations with panes 2×3 feet or smaller. Use ¹/₄-inch plate or crystal glass for larger panes. If glare is a problem, get glare-resistant glass. Always try to buy your glass in standard pane sizes in case you have to replace it someday.

Canvas

Canvas fencing offers many advantages in low wind areas. It is easy to install, is available in many colors, and can be painted. The canvas panel is installed on a basic fence frame with metal eyes and either screws or rope attaching it.

Bamboo

Bamboo can be gathered in many semiarid locations and cut into strips for fencing. Most people purchase bamboo strips already woven together with wire, and stretch them over the basic wood fence frame for the same effect. Bamboo fences are most popular around swimming pools and combined with tropical landscaping.

Open panel fences

There are many types and styles of open panel fences constructed from materials other than wood or masonry (FIG. 10-3). The most common are wrought iron, ornamental iron, and aluminum.

Wrought iron

Wrought iron fences provide security and beauty (FIGS. 10-4 and 10-5). However, they are expensive to construct and install, and they need repeated maintenance. A typical wrought iron fence may cost twice as much as a wood fence of the same length and height.

Wrought iron posts are usually 1-inch tubular steel and are set 4 feet apart in most appli-

Fig. 10-3 Unique fences can be built by combining wood and masonry. Val Ramos

Fig. 10-4 Wrought iron and masonry fence. Val Ramos

Fig. 10-5 *Wrought iron railing.*
Val Ramos

cations. The posts can be sunk 2 feet into the ground or built on floor flanges. Most wrought iron fences are simple to design, and are painted black.

Ornamental iron

Ornamental iron fences are more ornate, and include cast iron figures and scrolls. Because of the increasing costs, few ornamental iron fences are constructed today. Some are salvaged by fence builders and reinstalled at new locations (FIG. 10-6).

Aluminum

Aluminum is used in panels, tubing, caps, ornaments, siding, etc. Aluminum is replacing steel in the construction of many so-called wrought iron fences because of the lower cost and its ability to withstand weather. Aluminum can also be easier to maintain.

Fig. 10-6 *Wrought iron can be used to decorate a wood fence.* Val Ramos

Miscellaneous fencing materials

Fence builders are creative. Here are some materials that have been used to build barriers.

Railroad ties

Railroad ties are large timbers specially treated with creosote to withstand the elements and support railroad tracks. When ties are removed or replaced, the better ties are sold to wholesalers or directly to the general public for gardening and fence building (FIGS. 10-7 and 10-8).

Railroad ties are turned into short fences by simply stacking the ties in a tiered or zigzag fashion. They can be anchored to the ground by drilling a hole, driving a pipe through the

Fig. 10-7 *Used railroad ties can become the foundation of a sturdy wood fence.* Val Ramos

Fig. 10-8 *Railroad ties form a landscape barrier.* Val Ramos

hole and into the ground, and then spiking succeeding layers.

Junk

Many fences are literally made of junk: spare parts, bottles, cans, salvaged doors, and even trash. The bonding used can be a frame of chicken wire into which the junk is poured and compacted, mortor or an adobe mix. Fences and even homes in old mining towns of the West were woven together with discarded liquor bottles or bean cans from miners.

11

Gates

The gate is a very important part of any fence (FIG. 11-1). It's the functional and decorative door to your yard. The gate also shows the workmanship of your fence.

Gates allow passage in and out of the fenced area. The design and purpose of the fence somewhat dictates the design of the gate (FIG. 11-2). You can make the gate blend into the fence by using the same materials; or you can accent it, such as mixing a wrought iron gate with a masonry fence. There are dozens of possibilities.

The size of your gate will be determined by the height of the fence it serves and the amount of security you require. The gate should be on a scale with its surroundings. A low, inadequate front gate is an annoyance to adults and a temptation to children. Oversized gates may look ostentatious or institutional.

Some gates come preassembled and don't allow you much originality in design, such as gates for chain-link fences. Most gates can be designed to accent your yard and provide con-

trolled access to a fenced area (FIGS. 11-3 through 11-9).

Planning

Gates get more wear and abuse than any other part of the fence. Gates must be built solidly and fastened with top-quality, heavy-duty hardware. If a fence post isn't exactly plumb or a fence board is not quite perfect, only you may know the difference. But a few miscalculations or a little sloppy workmanship will result in a gate that doesn't open or close properly and soon must be replaced.

A good first step, particularly if the project is complex, is to make a sketch of your gate and show it to your lumber dealer. He or she can usually tell you whether your plan is feasible, how much it will cost, and whether there's some way to make the job easier by slightly modifying the design.

Before you make a sketch, however, you need to know something about gate construc-

Fig. 11-1 *No fence is complete without a gate.* Western Red Cedar Lumber Association

Fig. 11-2 *Gate design reflects the mood of the home.* Val Ramos

Fig. 11-3 *Even a minor design change will make the gate stand out from the rest of your fence.* Val Ramos

Fig. 11-4 *This gate is quite different than the surrounding fence.* Val Ramos

Fig. 11-5 *A gate can also be a simple opening in the fence.* Val Ramos

Fig. 11-6 *Your gate reflects both the fence design and the design of nearby structures.* Val Ramos

Fig. 11-7 *The vertical fence lines are broken by the horizontal lines of the gate.* Val Ramos

Fig. 11-8 *A wrought iron gate can enclose a courtyard.* Val Ramos

Fig. 11-10   *A close look at a simple wooden latch.*
Val Ramos

Fig. 11-9   A wrought iron gate can also enclose an entryway. Val Ramos

tion. There are three considerations: the latch, hinges, and the gate itself.

Latches

Sometimes you have to build the gate around the latch, unless it's a simple hasp or hook. A sliding bolt action latch may be too difficult to install on a gate with grape stake siding. Check hardware and lumber supply stores for latch ideas. Latches are commonly made of aluminum, steel or iron, and wood (FIGS. 11-10 through 11-12).

The latch must be able to take rough treatment. A flimsy latch put on with small nails or screws won't last long. If you want to keep children from opening the gate, get a latch that you can set up high or on top of the fence.

Fig. 11-11   Common metal gate handle. Val Ramos

Fig. 11-12   Simple metal latch used on many wood fences. Val Ramos

Hinges

The main reason gates fail is inadequate hinges. It's best to spend a couple extra dollars and buy heavier-duty hinges than you need for your gate (FIGS. 11-13 through 11-14).

Like latches, hinges should be considered in terms of the gate siding. It would be nearly

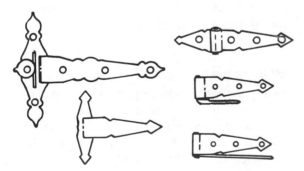

Fig. 11-13   Typical metal gate hinges. Arrowsmith

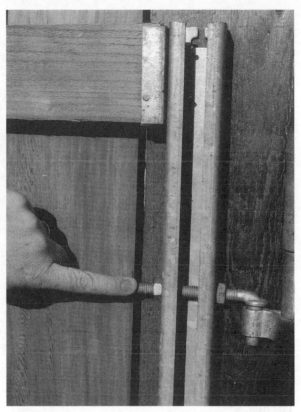

Fig. 11-14   Hinge for metal-framed wood fences. Val Ramos

impossible, for example, to mount heavy strap hinges on a gate paneled in translucent plastic. You'll probably want to buy hinges that match your latch, which may call for a revision in your gate design. When your fence is used to confine small children, self-closing hinges are a worthwhile investment. Springs in the hinge mechanism automatically close a gate that might otherwise be left ajar by visitors or delivery persons.

Here are a few hints about buying hinges for your gate:

- Lower-priced packaged hinges include screws that are too short for a heavy gate. Buy extra screws that go as far into the wood as possible without coming out the other side.

- Always use three hinges on gates more than 5 feet tall.
- Make sure your hinges have a weather-resistant coating such as cadmium, zinc, or galvanizing, unless you plan to paint them.
- Ask your building materials retailer for advice on the type of hinge you should use for your gate: butt hinge, T hinge, strap hinge, or common gate hinge.

Materials

There are many types of gate siding from which you can choose. Most wood gates have 2×4 frames covered with fencing materials. You can use lighter frames if the siding is exterior plywood or some other light material. These won't sag, but they usually need support on the flat sides to keep them from bowing and to give you a place to fasten hinges and latches.

Don't buy warped lumber. It doesn't take much of a warp to throw the whole gate out of line. Sometimes you might have to search through half a dozen pieces before you get a straight one. If you have to buy green lumber, let it dry flat outside for at least a week before you use it. Lay the green boards on blocks that let the air circulate around the wood.

Construction

Single gates run from 3 (36 inches) to 5 feet (60 inches) wide. Anything less than 3 feet wide won't be wide enough for wheelbarrows and larger outdoor furniture to pass through. Gates much wider than 5 feet need extra bracing to make sure they don't sag. Gate openings wider than 5 feet are best split into two gates: one that's commonly stationary and one that's easy to swing.

Your fence posts should be firmly embedded to withstand the gate's pull and weight. When possible, attach the hinge post to the house wall for added support. To accurately measure the opening, take your measurements at the top and bottom. If there's a considerable difference, you'll have to make the posts plumb before you can hang a gate between them.

Building the frame

The first step is to nail a temporary 1×1 stake onto the inside of the latch post. This will serve as the spacer to standardize the gap between the gate and frame and the latch post so that, once the gate is installed and the spacer is removed, the gate will swing without binding. The 1-inch nominal width of the spacer is actually about 3/4 inch.

Measure the distance between the latch post and gatepost. Hold the measuring tape as level as possible. Cut the 2×4s to that length. They will act as rails for the gate frame. Make sure you cut square corners on all frame members, because they are not always sawed square at the mill. Cut lap joints for all corners for strength. Redrill your nail and screw holes with a bit that's slightly smaller in diameter than the fasteners. Use galvanized or other treated hardware that won't corrode and discolor the face of your fence.

Installing the bracing

Brace your gate frame to prevent sagging. The most common brace is a 2×4 set diagonally from the bottom corner of the frame on the hinge post side to the top corner of the latch side (FIG. 11-15). This actually pushes up the frame from the bottom of the hinge post. You can't run a wood brace the opposite way and not have the gate sag. The amateur gate builder often has a hard time getting this brace in

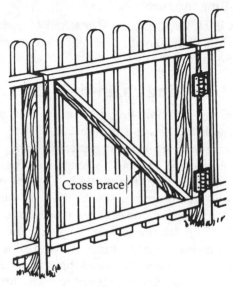

Fig. 11-15 *A cross brace.* Wolmanized pressure-treated lumber

Fig. 11-16 *Turnbuckle cross bracing.* Val Ramos

place. The solution is to hold the 2×4 in place and mark the angle with a pencil. A mistake of 1/8 inch will produce a loose-fitting brace. If the brace doesn't fit snugly, tighten it up with a wedge.

Another popular way to brace a gate is to install a turnbuckle and wire or metal rod from the top of the frame on the hinge side to the bottom on the latch side—just the opposite of the wood brace (FIG. 11-16). The turnbuckle brace pulls up the frame to the top of the hinge post. You can buy sets containing wire, a turnbuckle, and two metal angle plates that fit over the edges of the gate frame. Attach the wire to screw eyes set in the frame.

Wire or rod bracing (FIG. 11-17) has three advantages. It's easier and faster to install, easier to adjust if the gate sags, and is not as bulky or heavy as a wood brace. The cost is comparable.

Adding the siding

The gate siding can be identical to or vastly different from the siding used on your fence. A

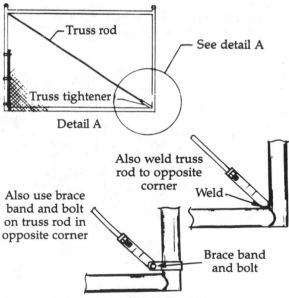

Fig. 11-17 *Typical truss rod and tightener installation.* International Fence Industry Association

solid board fence can be accented with a short picket gate or by a diagonal board gate, for example.

Lay the siding on the gate frame as it lies on the ground. If the gate requires a partial board, you might be able to widen or narrow the gaps to allow for it and reduce cutting. You can place the partial board in the center of the gate for a decorative effect. Install the siding from the hinge side of the frame. Make sure you also nail the siding into any diagonal wood bracing.

Hanging the gate

The simplest way to install a wood gate is to have someone help you hold it in place while you temporarily nail it to the gate and latch posts. Check for fit, and make sure it is level. Then install the hinges.

It's best to predrill hinge screw holes with a bit that's slightly smaller than the screw you'll be using. Use the longest screws that won't come out the other side of the wood.

Installing the latch

Each latch has a preferred method of installation. Install the female part first, then the male, for the best fit.

Installing chain-link gates

Preassembled chain-link gates are the simplest to install (FIGS. 11-18 through 11-21). After the entire fence has been completed, apply the male hinges to one of the gateposts. Position the top hinge with the pintle in a down position and the lower hinge with the pintle in an up position. This prevents the gate from being lifted off. Install the female hinges on the gate frame, insert the bolts and nuts, and slide the female hinges over the male hinges attached to the gate's post. Set the hinges to allow for the gate's full swing.

The gate should be set so that the top of the gate frame is even with the top rail. Tighten all hinges securely; this helps prevent sagging.

Position the fork latch on the frame. Install the center drop rod if required.

The butterfly latch, shown at bottom is a self-latching fitting used for self-closing gates. To make your single gate self-closing, install a butterfly latch and a self-closing hinge.

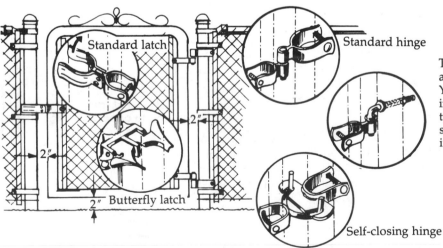

This is an illustration of an alternate type of hinge pin. You must drill a 1/2" hole in gate post to install this type pin, but it allows you some variation for adjusting the gate to the latch.

Fig. 11-18 *Hinges and latches for chain-link fencing.* Builders Fence Co., Inc.

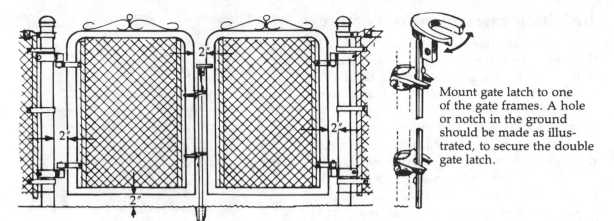

Mount gate latch to one of the gate frames. A hole or notch in the ground should be made as illustrated, to secure the double gate latch.

Fig. 11-19 *Hinges and latch for driveway double gate.* Builders Fence Co., Inc.

Fig. 11-20 *Larger gates can be installed on wheels.*
Val Ramos

Fig. 11-21 *Rails and rollers are also used for moving large gates.* Val Ramos

Installing gates on masonry fences

To install a gate on a masonry fence (FIG. 11-22), first make sure the masonry is solid and not hollow. If the masonry is hollow, fill it with concrete and let it cure before trying to hang the gate. You might be able to embed the anchors for the gate into the setting concrete.

Mark the locations of bolt holes and drill them out with a masonry drill larger than the bolt. Fill the hole with mortar and install the fastener. Let it set. Then install the metal or wooden gate as with other fences (FIGS. 11-23 and 11-24).

Fig. 11-23 *Typical metal-to-masonry installation.*
Val Ramos

Fig. 11-22 *Wrought iron gates can be installed on masonry fences.* Val Ramos

Fig. 11-24 *Gate hinge can be attached to masonry fences with an intermediate member of wood or metal.* Val Ramos

Variations

There are as many variations of gates as there are purposes for fences. Most variations are used on farms and ranches, such as in electric fences (11-25).

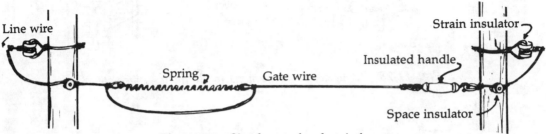

Fig. 11-25   Simple gate for electric fences.

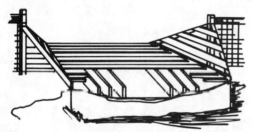

Fig. 11-26   Cattle guards allow vehicles to pass while restraining cattle.

Cattle guards

Cattle guards (FIG. 11-26) permit the passage of vehicles through the fence line while restraining livestock. A guard strong enough for heavy vehicles may be built of heavy planks set on edge, steel rails, small I-beams, or pipes 2 to 3 inches in diameter. It should be at least 8 feet wide, and the members should be spaced not more than 3 inches apart to prevent severe jolting of the vehicles as they are driven across.

If the guard is intended to restrain sheep or goats, there should be no smooth strip across its top. Sheep and goats will walk across a strip as narrow as 2 inches.

The pit beneath the cattle guard should be 12 to 18 inches deep. Use crankcase oil to control weeds and mosquitoes in the pit.

Floodgates

A floodgate may be used to restrain livestock where the fence line crosses a wide stream or gully (FIG. 11-27). Strong, well-secured end-

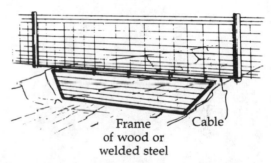

Fig. 11-27   Top hinged, wire, self-cleaning floodgate for narrow waterways.

post assemblies are required on each bank. Take precautions to prevent soil erosion around the posts. Keep floodgates free of debris to prevent the water from backing up and flooding the adjacent land.

Stiles and walk-throughs

A stile of a walk-through can easily be built where people cross a fence frequently. Figures 11-28A through 11-28C illustrate common stiles that allow pedestrians to safely climb over a short fence. Figures 11-28D and 11-28E are walk-throughs for narrow foot traffic. Stiles will turn all kinds and sizes of livestock, while a walk-through will turn only large animals.

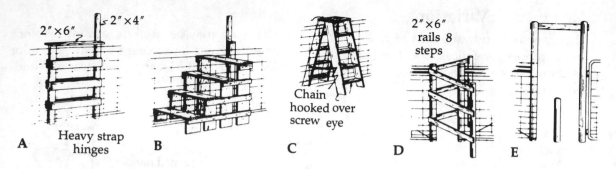

2" × 6"   2" × 4"

A   Heavy strap
        hinges

B

C   Chain
      hooked over
      screw eye

D   2" × 6"
      rails 8
      steps

E

Fig. 11-28 *Passageways for humans to eliminate some gates.*

12

Fence maintenance

Fencing is a major investment for the property owner. A wood fence built with preservative-treated posts will cost more to construct than one with non-treated posts, but the life of the fence can be extended 20 years or more. This is especially true if the fence is maintained properly. This chapter covers the preservation and the maintenance of wood, masonry, wire, and other fences (FIGS. 12-1 and 12-2).

Causes of decay in posts

Virtually all decay in wooden fence posts is caused by certain types of fungi. Fungi are forms of plant life that lack chlorophyll and are unable to produce their own food. They use food already prepared—such as that occurring in wooden fence posts.

Water is essential for decay to occur. Wood that can be maintained at a moisture content below its fiber saturation point—24 to 32 percent of the dry weight of the wood—will never rot. This is not possible with fence posts in ser-

vice because they are being constantly moistened by rain and surface water.

The amount of oxygen present in the air and soil surrounding the wood is also critical. If oxygen is too low, decay will be slowed.

The optimum conditions for growth of wood decay fungi in fence posts are within a zone a foot above and a foot below the ground-line. Here the moisture content is relatively constant, never dropping below the fiber saturation point, and sufficient oxygen is present to allow optimal growth of the fungus. It is in this zone that most decay occurs and where most wooden fence posts fail in service.

Almost any wood can be treated with a preservative to make it last longer. The sapwood of a tree is easier to penetrate with preservatives than is the heartwood. It usually retains a higher concentration of preservatives. Home treatments should be limited primarily to sapwood, although even slight penetration of preservative into heartwood posts will increase their life. Round posts, split wood, or

Fig. 12-1 *Semiannual inspection of your fence may reveal the need for minor repairs that may save major repairs later.* Val Ramos

Fig. 12-2 *Heavy winds can put stress on decay-weakened posts and topple a wooden fence.* Val Ramos

dimensional lumber can be treated equally well.

Choosing a preservative

The most generally used oil-soluble wood preservative for home and farm use is pentachorophenol, or penta. It is relatively low in cost, easy and comparatively safe to apply, and effectively prevents decay in posts. It is sold under several trade names and is available in either a dry, flaky powder or as a concentrated solution. The latter is preferred because the dust in the flakes is very irritating to mucous membranes.

The concentrated solution is usually mixed with a petroleum solvent, such as diesel oil, to give a final proportion of 5 percent penta (by weight). The 10 to 1 penta concentrate should be mixed using 1 gallon of penta to 10 gallons of oil.

Coal-tar creosote gives superior results, but its proper application requires equipment not readily available. It is an oily, brownish black, smelly liquid of indefinite composition and is obtained from the distillation of coal tar. It usually comes as a 97 to 100 percent formulation and should not be diluted. Some formulations are especially designed for open-tank soak treatments, but for most effective penetration all creosotes should be heated during the application period.

Copper naphthenate is formulated as a solution usually containing 1 to 8 percent metallic copper content. It could be diluted in mineral spirits or naphtha to a concentrate of 1 to 2 percent metallic copper content for treating fence posts.

Wood preservatives have been readily available to consumers for treatment of wood for many years. However, in 1985, the Environmental Protection Agency (EPA) proposed a ban on the retail sale of certain preservative chemicals that are creosote-, pentachlorophenol- and arsenic-based. The ban was later lifted indefinitely because of legal challenges brought against the EPA by certain industries. Therefore, check with local state officials for the current rulings on their sale use before attempting to use them.

The EPA did not propose a ban on the sale of lumber that is commercially treated by these substances or wood that has been pressure-treated by waterborne preservatives. Waterborne pressure-treated lumber can be identified by its distinctive greenish color and identifying label stamped on each board.

Preparing posts

There are several steps to preparing posts for wood fences from logs and dimensional lumber.

Peeling Remove bark from all wood for most treatment methods. Bark resists penetration by preservative solutions and favors decay and insect attack by keeping wood moist. Trees peel most easily during the spring and early summer. A barking spud, tire iron, or shovel with a flat or concave cutting edge will remove bark. A drawknife or other sharp cutting tool might be necessary to clean peel wood during the fall and winter when the bark is "tight." Remove as little sapwood as possible (FIG. 12-3).

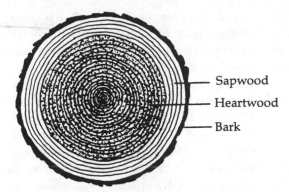

Fig. 12-3 Cross section of a typical tree showing sapwood and heartwood.

Seasoning Wood should be thoroughly air-dried before treating with oily preservatives. Green dimensional lumber doesn't absorb the preservative as well. Material to be seasoned should be loosely cross-piled on decay-free supports to permit air circulation (FIG. 12-4). Supports should be at least 18 inches high. The rate of drying can be speeded up by increasing the spacing between pieces. Although warm summer months are best for seasoning, wet wood will continue to dry slowly during winter months if stored under cover with good air circulation.

Posts and small poles can be dried in 1–3 summer months. Some woods such as lodge-

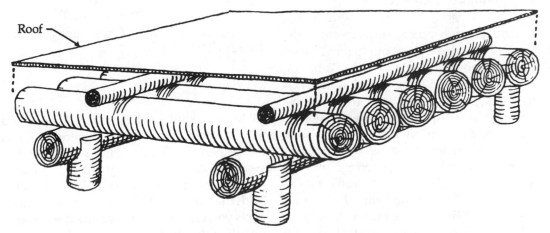

Fig. 12-4 A stack of peeled posts piled for seasoning.

pole pine, form a resinous glaze after peeling. Eliminating this surface condition might require incising, or seasoning through one winter exposed to the weather.

Incising Incisions aid penetration of preservative solution into the side grain of timbers. Many small incisions, staggered to prevent serious loss of strength, usually provide more uniform penetration than do a few large incisions. They can be made with a drill, ax, or saw, but more evenly spaced incisions can be made more quickly with an incising hammer. It should have sharp teeth capable of making incisions about 1/2 inch deep and less than 1 inch apart. An incising hammer can sometimes be rented or borrowed.

Framing All cuts or holes for fittings or fastenings should be made before treatment to prevent exposure of unprotected wood after treatment. Openings made through treated wood should be flooded with preservative.

Treating posts

The most convenient way to treat fence posts is to begin by embedding a 55-gallon drum into the soil—about a third to a half of its length. Only one drum is needed unless you're building a long fence on a farm. The top end or lid of the barrel should be removed.

Place the seasoned posts upright in the drums. Add enough preservative to cover the lower end of the drum to about ground level, and allow the posts to soak for 48 to 72 hours. Preservative may need to be added at intervals to replace that absorbed by the wood. Short soak periods are adequate for softer, easier-to-penetrate woods such as pine. Longer soak periods are needed for woods such as Douglas fir, that are more difficult to penetrate.

The drum should have a removable roof to prevent excessive contamination of the preservative mix by rain. Several inches of water in the drum may be desirable if easy-to-penetrate

woods are being treated with pentachlorophenol. The water, being heavier than the oil, sinks to the bottom of the drum. It is absorbed by the lower end of the post, thereby reducing excessive uptake and waste of the preservative by a portion of the post that very seldom decays in service.

Horizontal drums can also be used. Cut out about one-third of the circumference, lengthwise, of a 55-gallon metal drum. Cut out the ends that meet. Weld drums together, keeping a bunghole in each end for draining the preservative (FIG. 12-5). Two drums would be long enough for posts, although three or four may be welded together if long poles or lumber are to be treated. The top horizontal sections cut from the drums can be hinged to the lower portions and used as a lid to keep foreign matter out of the treating solution.

Other horizontal tanks can be made from old service station gasoline storage tanks or other suitable containers. Horizontal tanks can also be built with tongue-and-groove lumber and properly caulked.

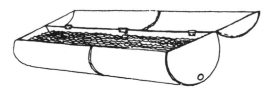

Fig. 12-5 Treatment of post using horizontal drums.

Costs

Table 12-1 includes rough estimates of the number of 6-foot posts that 50 gallons of ready-to-use penta will treat. Fifty gallons of ready-to-use penta comprise about 4.5 gallons of penta concentrate and 45 gallons of solvent. Add the costs and divide by the number of posts you can treat to determine the cost of preservative per post.

Table 12-1. Number of 6-Foot Posts Treated Per 50 Gallons of Ready-to-use Penta

Post diameter-inches	Number of posts
3	200
4	100
6	50
7	33
10	17

Creosote absorption rates will be given on the side of the creosote can. Coal-tar creosote is usually ready to use and should not be diluted.

Regardless of the preservative used, when the posts are removed from the drums, especially when the upright drum method is used, each should be inverted and placed in the preservative solution for several minutes. Tops are less subject to decay, but dipping the tops will provide added protection. After final removal, the posts should be stacked so that excess preservative solution dripping from the posts will be absorbed by the posts beneath them. The treated posts may be used immediately or may be stored until needed.

Anyone handling freshly treated wood should wear gloves and other protective clothing to prevent preservative from touching skin. Preservative that gets on the skin should be washed off at once.

Children, pets, and livestock are not normally harmed by contact with treated wood once it's dry. Although new plants may be damaged by touching or being near oil-type preservatives, plants are not likely to suffer from treated wood that has weathered for a few years unless the preservative continues to bleed from the wood.

Pressure-treated wood

While soaking wood in preservatives can be effective and extend the life of your fence, the most efficient method of preserving wood is pressure-treating (FIG. 12-6). Pressure-treated

Methods of treating wood	 Brush treatment	 Dip treatment	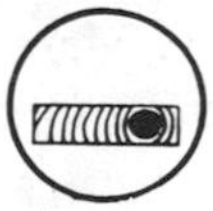 Pressure treatment
Protection	Surface with slight penetration	$1/10''$ to $1/8''$ penetration	Sapwood treated
Average amount solution required to treat 80-foot fence, made from 4×4 posts and $1'' \times 6'' \times 6'$ boards	6 gal.	23 gal.	120 gal.
Service life in ground contact	Unsatisfactory	Unsatisfactory	Long-lasting protection

Fig. 12-6 Methods of treating wood and their effectiveness.

wood has been impregnated with a preservative in a process that forces the chemicals under pressure deeply into the wood. The preservatives are locked permanently into the wood and are present in sufficient quantities to deter attack by insects and decay. The U.S. Department of Agriculture's Forest Products Laboratory has concluded that properly pressure-treated wood will last more than 50 years.

Pressure-treated lumber is available at most lumberyards and building supply centers. Most species and grades of lumber are available as pressure-treated lumber.

There are different depths of penetration and variations in the amount of preservatives injected into the wood. Two levels of treatment are available for outdoor home projects. LP-2 wood is recommended for above-ground use and definitely should not be used for portions of a fence in contact with the ground. LP-22 wood can be used in ground contact applications. LP-22 is recommended for all fences and outdoor home projects.

Pressure-treated wood can be painted or stained if dry. Many people allow the wood to weather to natural tones because it won't deteriorate.

Pressure-treated wood is recommended for fence posts, and preferred also for other wood in contact with the ground.

Finishes

Many finishes can be used to enhance your fence. Bleaches produce a weathered appearance quickly. Paints and stains are used for overall effect or for accent. Water repellent treatment is used to retain the wood's natural appearance. Table 12-2 has basic information on various paints, stains, weathering agents, and repellents.

Paints and painting White is the traditional color for fences, especially picket fences. It gives the appearance of neatness, comple-

ments floral displays, calls attention to the fence in dim light, and sets a positive boundary line. Colored fences are also popular.

For long fence life and infrequent repainting, use the best quality paints you can obtain. Apply a base coat for a superior finish and, after it dries, brush on two coats of outdoor paint. You will find the application easier if you paint the pieces before they are assembled. It's difficult to reach all parts and crevices with the brush after the fence is completed. When the fence is assembled, you can touch up hammer marks, handprints, and nailheads.

Fences that resemble house siding or those with large flat surfaces can be painted with an exterior-type paint roller. There are rollers designed to paint in V-grooved siding and for corner work, though you might have to touch up a few spots with a brush.

Your paint dealer can recommend the best finish for your particular climate. If you are planning to plant against the fence, watch for mildew deposits. You might use a mildewcide in your finish. Remember that some garden sprays will stain painted finishes. Flush the fence with water immediately if spray gets on it.

Fences in the country are often spray painted, but this method may not be appropriate in the city. Wind can carry the paint droplets some distance and deposit them on neighbor's cars and windows. Spray painting often does not give the lasting surface that a skillfully handled brush can provide. A surface that has been spray painted must be repainted more often.

Water repellents There are certain advantages to using a water repellent preservative when allowing the wood to weather. The water repellents do not alter the natural appearance of the wood, and they can be applied rapidly and easily. Water repellents modify the natural weathering process so the initial stage of darkening, which frequently occurs, is eliminated.

Table 12-2. Common Wood Finishes and Their Uses

Product	Finish to use	Instructions	Comments
Paints	Alkyd paints	Apply alkyd primer and 2 finish coats	Alkyds are quick drying, blister resistant and can be applied self-primed. Oil-base paints are not blister resistant unless applied over a zinc-free primer. Seal back of siding with water repellent.
	Oil-base paints	Use a zinc-free primer plus 2 finish coats	
	Latex paints	same as above	Product development in this field is rapid. Follow manufacturer's instructions.
Stains Solid, but somewhat soft color. Shoes wood texture, but little grain.	Heavy-body, oil-base stain	1 or 2 coats. Brush, dip or spray	Particularly suited for rough and saw-textured products.
	Semi-transparent oil base stain	2 brush applications. May be sprayed and smoothed with brush.	A natural for rough or saw-textured sidings. Gives transparent color which is durable and long lasting.
Light coloring, emphasis on wood grain show-through.	Creosote stains	1 or 2 brush applications	A durable finish. Some brands suitable for susbsequent painting after several years of weathering, if desired. Allows grain show-through.
	Semi-transparent resin stains	2 brush applications	Fast drying with good penetration and durability.
Weathering agents	Commercial bleaches	Brush 1 or 2 coats. Renew in 3 or 5 years if necessary.	Will give natural wood a weathered appearance.
Repellents	Water repellent	2 coats. Dip before installation, brush after.	Excellent for retaining the natural wood look. Pigmented or dye stain may be added.

The wood gradually changes from its original color and stabilizes at lighter shades. The water repellents also tend to minimize watermarks or surface checks on exposed wood.

Water repellents are an economical, easy-to-maintain type of treatment. In new construction the water repellent may be used as a back, end, and edge primer as well as a face treatment. It may be applied by giving the siding a 3-minute dip. If dipping is not feasible, apply the water repellent liberally with a brush to the face, back, and ends of the boards. In either event, freshly cut surfaces that develop during construction should be given a liberal brush coating. The second application of the water repellent should be made after the siding is in place.

Begin with a two-coat application for existing construction. Subsequent maintenance coats need be applied only when the wood no longer shows ability to shed water. No special surface preparation is needed prior to application, and one coat is sufficient.

The cost of the material is considered eco-

Paints, stains, or bleaches may be used over paintable water repellents without difficulty if you decide to change the exterior finish effect of the fence. Paintable water repellents contain a mildewcide.

Bleaches Use a bleach if you want a gray, long-weathered look without waiting the time necessary to achieve it through unassisted weathering. A bleach will hasten the natural color changes in the wood and will provide a more uniform appearance than occurs when the wood is untreated. It will also eliminate the initial darkening of the natural process in many woods.

Use one or two coats of wood bleach according to the manufacturer's recommendations for the original application. Reapplication of the bleaching oil is necessary only if the wood shows a tendency to darken. No surface preparation is necessary before reapplication other than washing off dirt. Because the bleaching application depends both on moisture and sunlight, it's helpful to spray the surface with water occasionally. To eliminate the possibility of streak areas developing after a rainstorm, flush the siding from top to bottom with a hose. Occasional flushing will also clean off dirt and grime.

Masonry finishes Concrete masonry walls can be painted with a special Portland cement-base paint available at most building material outlets. Follow directions on the can.

The masonry surface must be clean of oil, dirt, or any substance that could prevent the paint from adhering. Check the wall thoroughly for cracks and repair them before painting the surface.

Spray the wall with a garden hose. Make sure it's uniformly damp but not soaked. Mix your paint by adding water as recommended by the manufacturer. Make sure it's thoroughly mixed before and during application to avoid settling. Apply with a stiff brush. See that the paint gets into the pores of the concrete. Exterior concrete walls and fences should be given two coats.

Cement-base paints must cure slowly. To keep your wall's paint from drying too fast in the sun, keep the first coat moist for at least 12 hours and the second coat moist for about 48 hours.

Replacing rotten fence posts

Most fences can be repaired more easily and economically than they can be replaced. All it takes is a few tools and some know-how.

Because of the highest combination of moisture and oxygen, posts usually rot right at ground level. Preventive maintenance steps include using pressure-treated posts and crowning the posthole fill so water runs off easily and doesn't collect at the base of the post.

The easiest way to replace a rotten fence post is to add a reinforcement post next to it and cut the old one off above the rot. Use scrap lumber to prop the rotting post into place. Dig the old posthole out and remove the bad section of the post. Lay the new post beside it, pour and pack concrete for the new posthole, then attach the two posts with lag screws or carriage bolts. Remove the supports and you're back in business.

Maintaining picket fences

Picket fences are pretty to look at but a pain to maintain. If you catch a fence in time, a minor touch-up may be enough. Give healthy posts a coat of penta, especially around the base, and repaint.

If your picket fence is in rough shape, you can still save it with some work. Set up an outside work area if it's good weather, or open up the garage and clear a space if it's not. A 4×8 sheet of plywood on sawhorses makes an excellent worktable for picket fence sections. You can lay two out at a time.

Check each picket, rail, and post for rot. If the material is either dry and brittle or wet and soggy, replace it. Remove it from the line up. With any luck, your fence was built of standard dimensional lumber, and the picket design won't be too difficult to duplicate. Fancy cuts can be copied with a handsaw, radial arm saw, or saber saw as described in chapter 5.

Replace or reinforce all rotten pots (FIG. 12-7). Rails rarely rot. Use preservative on the new and old materials as needed. Apply the first coat of paint to the picket fence before installing it. Dig new postholes or pull out the casings in the old ones. Brace your fence and attach temporary supports until the concrete is poured and cured (FIGS. 12-8 and 12-9). Apply the second coat of paint to your renewed picket fence.

Fig. 12-8 A temporary support can be placed against a weak fence until repairs can be made. Val Ramos

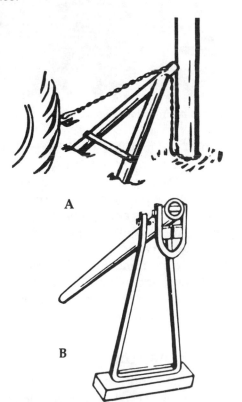

Fig. 12-7 Post pullers. (A) tractor-powered. (B) hand-operated.

Repairing masonry walls

If a brick masonry wall is properly constructed, it will require little maintenance or repair. The proper repair of old masonry can be more expensive than the complete removal and replacement of the disintegrated portion. The use of good mortar, proper finishing joints, and adequate flashing adds little to the initial cost and reduces the cost of maintenance throughout the life of the masonry.

Tuck-pointing involves cutting out all loose and disintegrated mortar to a depth of at least $1/2$ inch and replacing it with new mortar. If leaks are to be stopped, all the mortar in the

Fig. 12-9 *Temporary supports are used to lift a fallen fence into position for repair.* Val Ramos

affected area should be cut out and replaced with new mortar. Tuck-pointing is done as routine maintenance only.

To prepare the mortar joint, all dust and loose material should be removed by brush or by a water jet after the cutting has been completed. A chisel with a cutting edge about 1/2 inch wide is suitable for cutting. If water is used to clean the joints, no further wetting is required. If not, the surface of the joint must be moistened.

The mortar to be used for tuck-painting should be Portland-cement-lime, prehydrated type-S mortar, or prehydrated prepared mortar made from type II masonry cement. The prehydration of mortar greatly reduces shrinkage.

Sufficient time should be allowed for absorption of the moisture used in preparing the joint before the joint is filled with mortar. Filling the joint with mortar is called repointing and is done with a pointing trowel. The prehydrated mortar that has been prepared is packed tightly into the joint in thin layers about 1/4 inch thick and finished to a smooth concave surface with a pointing tool. The mortar is pushed into the joint with a forward motion in one direction from a starting point to reduce the possibility of air pockets forming.

Repairing gates

If your gate sags, binds, or won't latch, check the hinge post to see if it is still solid and plumb. Sometimes a wire from the hinge post to a more solid post down the line will correct the tilt. If the gate still binds, see if the hinge is pulled out slightly. When posts and hinges are in good order, try tightening the turnbuckle or wedging up the wood brace.

Sometimes a poorly latching gate is caused by a sagging gate frame. The whole gatepost may sink slightly, causing the latch bar to miss the catch. Reset the hinges or the latch. If screws and nails pull out of the wood, remove the gate and hinges, fill the holes with wood glue, and reset the hinges when the glue is dry, or change the location of the hinges using longer screws.

A wooden gate may bind in wet weather and work fine when it's dry. Plane off a little of the latch post or gate frame. You can frequently restore an old gate by simply replacing a wooden brace with a wire and turnbuckle brace.

Grounding metal fences

Many owners of metal fences should consider installing a lightning protector, especially in areas where lightning is a problem. Livestock can be killed instantly if they are near an ungrounded or improperly grounded wire fence that receives a lightning discharge. Wire fences attached to trees and buildings are most likely to receive lightning discharges, but any wire fence can be a hazard.

Properly grounded fences greatly reduce the chance of electrocution. Because lightning is so highly erratic, there will always be some danger.

All steel fence posts will ground a wire fence if they are in contact with wet or moist soil. Unless you can be sure that your posts are in contact with wet soil, you should use extra long posts set at least 5 feet in the ground or install special ground rods as recommended for wood posts.

Figure 12-10 illustrates the recommended way to ground a wire fence with wood posts. Drive the 1/2- or 3/4-inch steel rod at least 5 feet into the ground. Allow it to extend a few inches above the post. Fasten the rod to the post with the pipe straps so it touches all the wires. Ground the fence in this manner every 150 feet. Another way to ground the fence is to use an extra long steel post, set 5 feet into the ground, every 150 feet.

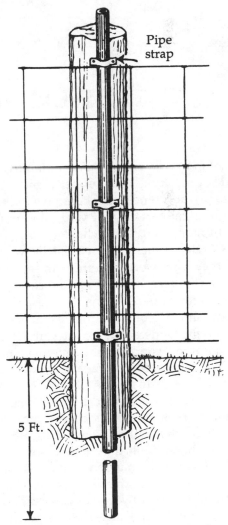

Fig. 12-10 Grounding woven wire fences.

13

Fence landscaping

Fences and walls are elements of landscaping. Besides protecting your property and increasing its privacy, fences can become a backdrop, or an integral part of your yard's design (FIGS. 13-1 through 13-9). This chapter looks at the fence's related elements within the yard and how they can work together: trees, shrubs, hedges, climbers, flowers, ground cover, rocks, and man-made decorations.

You should consider four elements when you plan the landscaping around your fence: nature, harmony, concealment, and maintenance.

Considering nature means looking at the natural elements to decide what effect they will have on the mood created by your fence. Will the fence, trees, or shrubs change the amount of sunlight that enters your yard? Will they increase shade? Will they redirect or stop the wind? How much change will they cause, and during what part of the year? Is this change a benefit or liability to your yard's intended use?

Will a tree drop leaves into the pool? Will a tall, windbreaking fence cast too much shade into your garden area? Will the shrubs next to the fence receive adequate light and water?

Harmony of purpose and of design is the main goal to be sought in landscaping. Will the ground cover blend in with your stone wall or will it detract? Are the colors of the flowers complementary to your fence and home?

Concealment applies to landscape elements that cover something else: a fence, rock, or a view. Ivy may be grown to conceal a fence. A tree could be planted to conceal a view. Make sure that concealment serves its intended purpose. It's a waste of time and money to install a quality fence then plant climbers that completely cover it.

Whether the landscape element is a fence, hedge, or ground cover, it should not require undue maintenance. Some plants, for example, can be a chore to maintain; others thrive on neglect. You must also consider soil, water, and local growing conditions.

Fig. 13-1 *A well-designed and built fence can be a beautiful addition to your landscape.* Western Wood Products Association

Fig. 13-2 *Brick fences offer security, privacy, and beauty.* Brick Institute of America

Fig. 13-3 *Fences are a popular landscaping accent.* Val Ramos

Fig. 13-4 *A split fence easily follows land contours.* Val Ramos

Fig. 13-5 *A fence can be an outdoor room divider.*
Val Ramos

Fig. 13-6 *Fences can serve as a backdrop for land-scaping.* Val Ramos

Fig. 13-8 *Rocks and shrubs highlight this masonry and wood fence.* Val Ramos

Fig. 13-7 *Landscaping and fences should reflect the mood of your home.* Val Ramos

Fig. 13-9 *Shrubs and trees are contained with a rustic fence.* Val Ramos

Fig. 13-10 *Deciduous trees are best for the south side of your home.* Val Ramos

Trees

Trees are natural barriers that add beauty and function to a fenced yard (FIGS. 13-10 and 13-11). Trees can provide effective noise control and shade.

Keep in mind the mature height and spread of the tree. Shade trees ideally should be sturdy, long-lived species that grow relatively fast and produce the size and shape desired. If yours is a one-story house on a

Fig. 13-11 *These trees were planted here to accent the vertical lines of the fence.* Val Ramos

small lot, you should plant small trees. If you have more space, plant a larger tree.

Trees for small yards

Trident maple (Acer buergerianum)
Hornbeam maple (Acer carpinifolium)
Full moon maple (Acer japonicum)
Manchurian maple (Acer nikoense)
European hornbeam (Carpinus betulus "Globosa")
American hornbeam (Carpinus caroliniana)
Eastern redbud (Cercis canadensis)
Flowering dogwood (Cornus florida)
Russian olive (Elaeagnus angustifolia)
Balkan ash (Fraxinus ornus)
Golden rain tree (Koelreuteria paniculata)
Sourwood (Oxydendrum arboreum)
Chinese elm (Ulmus parvifolia)

Trees for larger yards

European beech (Fagus sylvatica)
Sugar maple (Acer saccharum)
Littleleaf linden (Tilia cordata)
Red maple (Acer rubrum)
Northern red oak (Quercus borealis)
Tulip tree (Liriodendron tulipifera)
Pin oak (Quercus palustris)
White oak (Quercus alba)
Cucumber tree (Magnolia acuminata)

Consider the planting site and its soil, compaction, and drainage. Select only species that are hardy enough to survive summer heat and winter cold in your area. Many species are killed by early fall or late spring frosts when planted north of their adapted range. U.S. Agriculture Handbook 425, *Shade Trees for the Home*, lists the adaptive range of shade tree species. Your local garden shop or landscaper can give you information about your region.

The most frequent cause of death to newly established trees is the lack of ample water. There is a critical period following transplanting, before an adequate root system is established, during which ample water must be provided to allow maximum efficiency of these roots that are functional.

The soil around each tree should be saturated deeply but not flooded. The number of times you water will depend on rainfall and soil conditions. It might be necessary to water twice a week for the first two months following planting. Soil around the root system should be kept moist.

Even after your plants are established, you will have to water them during periods of drought. Permanent irrigation systems are recommended in arid regions.

In newly established yards it's a good idea to fertilize your plants every year until they are established. Liquid premixed fertilizers are available at garden centers. These fertilizers are available immediately to the plant, and no fertilizer residue is left to burn the plant's roots or grass. Follow the directions on the label when you apply these fertilizers.

Shrubs

Shrubs can be planted for the same reasons as trees: to define your property, reduce noise, and add beauty to your yard (FIGS. 13-12 and 13-13). Evergreen plants generally keep their leaves year-round and often make the best hedges. Semi-evergreens might lose some of their foliage during the fall and winter. Deciduous plants drop their leaves during colder months and are used where winter shade is not needed. Plant evergreen shrubs in the fall or spring and deciduous shrubs in the spring.

Fig. **13-12**   *Shrubs should not be planted too close to fences and walls.* Val Ramos

Fig. **13-13**   *Shrubs should be chosen carefully to make sure they won't grow over fences.* Val Ramos

Evergreen shrubs

Bog rosemary (Andromeda polifolia)
Aucuba (Aucuba japonica)
Korean boxwood (Boxus microphylla koreana)
Bottlebrush (Callistemon citrinus)
Natal plum (Carissa grandiflora)
New Jersey tea (Ceanothus americanus)
Blue blossom (Ceanothus thyrisflorous)
Heather (Erica canaliculata)
Japanese aralia (Fatsia japonica)
Cape jasmine (Gardenia jasminoides)
Veitch wintergreen (Gaulteheria veitchiana)
Japanese holly (Ilex crenata)

Common juniper (Juniperus communis)
Mountain laurel (Kalmia latifolia)
Sweet bay (Laurus noblis)
Oleander (Nerium oleander)
Chinese photinia (Photinia Serrulata)
Japanese andromeda (Pieris japonica)
Japanese pittosporum (Pittosporum tobira)
Yeddo hawthorn (Raphiolepis umbrellata)
Japanese skimmia (Skimmia japonica)
Athel tree (Tamarix aphylla)
Canada yew (Taxus canadensis)

Semi-evergreen shrubs

Glossy abellia (Abelia grandiflora)
Spanish jasmine (Jasminum grandiflorum)

Common white jasmine (Jasminum officinale)
Creeping mahonia (Mahonia repens)

Deciduous shrubs

Shablow, service berry (Amelanchier canadensis)
Japanese barberry (Berberis thunbergii)
Butterfly bush (Buddleia davidii)
Summer sweet (Clethra alnifolia)
Cornelian cherry (Cornus mas)
Fragrant daphne (Daphne odora)
Russian olive (Elaeagnus angustifolia)
Silverberry (Elaeagnus pungens)
Winged euonymus (Euonymus alata)
Early forsythia (Forsythia ovata)
Large fothergilla (Fothergilla major)
Spring with hazel (Hamamelis vernalis)
Shrub althaea (Hibiscus syriacus)

Beauty bush (Kolkwitzia amabilis)
Amur privet (Ligustrum amurense)
Witner honeysuckle (Lonicera fragantissima)
Tatarian honeysuckle (Lonicera tatarica)
Cinquefoil (Potentilla fruticosa)
Flowering currant (Ribes sanguineum)
French pussy willow (Salix caprea)
Bridal wreath spiraea (Spiraea prunifolia)
Late lilac (Syringa villos)
Arrowwood (Vivurnum dentatum)
Wayfaring tree (Viburnum lantana)
Eurpoean cranberry bush (Viburnum opulus)
Cranberry bush (Viburnum trilobum).
Chaste tree (Vitex agnus-castus)

Vines

A climbing vine can add a sense of permanence to any fence, wall, or trellis. Vines grow quickly, are easy to care for, and can provide shade, privacy, and beauty.

Your choice of vines depends partly on the location of the barrier you want the vines to climb (FIG. 13-14). Some varieties thrive best in the direct sun, others prefer shade.

Fig. 13-14 *A lattice screen is the perfect place to plant a rose bush or ivy plants.*

Val Ramos

Sun vines

Coral vine (Antigonon leptopus)
Evergreen clematis (Clematis armandi)
Morning glory (Ipomoea purpurea)
Scarlet kadsura (Kadsura japonica)
Sweet honeysuckle (Lonicera caprifolium)
Chilean jasmine (Mandevilla suaveolens)

Passion flower (Passiflora caerulea)
Scarlet runner bean (Phaseolus coccineus)
Plumbago (Plumbago capensis)
Rambler rose (Rosa)
Japanese wisteria (Wisteria floribunda)

Partial shade vines

Five-leaf akebia (Aleboa qiomata)
Blueberry climber (Ampelopsis
    previpendunculata)
Dutchman's pipe (Aristolochia durior)
Cross vine or trumpet vine (Bignonia
    capreolata)
American bittersweet (Celastrus scandens)
Wintercreeper (Euonymus fortunei)
Creeping fig (Ficus pumila)
Carolina jasmine (Gelsemium sempervirens)

Climbing hydrangea (Hydrangea petiolaris)
White jasmine (Jasminum officinale)
Burmese honeysuckle (Lonicera
    hildebrandiana)
Hall's honeysuckle (Lonicera japonica)
Virginia creeper (Parthenocissus quinquefolia)
Kudzo vine (Pueraria thunbergiana)
Horse brier (Similax rotundifolia)
Star jasmine (Trachelospermum jasminoides)
Glory grape (Vitis coingnetiae)

Shade vines

English ivy (Hedera helix)

An *espalier* is a shrub or tree trained to grow on a trellis or fence (FIG. 13-15). The trellis can actually be a fence, wall, woven lattice trellis, or even a mound of dirt or rock. Espaliered

Plants to espalier

Japanese camellia (Camellia japonica)
Chinese rosebud (Cercis Chinensis)
Chinese quince (Chaenomeles sinensis)
Border forsythia (Forsythia intermedia
    spectabilis)

Winter jasmine (Jasminum nudiflorum)
Korean stewartia (Stewartia koreana)
Spreading English yew (Taxus baccata
    repandens)
Japanese yew (Taxus cuspidata)

Fig. 13-15 An espalier; a plant is trained to decorate a trellis.

Val Ramos

plants are also trimmed to the desired shape.

Espaliered plants can be grown in the ground or in containers placed close to the fence or support. Shoots can be trained with string tied between nails or hooks on the fence or wall. They can also be shaped by pruning.

Flowers

Fences can be emphasized or camouflaged by the beauty and color of flowers. You can tie together the color of the house and outdoor living area or separate them through the appropriate selection of perennials, annuals, and bulbs.

Perennials are long-lived, strong growers that produce richly colored flowers. Popular perennials include: aster, baby's breath, chrysanthemum, columbine, delphinium, carna-

tion, primrose, hibiscus, iris, lily of the valley, peony, sunflower, and violet.

Annuals can bring colorful blooms to your yard on little notice, especially during seasons when perennials are dormant. Common annuals include: African daisy, baby blue-eyes, California poppy, everlasting, forget-me-not, French marigold, nasturtium, petunia, snapdragon, sweet pea, and tassel flower.

Bulbs are the trumpets of spring, producing bright colors and varied designs. Common bulbs includes: crocus, dahlia, glory-of-the-snow, hyacinth, lily of the nile, narcissus, star-of-Bethlehem, tulip, and wind-flower.

Ground covers

Ground covers serve as natural carpeting for outdoor activities and help fill in the landscape with easy-maintenance beauty. Ground covers include bog-rosemary, carmel creeper, cinquefoil, creeping mahonia, dwarf rosemary, English ivy, ground holly, ground ivy, Hall's honeysuckle, ice plant, periwinkle, rock spray, Scotch heather, star jasmine, sweet fern, thyme, wild strawberry, and wintercreeper.

The most popular ground cover is grass. Grass is classified into two groups: cold-season (for areas with winter frost and snow) and subtropical (for areas with milder winters). Cold-seasons grasses include bents, blue grasses, clover, coarse fescues, fine fescues, red top, and rye grasses. Subtropical grasses include Bermuda grasses, Saint Augustine grass, and zoysia grasses.

When planting grasses or ground cover near fences, make sure the fence will not interfere with subsequent maintenance and cutting of the covers as they grow (FIGS. 13-16 and 13-17).

Fig. 13-17 *Low shrubs and ground cover should periodically be trimmed back.*

Rocks

Rocks can be used as landscaping elements in many ways (FIG. 13-18). They can be grouped to form rock gardens. Flat rocks can be buried to become the tops of walkway steps. Rocks can be the central point of a landscape design (FIG. 13-19).

A true rock garden is not a haphazard collection of rocks sprinkled with plants, but has distinctive characteristics. The principal rocks should be native to your locality and blended with natural plants.

A large rock can be set in front of a tall board fence to break the monotony of the design. You can add ground cover to accent the rock.

Sometimes you'll run across a large rock when building your fence that can be integrated into the fence's design. Go over or

Fig. 13-16 *Sometimes an ivy or other ground cover decides to take over a fence.* Val Ramos

Fig. 13-18 *Rocks can be used to build a short retaining wall for your fence.* Val Ramos

around the rock rather than remove it, as long as your fence remains within your property line.

Man-made decorations

A fence lends itself to many decorative possibilities, especially when it serves as the wall of an outdoor room. The decoration adds color, interest, and makes the fence seem more like a real wall, extending the size and function of the home. Many man-made decorations can be used to beautify your fence (FIG. 13-20).

There are some real differences between decorating indoor and outdoor areas. A picture that is just the right size for a wall in your home might look too small on a 40-foot fence. You normally sit farther away from a fence than you do an indoor wall, so your outdoor decorations should be larger.

Another consideration is the weather. Your decorative materials need to take extremes of sun, wind, rain, and temperature well. The material should be predictable and beautiful in its discoloration. Wood, copper, brass, bronze, and brick become more beautiful as they weather.

The materials available for decorating

Fig. 13-19 *Rock stream.* Val Ramos

Fig. 13-20 *Accent can be added with man-made designs, or living plants.* Val Ramos

fences and walls are limitless. They can be of wood, metal, plastic, concrete, tile, stone, clay, or other materials. Some unique decorations used on fences and walls include old farm implements, scrap metals, glass floats, clay tiles, used brick, plywood scraps, wires, cans, pottery, cast blocks, and plastics. Your imagination is your only limitation.

Lighting

One of the most dramatic decorations you can add to your fence and yard is lighting (FIGS. 13-21 and 13-22). You can use your fence as a backdrop or screen for many shadows and designs by running underground wires and setting spotlights. You can accent the wood or ma-

Fig. 13-21 *Lamp posts offer decoration and outdoor lighting.* Val Ramos

Fig. 13-22 *Floodlights help accent landscaping.*
Val Ramos

sonry texture, silhouette plants or decorations, spotlight a fountain, or even add color lighting for special effects.

Electric wiring for outside lighting must be weatherproof and in accord with the National Electrical Code and local regulatory agencies.

Incandescent lamps or fixtures are simple and inexpensive. The gooseneck fixture, a porcelain reflector fastened to a pipe curved like a gooseneck, is still in use and is mounted to the vertical side of buildings or poles.

New installations use a floodlight holder for incandescent lamps with built-in reflectors. Some completely shield the lamp, permitting the use of indoor lamps. Others shield only the lamp base, and outdoor or weatherproof lamps must be used. Although not as efficient as higher wattage lamps, incandescent lamps are used where the lamps are turned off and on frequently or where color rendition is important.

Tungsten-halogen incandescent lamps have a longer life and are used in larger wattage floodlights. Tungsten-halogen is normally a tubular lamp with electric contacts at each end, although some are available in reflector types with regular screw bases.

Fluorescent lamps can be used for outdoor lighting provided that a weatherproof fixture is used, the lamps are enclosed with a transparent cover for temperatures below 50 degrees, and special ballasts or fixtures are used for operation at below-freezing temperatures. A fluorescent lamp's light output efficiency at indoor temperatures is normally two to three times that of an incandescent. The efficiency is only slightly more than incandescent lamps for outdoor temperatures of freezing or below.

Torches burning kerosene or similar fuels are decorative and portable for occasional outdoor use in patios and gardens. For frequent use or unattended operation, camping lanterns are preferred because of convenience and safety in operation. Open torches should be kept remote from combustible materials.

Hiring a landscaper

You might decide to have some or all of your landscaping done by professionals. You could design it yourself and have a landscape contractor do the work, or have it designed by a landscape architect or designer and let him subcontract the job to a landscaper.

The cost of full landscaping is usually figured at about 10 percent of the home's value. A $75,000 home will probably need about $7,500 in landscaping to bring up the quality of the home. This figure might be on the high side depending on the size of the lot, whether the construction of a fence or masonry walls is included, and what outdoor structures are planned.

Make sure the firm landscaping your property is reputable and experienced. Ask for references. Make sure the contractor is bonded and has adequate liability insurance in case your property is damaged or any workman is hurt on the job.

Know what you're getting. A reputable landscape contractor, designer, or architect will have detailed plot drawings, artist renditions, and a list of plants, shrubs, and trees to be installed. Make sure you include in the contract when work will begin, when it will be completed, what happens if it isn't completed on time (forfeiture of partial funds), how it will be paid for, and who has final say-so. Depending on the complexity of the job and price, you might want a lawyer to look over the contract.

While no contractor likes a "sidewalk supervisor," most will work more conscientiously if they know you're nearby. Also, they might have questions you can answer that will help them do the job faster or more to your liking.

14

Decks

Few home improvements can match a wood deck for usefulness, beauty, and enhanced value to a home. Decks provide outdoor living space for entertaining, sunbathing, and dining. They provide an excellent outdoor play area for children. No advanced carpentry skills or sophisticated tools are needed to build a deck. If you can hammer a nail, saw a straight line, and read a level, building a deck should present no major problems.

Figure 14-1 illustrates a popular 12-foot × 12-foot sun deck, complete with construction details and materials list.

Planning

The location and design of your deck should be influenced by several factors. Consider, for example, the use to which you expect to put your deck. Will you use it for private sunbathing, large parties, family recreation, outdoor cooking, etc.? Consider how air currents allow the flow of gentle breezes and block out prevailing winds, and sunlight will create sun or shade. For privacy, you may want to screen certain areas and avoid street noise through landscaping. You may want to emphasize a good view or mask a poor one. You should consider safety to children and senior citizens. You will also want to consider the access to your home from the deck. Should it adjoin the kitchen, living room, or bedroom? Your terrain: elevated deck, ground level, or split level, will also make a difference (FIG. 14-2). And you may have other personal needs and preferences.

Decks can be built just inches high or elevated well above the ground (FIG. 14-3). They may be freestanding or attached to the home or other building. They can even be built in a second story above a garage, carport, or other roofed structure.

Make certain the deck does not block access to any utility or drainage lines. If you aren't sure of the location or depth of buried electric, telephone, gas, water, or sewer lines, ask your utility companies.

Keep in mind how you intend to use your deck. Will it accommodate benches, lounge

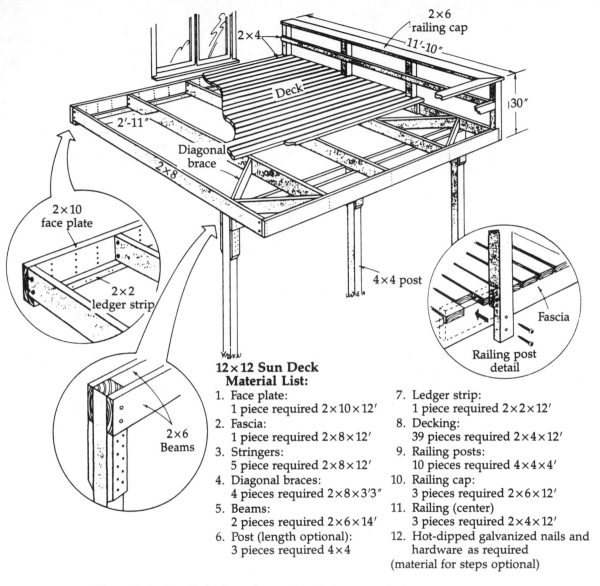

2×6 railing cap

2×4

11'-10"

Deck

30"

2'-11"

Diagonal brace

2×8

2×10 face plate

2×2 ledger strip

4×4 post

Fascia

Railing post detail

2×6 Beams

12×12 Sun Deck Material List:

1. Face plate:
   1 piece required 2×10×12'
2. Fascia:
   1 piece required 2×8×12'
3. Stringers:
   5 piece required 2×8×12'
4. Diagonal braces:
   4 pieces required 2×8×3'3"
5. Beams:
   2 pieces required 2×6×14'
6. Post (length optional):
   3 pieces required 4×4

7. Ledger strip:
   1 piece required 2×2×12'
8. Decking:
   39 pieces required 2×4×12'
9. Railing posts:
   10 pieces required 4×4×4'
10. Railing cap:
    3 pieces required 2×6×12'
11. Railing (center)
    3 pieces required 2×4×12'
12. Hot-dipped galvanized nails and
    hardware as required
    (material for steps optional)

Fig. 14-1 *Detailed plans for a 12×12-foot sun deck.* Wolmanized pressure-treated lumber

chairs, or perhaps a table for outdoor dining? How many people will be using the deck at any given time? These are elements that must be considered in planning for proper size and design.

When you've decided on the basic size, shape, and location of your deck, check local building codes. You might find there are re-strictions as to height and size within your sub-division or community. A construction permit will probably be needed, but don't apply for one until you've finalized your plans.

Basic deck design

Decks consist of six parts: footings, posts, beams, joists, decking, and railings (FIG. 14-4).

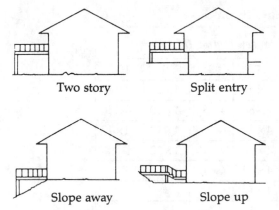

Two story   Split entry

Slope away   Slope up

Fig. 14-2 *Locating your deck.* Wolmanized pressure-treated lumber

When you plan your deck, you might consider three basic factors: function, structural stability, and appearance.

The aesthetics of your deck depends upon your choice of railing and decking. And the location of posts and beams affect the appearance of a deck.

You must choose between using many small pieces of lumber or fewer large ones for each component of your deck. A railing may be held by 2×4 posts spaced every 16 inches or closer, or you may use 4×4 posts spaced as far apart as 8 feet capped by a 2×6.

Fig. 14-3 *Planning decks over a slope.*
Wolmanized pressure-treated lumber

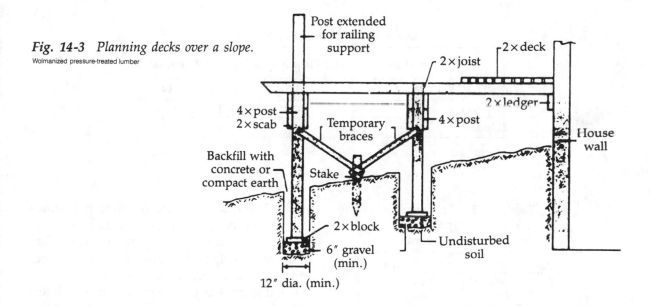

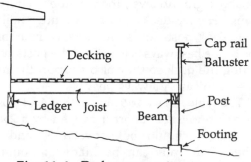

Fig. 14-4 *Deck components.* Georgia-Pacific Corp.

You'll make similar choices when you choose decking. A popular choice is 2-inch-thick lumber in widths of 4 or 6 inches. (Wider boards may present warping problems.) These can be alternated to make interesting patterns. Use pressure-treated wood and rustproof galvanized fasteners.

Tables 14-1 through 14-4 will help you design your deck, using lumber with 1200 psi (pounds per square inch) bending stress rating

Table 14-1. Minimum Beam Sizes

Length of span (ft.)	Spacing between beams (ft.)						
	4	**5**	**6**	**7**	**8**	**9**	**10**
6	4×6	4×6	4×6	4×8	4×8	4×8	4×10
7	4×8	4×8	4×8	4×8	4×8	4×10	4×10
8	4×8	4×8	4×8	4×10	4×10	4×10	4×12
9	4×8	4×8	4×10	4×10	4×10	4×12	*
10	4×8	4×10	4×10	4×12	4×12	*	*
11	4×10	4×10	4×12	4×12	*	*	*
12	4×10	4×12	4×12	4×12	*	*	*

*Beams larger than 4×12 recommended. Consult a designer for appropriate sizes.

Table 14-2. Minimum Post Sizes

Height (ft.)	Load area (sq. ft.) = beam spacing × post spacing				
	48	**72**	**96**	**120**	**144**
Up to 6	4×4	4×4	6×6	6×6	6×6
Up to 9	6×6	6×6	6×6	6×6	6×6

Vertical loads figured as concentric along post axis. No lateral loads considered.

Table 14-3. Maximum Allowable Spans for Spacing Deck Boards

Laid flat		Laid on edge
2×4	2×6	2×4
32	48	96

Table 14-4. Maximum Allowable Spans for Deck Joists

Joist size (inches)	Joist spacing (inches)		
	16	**24**	**32**
2×6	9'9"	7'11"	6'2"
2×8	12'10"	10'6"	8'1"
2×10	16'5"	13'4"	10'4"

and a live load of 24 psf (pounds per square foot). This design and construction information is for normal use. If special load conditions are anticipated or unusual circumstances exist, consult a competent designer.

Let's say that your deck will extend 8 feet from the house and be 14 feet long. If it's to be just above ground level, there's little need for a railing. Higher decks call for a sturdy railing using 4×4 posts or something comparable. One of the best ways is to extend the posts supporting the deck so they also support the railing, but this isn't always possible.

The table in FIG. 14-5 shows that 4×4 posts can be up to 6 feet apart if capped by a 2×6. Rail height should be between 30 and 40 inches. Side rails can be made of nominal 2-inch lumber. The fastening system you use

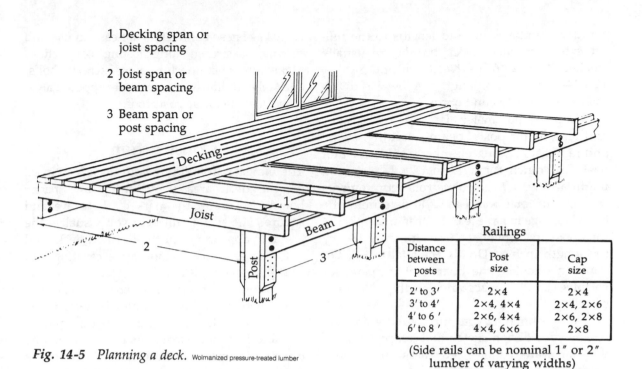

1 Decking span or joist spacing

2 Joist span or beam spacing

3 Beam span or post spacing

Railings

Distance between posts	Post size	Cap size
2' to 3'	2×4	2×4
3' to 4'	2×4, 4×4	2×4, 2×6
4' to 6 '	2×6, 4×4	2×6, 2×8
6' to 8 '	4×4, 6×6	2×8

Fig. 14-5 *Planning a deck.* Wolmanized pressure-treated lumber

(Side rails can be nominal 1" or 2" lumber of varying widths)

will depend on how rigid you want the rail to be, especially when anchoring to stub cantilevered posts.

Table 14-1 shows the appropriate beam size. The distance between the house and the beam is 8 feet. A 4×8 beam allows a span of 7 feet between posts, which is a convenient figure for a deck 14 feet long. A beam can be a single piece of the dimension specified or built up from two smaller pieces, either nailed together or placed a few inches apart on either side of a post. Note, however, that two 2×8s are not equivalent to a 4×8 in actual dimensions.

To calculate the size post you need, multiply the beam spacing (8 feet) by the post spacing (7 feet). This gives you the load area: 56 square feet. Table 14-2 shows that a 4×4 post is adequate for a load area less than 72 square feet and a post height under 6 feet.

In this example, decking will be 2×6 boards laid flat. Table 14-3 shows the safe spans for decking.

Your joists must span the 8 feet between the house and the outer beam. That can be achieved with 2×8 joists spaced 32 inches apart. The 32-inch spacing is within the maximum span of 48 inches allowable for the 2×6 decking (refer to TABLE 14-4).

Estimating materials and costs

After deciding the type, place, and size of deck you'll build, the next step is to estimate the materials you'll need. If you use a ready-made design with a materials list, this work is already done for you. If you design your own deck or vary a standard plan, you'll have to estimate material requirements. It's better to overestimate because you can always use any excess material in other projects, such as benches or planter boxes.

Draw a simple sketch of the deck—decking, rails, footings, posts, and beams. The best scale is 1/4 inch per foot. To save money, stick to standard lumber sizes and lengths to the fullest extent possible. Deck boards are usually stocked 2×4, 2×6, or 2×10-inch and 8-, 10-, 12-, 14-, and 16-foot lengths. Allow 1/4- to 1/2-inch spacing between boards.

Prepare your materials list by dimensions and lengths for posts, beams, decking, stairs, and railings. Although lumber is sold on a unit basis—so much for a 12-foot 2×4, etc.—you might also want to calculate your requirements in terms of total board feet. To determine the board footage in a piece of lumber, multiply the thickness in inches by the width in inches by the length in feet. Divide the total by 12. Or, you can calculate the board-feet measure for various standard sizes and lengths of lumber by using TABLE 14-5.

After estimating your lumber requirements, review your design sketch and compile a list of the hardware you'll need: nails, bolts, joist hangers, and other fasteners, as well as the quantity of gravel and concrete needed. It's better to overestimate so you won't have to interrupt work for a trip for additional supplies.

Some special connectors and accessories that you should be familiar with are shown in

FIG. 14-6. These connectors are easy to use and provide a strong, long lasting connection. Make sure all connectors, nails, screws, bolts, and related hardware are hot-dipped galvanized, or otherwise rustproof.

Construction

The first step in building your deck is to mark off the deck area using string and batter boards. Make sure the marked area is level and square. The string will help you visualize the size and appearance of the finished deck, and will also serve as a guide for excavating and post placement (FIG. 14-7).

To square the site with a string, first attach the string to the house and/or batter boards. Make sure it's level. Then use a felt tip marker to mark the string 3 feet from the corner in one direction and 4 feet from the corner in the other direction. When the diagonal connecting these two points is 5 feet, you have a right triangle. The angle at the corner will be 90 degrees.

The second step is to prepare the site. With a spade or sod cutter, remove sod to a depth of

Table 14-5. Lumber Scale or Board Feet Per Timber

Length of Timber	8	10	12	14	16	18	20	22	24
1×4	2²/₃	3¹/₃	4	4²/₃	5¹/₃	—	—	—	—
1×6	4	5	6	7	8	—	—	—	—
1×8	5¹/₃	6²/₃	8	9¹/₃	10²/₃	—	—	—	—
2×4	5¹/₃	6²/₃	8	9¹/₃	10²/₃	12	13¹/₃	—	—
2×6	8	10	12	14	16	18	20	—	—
2×8	10²/₃	13¹/₃	16	18²/₃	21¹/₃	24	26²/₃	—	—
2×10	13¹/₃	16²/₃	20	23¹/₃	26²/₃	30	33¹/₃	—	—
2×12	16	20	24	28	32	36	40	—	—
4×4	10²/₃	13¹/₃	16	18²/₃	21¹/₃	24	26²/₃	—	—
4×6	16	20	24	28	32	36	40	—	—
6×6	24	30	36	42	48	54	60	66	72

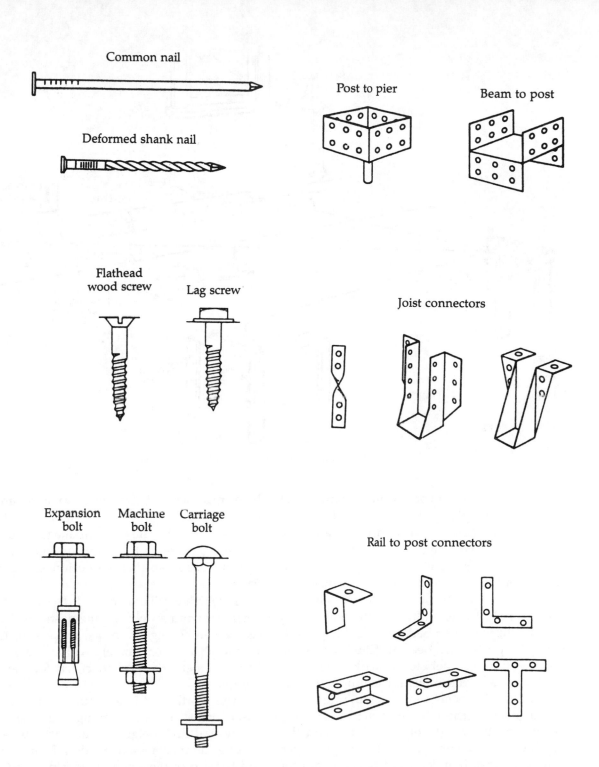

Common nail

Deformed shank nail

Post to pier

Beam to post

Flathead
wood screw

Lag screw

Joist connectors

Expansion
bolt

Machine
bolt

Carriage
bolt

Rail to post connectors

Fig. 14-6 *Accessories and connectors used in constructing decks and fences.*

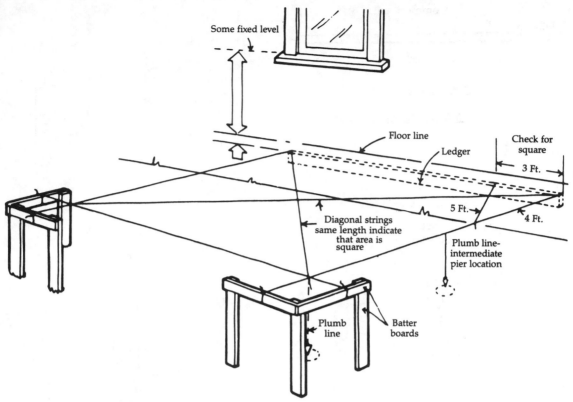

Some fixed level

Floor line

Ledger

Check for square

3 Ft.

5 Ft.

4 Ft.

Diagonal strings
same length indicate
that area is
square

Plumb line-
intermediate
pier location

Plumb
line

Batter
boards

Fig. 14-7 *How to measure and lay out your deck.* Georgia-Pacific Corp.

2 or 3 inches. Uncover an area about 2 feet larger than the planned deck. It's unlikely that grass will be able to grow in the shadow of your deck, so you might transfer the sod to a bare spot in your yard where it will be useful. To prevent weeds and unwanted vegetation from growing up through the deck, spread a sheet of polyethylene film over the area. You'll have to slit this to embed posts in the ground. After the posts have been installed, cover the sheet with gravel, pebbles, or bark chips.

Locate and dig holes for footings. In normal soil the holes should be a minimum of 24 inches deep, although the actual depth will depend on the height of the column and the depth of the frost line. Posts should go deeper than the frost line to avoid heaving during freeze and thaw cycles. In the bottom of the

holes place a 6-inch layer of gravel and tamp it firm, or pour a 3-inch concrete footing and top it with gravel to allow for drainage. You can also use a pressure-treated wood footer plate. Upright posts can then be positioned on this base.

If concrete collars are used, taper the tops downward and away from the posts for drainage. When setting the posts, make sure they are plumb and in alignment with one another. Use a carpenter's level to check for vertical alignment.

The fourth step is to secure beams to the posts (FIG. 14-8). Using a string and level, find the desired deck height on the posts. By subtracting the thickness of the deck board, joist, and beam (use the actual dimensions and not the nominal one), you'll have determined the

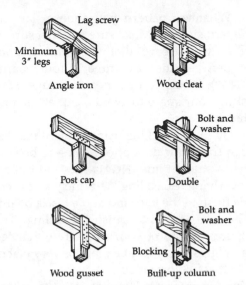

Fig. 14-8 *Six ways to attach beams to posts.* Georgia-Pacific Corp.

correct spot for the bottom side of the beam. Cut the post at that point and fasten the beam on top by one of the methods in FIG. 14-8. If the posts are also serving as railing supports, they cannot be sawed off. Beams should be fastened to their sides. Double beams equaling a single beam of their combined thickness, can be installed instead of single beam supports.

Step five involves attaching the joists to the house and beams (FIG. 14-9). Joists are attached to the house with joist hangers or supported by a ledger strip—a board secured to the house. The placement of the ledger determines the level of the deck floor, so position it at the correct height and make sure it's horizontal (FIG. 14-10).

When fastened to wood, ledgers can be held securely with lag screws. Predrill a pilot hole before driving the screws. If you have lapped siding, a strip of the siding can be inverted and used as a shim to hold the ledger perpendicular. Expansion shields and lag bolts are needed for masonry construction.

Install posts for the railing. This can be a continuation of the posts that support the

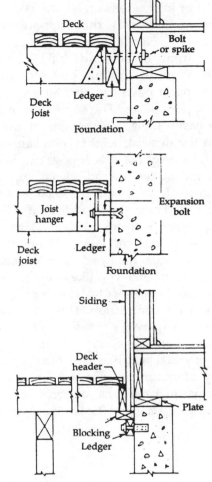

Fig. 14-9 *Various ledgers and deck components, and how ledgers are installed.* Wolmanized pressure-treated lumber

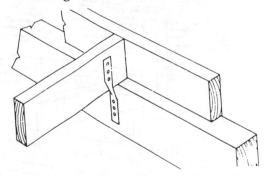

Fig. 14-10 *Attaching the deck to the ledger.* Wolmanized pressure-treated lumber

deck, or railing posts may be bolted to the outside joist or joist extension (FIG. 14-11).

When using posts, they support the deck as in FIG. 14-11. Notice how the main posts continue up from the actual deck floor level and provide a sturdy railing post. Intermittent posts or spacer posts can be used between the main support posts. The top railing member can be easily nailed to the side of the main posts at the desired height. Posts can then be cut off. The height of spacer posts can be determined and added for additional support or appearance. Railing caps of suitable size can now be added along with additional side rails.

Step seven is to install deck boards using hot-dipped galvanized coated 12-penny nails. Examine various nailheads and choose one with the appearance you like best.

Separate boards 1/4 to 1/2 inch to allow for expansion and contraction. This can be quickly done using a spacer of the desired thickness.

Make your deck surface simple, using boards of equal width set on joists, or experiment by alternating boards of different widths, making parquet patterns, diagonal or herringbone designs, or using 2×4s set on edge (FIG.

14-12). Whatever pattern you choose, lay the deck board side up. Make sure you measure as you go. If you discover that your spacing is off, adjust between the next three or four boards (FIG. 14-13). When you get near the edge, start adjusting your space to avoid a gap at the end of your deck.

If you install decking using straight planks, you can trim your deck after nailing to be sure you get a straight line (FIG. 14-14). Don't allow any overhang exceeding 1 1/2 inches, or cut boards flush to the joist and add a fascia board.

The next step is to finish the railing. The safety and beauty of your deck are enhanced by its railings. They can be plain or very elaborate (FIGS. 14-15 through 14-17).

You can integrate benches into the railing on one or all sides (FIG. 14-18). Bench seats should be at least 15 inches wide and 15 to 18 inches above the deck floor.

Privacy screens can enhance the beauty of your deck and provide privacy. They can also be used effectively under an elevated deck to create a storage facility or hide an unsightly hillside.

The final step is to install steps. Measure

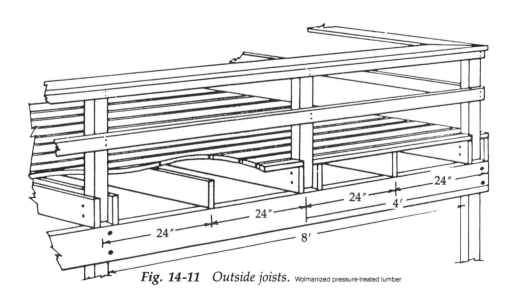

Fig. 14-11 Outside joists. Wolmanized pressure-treated lumber

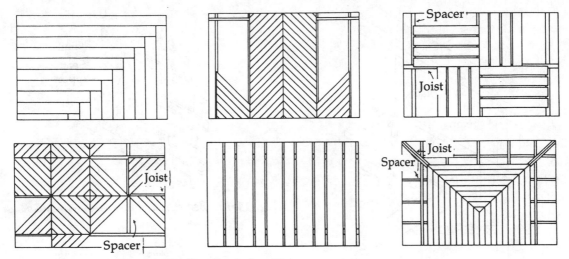

Fig. 14-12 *Popular deck patterns.* Wolmanized pressure-treated lumber

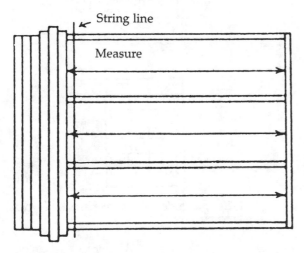

Fig. 14-13 *Measure after installing every third or fourth board to make sure your deck will be square.*
Wolmanized pressure-treated lumber

the vertical rise and decide on the best riser size for each step. This will determine the number of steps needed. Figure 14-19 shows some recommended ratios of tread length to find the overall run of the stairs. Figure 14-20 shows stair construction.

Figure 14-21 illustrates two types of stairway stringers: open, in which the treads are placed

Fig. 14-14 *Once boards are installed, lay a straightedge and trim the edge of your deck.* Wolmanized pressure-treated lumber

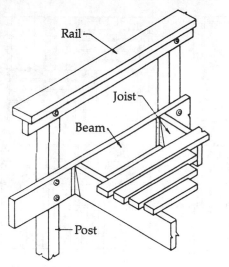

Fig. 14-15 *Typical post and railing.* Wolmanized pressure-treated lumber

Rail
Joist
Beam
Post

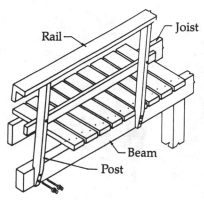

Fig. 14-16 *Slant railing.* Wolmanized pressure-treated lumber

Rail
Joist
Beam
Post

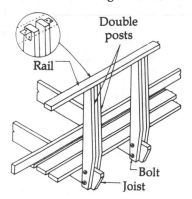

Fig. 14-17 *Double post railing.* Wolmanized pressure-treated lumber

Double posts
Rail
Bolt
Joist

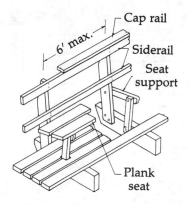

Fig. 14-18 *Bench rail plans.* Wolmanized pressure-treated lumber

Cap rail
Siderail
Seat support
6' max.
Plank seat

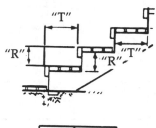

"T"
"R"
"R"
"T"

"R"	"T"
7"	11"
6"	15 1/2"
5 1/2"	16"
5"	17"
4 1/2"	18 1/2"
4"	19 1/2"

Fig. 14-19 *Suggested ratios for risers and treads.* Wolmanized pressure-treated lumber

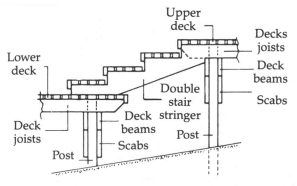

Fig. 14-20 *Stair construction for deck to deck and ground to deck.* Wolmanized pressure-treated lumber

Upper deck
Decks joists
Deck beams
Scabs
Lower deck
Double stair stringer
Deck beams
Post
Deck joists
Scabs
Post

Steps on cleats

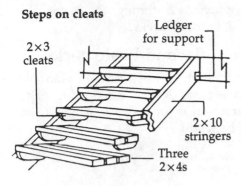

2×3 cleats

Ledger for support

2×10 stringers

Three 2×4s

Step supports sawed into stringers

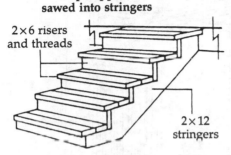

2×6 risers and threads

2×12 stringers

Fig. 14-21 Two types of stairway stringers. Wolmanized pressure-treated lumber

on sawed cuts; or closed, where concealed cleats support each tread. Figure 14-22 illustrates designing the stair stringer.

You can purchase precut steps at many lumberyards. A call ahead might eliminate some of the more difficult angle cutting you need to do.

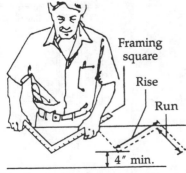

Framing square

Rise

Run

4″ min.

Fig. 14-22 Designing your stair stringer. Wolmanized pressure-treated lumber

Additional construction tips

- Always nail a thinner member to a thicker member.
- Drive nails at a slight angle toward each other for greater holding power.
- When toenailing, stagger opposing nails so they pass each other.
- Use annular- or spiral-shank nails for maximum holding power.
- To reduce splitting, drill a pilot hole about three quarters of the nail's diameter. For dense or brittle wood, grind sharpness from nails or blunt the points by striking them carefully with a hammer. Blunt nails cut through; sharp ones pry apart.
- Place nails no closer to the edge than about half the board thickness and no closer to the end than the board's thickness. When nailing closer to an edge, use predrilled holes.
- Use 12d nails on nominal 2-inch decking. Use two at each joist with 2×4s laid flat; use three for 2×6s laid flat and just one for nominal 2-inch lumber on edge.
- Use a flat washer under the head with lag screws.
- Use washers under the nut of machine bolts and just under the nut of carriage bolts.
- When sanding or sawing treated or untreated wood, avoid inhaling dust. The fine dust particles are air pollutants and could cause nose and throat irritation. Avoid getting dust or wood chips in your eyes. Pounding nails should be done cautiously; small flying particles of metal can cause serious eye damage. Ask your dealer about dust masks and eye protection devices.
- Wear gloves to help avoid splinters.
- Maintain a clean shop. Don't leave sawdust or scrap lumber lying around; they are fire and accident hazards. Pressure-

treated wood should not be burned either indoors or outdoors. Any scrap should be disposed of in a government-approved landfill or buried.

• Tops of upright structural components and joist ends should be beveled to a 30- to 45-degree angle for drainage to minimize moisture absorption.

Figures 14-23 through 14-25 are plans for several kinds of decks.

Beyond basic decks

Now that you've seen how to plan and construct a basic deck, the following pages will illustrate ideas for decks that might better fit your backyard.

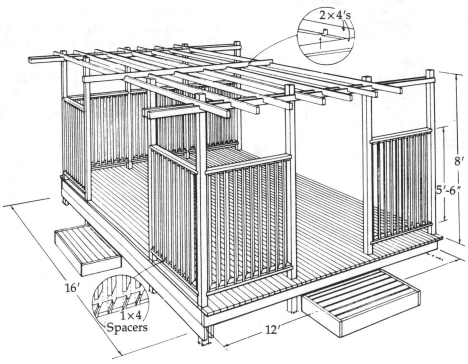

Material List

1. Main support posts: 10 pieces required. Cut to fit terrain of your deck (approx.) 10 pieces 4×4×10'
2. Materials for header boards: 3 pieces required 2×8×16'
3. Fascia boards: 2 pieces required 2×8×12'
4. Joists: 7 pieces required 2×8×12'
5. Decking: 36 pieces required 2×4×16'
6. Trellis materials: Support beams: 5 pieces required 2×4×14' Trellis boards: 7 pieces required 2×4×18'
7. Privacy screen as per your requirements.
8. Nails and accessories as required.

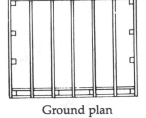

Ground plan

Fig. 14-23 *Detailed plans for 12×16-foot trellis-covered privacy deck.* Wolmanized pressure-treated lumber

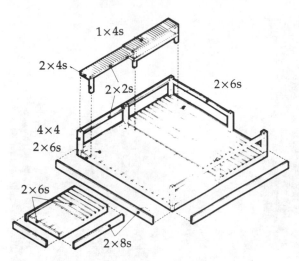

Fig. 14-24 *Floating deck sits on the ground.* Georgia-Pacific Corp.

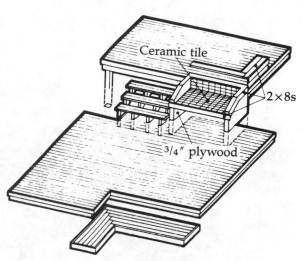

Fig. 14-25 *Deck has built-in planting table.* Georgia-Pacific Corp.

Multi-level deck Is your lot too steep for a traditional yard or too shaded for grass? Let a deck do the impossible—create a "yard."

It's a mistake to think of a deck as just a wooden patio attached to the back of a house. Decks can take any shape or size and be sited almost anywhere—overhanging a steep slope, for example, or tiered in multiple levels away from the house.

Let your needs dictate the design, as the owners of the home shown in FIGS. 14-26 through 14-28 did when they built a multi-level

Fig. 14-26 *Tri-level deck.* Wolmanized pressure-treated lumber

Fig. 14-27 Raised deck. Wolmanized pressure-treated lumber

deck that wraps around their steep property. A 16-foot-long staircase descends from an upper level deck overlook to an octagonal deck nestled in the woods below. A large sun deck at another level includes a small cactus garden platform in a sunny spot. The design complements and preserves the natural wooded setting.

Each of the decks is supported on rough-sawn 4×8 posts with pressure-treated joists and beams. Cedar decking was used for the deck surfaces.

Small two-tier deck Spacious and inviting, the two-tier deck (FIGS. 14-29 and FIG. 14-30) is a private world. It's a place to retreat, alone or with friends, for welcome relaxation.

Fig. 14-28 *Two-level step-up deck.* Wolmanized pressure-treated lumber

Fig. 14-29 Two-tier deck. <small>Georgia-Pacific Corp.</small>

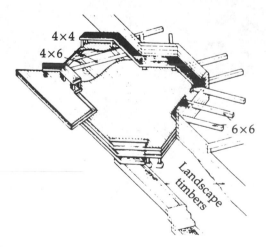

Fig. 14-30 Construction of two-tier deck. <small>Georgia-Pacific Corp.</small>

Nestled into a steeply sloping hillside, the deck system wraps around the house with walkways, retaining walls, and built-in benches forming an integral part of the design.

The angled retaining walls helped turn a problem zone into an eye-pleasing focal point. Pressure-treated 6×6s make up the 4-foot-high walls that solved erosion and drainage problems on the steep lot. Benches were built along the walls to provide extra seating. More pressure-treated 6×6s line the gravel-filled paths that lead around both sides of the house to the backyard hideaway.

Cedar 2×4 decking spans the 4×4 joists and 4×6 beams of the framing system. A

5-foot-wide upper deck with cedar benches adjoins the house, while the main deck is one step lower, giving extra dimension and a sense of depth to the landscape. Plans for a similar two-tier deck system will be covered later in this chapter.

Completing the landscape design, a pathway of pressure-treated landscape timbers links the house to lower terrain. (Smaller than railroad ties, timbers are rounded on two opposite sides.)

To make the walkway, the homeowners simply nailed the timbers to 2×4 cross-pieces, forming separate sections of the walk. These sections were then laid in position and nailed to one another. Each of the steps is made of three landscape timbers nailed together.

Poolside deck If you're lucky enough to have a backyard pool, or plan to add one to your landscape, the perfect poolside setting is an imaginatively designed deck.

Figures 14-31 through 14-33 illustrate many creative ideas worth copying—flowing free-form styles, cleverly designed built-in seating and storage, and an unusual table and benches.

The deck designed for poolside activities

Fig. 14-31 Poolside deck for entertaining. Georgia-Pacific Corp.

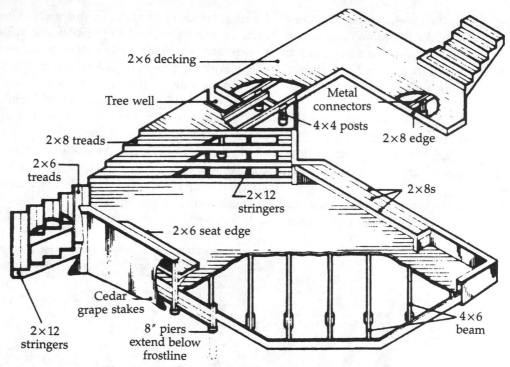

Fig. 14-32 *Construction of poolside deck.* Georgia-Pacific Corp.

2×6 decking

Tree well

Metal connectors

4×4 posts

2×8 edge

2×8 treads

2×6 treads

2×8s

2×12 stringers

2×6 seat edge

Cedar grape stakes

2×12 stringers

8″ piers extend below frostline

4×6 beam

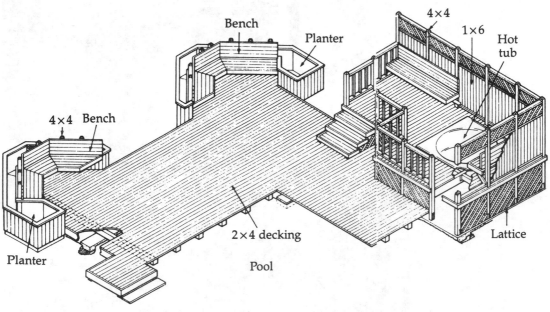

Fig. 14-33 *Pool and hot tub deck.* Georgia-Pacific Corp.

Bench

Planter

4×4

1×6

Hot tub

4×4 Bench

2×4 decking

Planter

Pool

Lattice

has a spacious stair-step pattern with room for sunbathing and entertaining. The deck and semicircular benches seem to flow around the trees and down the slope, enhancing the landscape and making good use of every square foot of space.

Built entirely of 2×4s, the curved bench is a simple project that a beginner can duplicate. The spiral-shaped table is composed of three separate parts: two quarter-circles and a smaller half-circle. Each piece can be used individually or together. A trio of benches, two semicircles and one straight, complete the set. All the pieces are made entirely of 2×4s.

Hot tub deck Nothing is quite as relaxing as a long soak in a hot tub. Figure 14-33 illustrates a raised deck perfect for the installation of a hot tub. Pressure-treated lumber is ideal for this deck because of its resistance to moisture damage caused by soil contact. Built-in benches and planters add additional function and beauty.

Tri-level deck Maybe your yard doesn't have the slope and space problems solved by the previous decks. The tri-level deck (FIGS. 14-34 and 14-35) might suit your needs better. A tri-level deck uses construction techniques that you can easily adapt to build the multi-level,

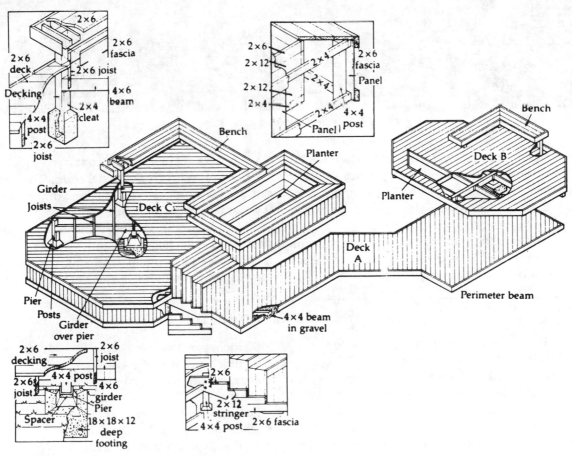

Fig. 14-34 Tri-level deck. Georgia-Pacific Corp.

Fig. 14-35 Sectionalized deck. Georgia-Pacific Corp.

two-tier, poolside, hot tub and other decks. These designs were built with pressure-treated lumber, but you can also build them with red-wood or cedar. Materials cost for this 800-square-foot deck was less than $2000.

To simplify matters, the deck construction will be referred to as deck A, deck B, and deck C, as shown in the figure.

For deck A, first design your deck 5 inches off the ground for easy installation. Then lay out the deck on the site, adjusting dimensions if necessary. Square corners.

To prepare the site, dig trenches 2 to 3 feet deep, 8 to 12 inches wide, and 3 feet on center for the 4×4 base under structure. It is necessary to allow drainage in the trenches to flow

Tri-Level Deck Materials List

- 2600 feet of 2×6-inch pressure-treated lumber
- 200 feet of 4×4-inch pressure-treated lumber
- 200 feet of 2×4-inch pressure-treated lumber
- 100 feet of 2×12-inch pressure-treated lumber
- 50 feet of 4×6-inch pressure-treated lumber
- 4 concrete piers
- 25 90-pound bags of concrete mix

- 30 inches of 1×6-inch cedar fence wood
- 1 cubic yard of pea gravel
- 4 gallon linseed-oil-based, semi-transparent stain
- 20 2×6 joist hangers
- 50 pounds 16d galvanized nails
- 5 pounds 6d galvanized nails
- 50 $3/8 \times 4$-inch coated lag bolts
- 50 $3/8$-inch coated washers

with the natural slope of the land and away from the house. Replace the soil removed by digging with gravel.

Level one pressure-treated 4×4 in the first trench. Work away from this first, leveled, 4×4. Make sure all 4×4s are not only level, but leveled with each other. Finish the framework by nailing 2×4s to the ends of the 4×4s or butted to the 4×4s. Finish leveling by knocking down the high spots with a sledge hammer.

Kill or remove grasses and weeds. Lay the 2×6 decking and nail in place. Begin with a straight board and continue with subsequent boards laid with 1/8-inch spacing between. Using a chalk line, strike the cutting line, making sure you are outside the substructure.

Trim off the decking along the edges and attach the fascia board for a finished appearance.

For deck B, lay out the deck corner points and bench posts, making sure all corners are square.

Dig postholes and set pressure-treated lumber posts in cement. Bench posts are the same, but 18 inches longer. Set the pier as indicated on the plan in an 18×18×12-inch-deep footing. Allow all cement to dry at least 12 hours.

Tack the outside perimeter beam to the posts, maintaining level all the way around. Set the 4×6 beam to the exact height as the perimeter beam and bolt into position. Tack the 2×6 joists in place, 2 feet on center, using joist hangers wherever possible. Finally, nail all joists and the perimeter beam.

At this point, follow the last four steps in the deck A instructions.

To build the planter, let the first and second joists act as the sides. Cut the two end pieces from a 2×6, one straight, the other angled. Run additional boards to the ground, if necessary, to form a box and nail all in place. While nailing the decking in place, allow every fifth board to run continuously across the planter to help maintain parallel lines, then trim the decking

around the planter edge. Fill the planter with soil.

Trim the bench posts 16 1/2 inches above the finished deck. Tack pre-cut bench brackets to the 4×4 posts, allowing room for bolting. Bolt or lag-bolt brackets to posts. Place boards on bench brackets, overlapping for miter cuts.

Draw lines where boards intersect, then cut through the top row of boards, allowing the saw blade to mark the bottom row of boards. Cut the bottom row and nail down to brackets. Mark end cuts of benches and trim them with a saw. Add fascia.

For deck C, follow the instructions for building deck B with these exceptions:

Cut beams on 45-degree angles as shown in the diagram. Beams should be nailed and/or bolted as well as fastened to the post with a cleat. Some beams require cutting a double 45-degree angle where they come together in a notch.

Place joists on top of beams rather than hung on beams.

Install skirting, following these instructions: Trim decking past the ledger joist to allow for the thickness of the skirt board. Add an additional 2×4 ledger 1 or 2 inches off the ground. Cut skirt boards to length. Nail skirt boards, maintaining equal spacing and plumb. Add fascia and bottom skirt face.

In some cases, you might want to have short stair runs in your deck. Here's how: Build deck C 22 inches higher than deck A to eliminate the need to rip lumber. Then cut stair stringers with a rise of 5 1/2 inches and a run of 17 inches from 2×2 stock. Fasten stringers to deck C posts with metal hangers at the top end, and rest them on deck A at the bottom. Lay decking for treads, bark side up, then trim flush with the stringer. Add fascia.

Follow these steps for building a planter box: Set posts as described above. Use pressure-treated lumber 2×12 boards for sides and bottom of box. Line the box with plastic before filling with a layer of gravel and planting soil. Finish edges with 2×6 decking and fascia as shown in the plan.

Planning a deck

A deck is a major element in the design of your yard. Let's see how you can easily improve your backyard landscaping with careful planning and the addition of a deck.

It's easy to rearrange furniture indoors to get the look and functional design you want. But outdoor living spaces aren't so readily transformed. Before you buy a truckload of lumber and begin laying out your new deck, take time to define what it is you really hope to achieve in your outdoor remodeling. Decide what your goals are—and the purpose for remodeling. Then investigate how a landscape plan can help you meet your needs attractively. Take into account individual preferences for sun worship or shade, open play space or secluded privacy, lavish outdoor entertaining or small family gatherings.

Also be realistic about your gardening abilities. Remember that there is no such thing as maintenance-free landscaping, but there are various degrees of maintenance. Specific landscaping recommendations are found in chapter 13.

Analyze your space

Once you've outlined your goals, analyze your existing space. Figure 14-36 will help you get started. It has many of the common flaws and assets you may find in your own yard. Consider the existing features and your preferences.

As you start your plan, note factors such as those on the sketch: direction of winter winds, direction and angle of morning and afternoon sun (who wants a deck that gets hot, late afternoon sun?), unattractive views of the neighbor's garage, a too-narrow drive from the street to garage front entrance, an unattractive view of an apartment house to the northwest of the house, the proximity of the lot line to the neighbor's drive, a direct view of the street from the living room, a lack of privacy at the rear of the house.

Some clear assets shown on this plan are a view of distant hills and an existing oak at the rear of the house with about a 10-foot-diameter shading area, including the dining and kitchen areas.

Be sure to locate underground water or power lines, the septic tank and its field on your plan.

Redrawing your yard

Start with graph paper. The 1-inch squares on graph paper are divided into smaller segments to give you 10 squares to the inch. The larger squares will represent 10 feet on the ground, the smaller squares will be equivalent to 1 foot on the ground. After you have established the lot lines and the position of your house on the graph paper, locate and accurately record the various features on the plan—trees, walks, and garages.

Take your ground measurements with a flexible 25- or 50-foot tape—one that winds up on a reel. Use a ruler when you transfer information to your plan. Indicate door and window locations on the diagram: they will help later when you're ready to design plantings near the house.

Now you're ready to inspect your land. Begin by measuring out from the corners of your house and projecting lines with stakes set at 10-foot intervals. These will be the base lines for your diagram. Next measure from the base lines at right angles, running out to your property lines.

Draw walks, drives, walls, fences and all other structures on your lot plan. Seeing their proximate relationships on a diagram will help you visualize what you'll add or change later.

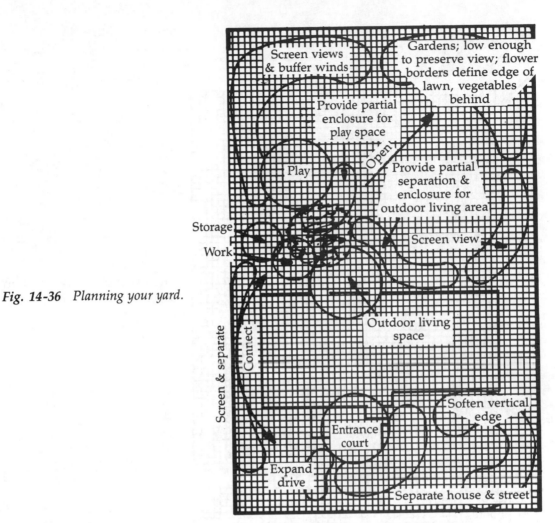

Within the figure:

Screen views & buffer winds

Gardens; low enough to preserve view; flower borders define edge of lawn, vegetables behind

Provide partial enclosure for play space

Play

Open

Provide partial separation & enclosure for outdoor living area

Screen view

Storage

Work

Screen & separate

Connect

Outdoor living space

Soften vertical edge

Entrance court

Expand drive

Separate house & street

Fig. 14-36 *Planning your yard.*

Dream on paper

Now compare FIG. 14-36 with FIG. 14-37 to see what has been changed to capitalize on the assets and minimize the defects that existed before a landscape plan was developed.

Both structural and planting changes have been indicated. Plantings in the right places have accomplished more privacy for the front of the house from the street, as well as from the neighbor's property at left. Plantings also have helped screen out the view of the neighbor's garage on the right and of the more distant apartment house to the rear. They also protect against winter winds.

Structural changes have been used to widen the drive with a parking area, to partially enclose play space, and to provide some separation and enclosure for outdoor living areas. Enclosed work and storage space at the rear has been added in a convenient spot.

The shade of the oak tree has been used effectively by putting play and outdoor living space at the rear of the house. To take advantage of the attractive view of hills, plantings

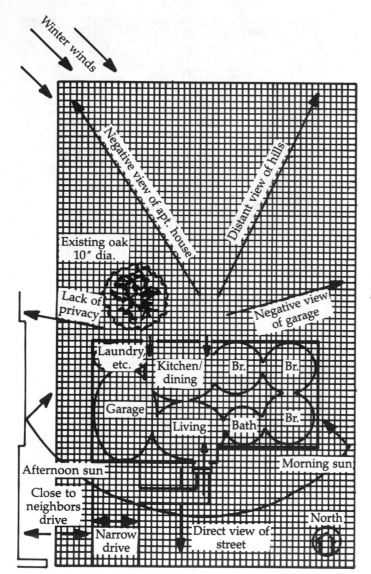

Winter winds

Negative view of apt. house

Distant view of hills

Existing oak
10″ dia.

Lack of
privacy

Negative view
of garage

Laundry,
etc.

Kitchen/
dining

Br.

Br.

Garage

Living

Bath

Br.

Afternoon sun

Morning sun

Close to
neighbors
drive

North

Narrow
drive

Direct view of
street

Fig. 14-37 *Planning can overcome many problems.*

and landscaping near the edge of the lot have been kept low.

Make tentative alterations on the plan of your existing property, using structural and plant changes to see what solutions you create.

As you plan, dream, and sketch, don't settle for the first idea that comes to mind. Look at alternatives before you decide. You'll then be certain to create a plan that will prove versatile and attractive for years to come.

Deck plans

Small patio deck

Figures 14-38 through 14-41 illustrate a small deck designed to adjoin an entry or garden doorway. It can also be a freestanding platform, or combine with a fence or retaining wall. Build it from garden grades of redwood, from cedar, or from pressure-treated lumber.

This design is, ideally, a ground-hugging

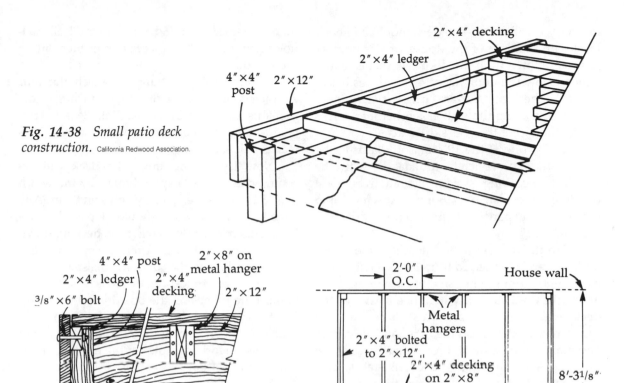

Fig. 14-38 *Small patio deck construction.* California Redwood Association.

2"×4" decking

2"×4" ledger

4"×4" post   2"×12"

Fig. 14-39 *Cross section of small patio deck.* California Redwood Association

4"×4" post

2"×4" ledger

3/8"×6" bolt

2"×8" on metal hanger

2"×4" decking

2"×12"

Fig. 14-40 *Laying decking.* California Redwood Association

2'-0" O.C.

House wall

Metal hangers

2"×4" bolted to 2"×12"

2"×4" decking on 2"×8" joists

8'-3 1/8"

10'-00"

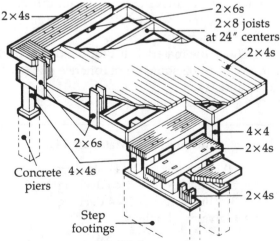

2×4s

2×6s

2×8 joists at 24" centers

2×4s

2×6s

4×4

2×4s

Concrete piers

4×4s

2×4s

Step footings

Fig. 14-41 *Small back door deck.* Georgia-Pacific Corp.

deck with the 2×12 skirting lying near enough to the ground to create a boxed-in effect.

The drawings show the use of posts to support the deck, and posts might be necessary where the ground slopes or where the deck is to meet a high doorway. However, if the floor level at the doorway is between 12 and 25 inches above the ground, and the ground is fairly level, posts can be eliminated and the skirtboards attached directly to the footings.

The first step in construction is to decide the placement and height of the deck relative to the doorway it will serve. The deck should be nearly level with the floor of the house, or else have an easy step down from the doorway: that is, either 1 inch below the doorway or 4 to 7 inches below it. With the deck surface height determined, draw a line along the wall as a benchmark. This marks the top of the rear skirtboard.

Anchor one of the 10-foot skirtboards to the house studs or concrete foundation with the simplest anchoring system permitted by local building codes—such as 6-inch lag screws into the studs or expansion bolts into holes drilled in the concrete.

With the rear skirtboard attached, the deck's outlines can be projected from it by establishing a right angle from the house and measuring 8 feet 3^{1}/$_{8}$ inches outward to where one corner of the deck will extend. Mark this corner with a wooden stake. Establish the other outside corner and mark it with a stake. Prove squareness of the projections by measuring between stakes, and between stakes and the house, then measure diagonally between the farthest corners. If these lateral measurements are equal, the corners of the deck are properly marked.

With corners and squareness established, the three footings of precast concrete should be firmly seated.

If posts are used, post lengths will vary with the unevenness of the ground. Accurate measurement of the posts can be achieved by extending a board out from the anchored skirtboard and even with its top, leveling it with the aid of a carpenter's level, and measuring the height from the top of the footing to the top edge of the board. Now subtract 1^{9}/$_{16}$ inches from this measurement and cut the post to that length.

Attach skirtboards to posts with ^{3}/$_{8}$× 6-inch-long screws, and toenail posts to the nailing blocks in the footings. If posts are not used, measure from the bottom of the leveled skirtboard to the ground to determine how deeply to seat the footings.

With the skirtboards level and in place, nail them together with 16d nails. Predrill all nailholes near the ends of pieces to prevent splitting the wood.

Using metal joist hangers, attach the four 2×8 joists on 2-foot centers, 1^{9}/$_{16}$ inches below the tops of the skirtboards. Bolt 2×4 ledgerboards along each of the 8-foot skirtboards, 1^{9}/$_{16}$ inches below their tops.

Now lay the decking. The deck will accommodate 26 2×4s spaced apart by the width of a 16d nail inserted loosely between them. Any large knots in the wood should be placed over a joist. This might mean laying the decking down loosely to check the best arrangement of pieces.

Depending on the cut of the millsaw, boards may have a vertical grain—which shows as parallel grain lines on the board—or a flat grain. Lay flat-grain deck boards bark side up to avoid raising grain and splinters. Nail into joists with 16d nails, predrilling holes at the ends of pieces to prevent splitting.

Your small patio deck is complete.

Patio deck over concrete

Building a deck over an existing concrete slab is an easy way to get the complete enjoyment of a deck for a fraction of the labor and cost. Concrete slabs that have been around for years are often cracked, uneven, or just plain unsightly. A well-designed wood deck can cover all these defects beautifully.

Check the materials list for building a deck on a typical 100-square-foot concrete slab (FIGS. 14-42 and 14-43).

Concrete Deck Materials List

- 60 linear feet of 2×4 "sleepers"
- 210 linear feet of 2×6 decking
- 326 linear feet of 2×4 decking
- Galvanized nails

Fig. 14-42 *Deck over concrete.*

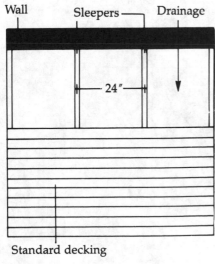

Fig. 14-43 *Deck construction.*

First, lay the sleepers down roughly in the spots they will be attached. They should be spaced 24 inches on center. The sleepers may be random lengths because the concrete slab will support the full length of the sleeper. This can be a savings because short lengths are often less expensive. If the concrete slab is cracked or uneven, level the sleepers with shims or small pieces of wood. If the concrete slab is adjacent to the wall of a house, sleepers should run perpendicular to the wall for best drainage.

The best way to attach sleepers to the concrete slab is with a power hammer which uses explosive charges to shoot special nails into the concrete. Power hammers are available at building supply and tool rental centers. They are easy to use and designed with safety features to help prevent accidents. Follow manufacturer's directions for safe operation.

Lay the decking in place before nailing. Random lengths of wood can be used for decking as long as butt joints meet over the sleepers. It is good practice not to have two butt joints adjacent to each other on the same sleeper. Trim and nail boards individually, as opposed to trimming them all at once. This helps prevent mistakes and offers leeway to cover for miscalculations in measurement.

Use stainless steel or aluminum hot-dipped galvanized nails and fasteners that are of top quality. Cheaper corrosive or electroplated nails can react with the wood, causing stains.

For 2-inch decking, use 10d nails. Decking nails should penetrate 1½ inches into the sleepers. Predrill holes at the ends of boards to prevent splitting. To allow for water drainage, decking boards should be spaced about ⅛ inch apart.

Hot tub deck

An outdoor hot tub is made more practical and more beautiful with a deck. Figures 14-44 through 14-49 illustrate the construction of a 12×16- and a 10×20-foot deck for a 6-foot-diameter hot tub. Materials are listed in TABLE 14-6. The models are made out of redwood.

The hot tub deck is built from the ground up. The footings—the concrete "anchors" dropped in the ground below the frost line—

Fig. 14-44 *Elaborate hot tub deck.* Wolmanized pressure-treated lumber

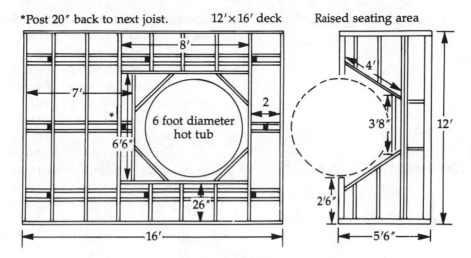

*Post 20″ back to next joist.   12′×16′ deck   Raised seating area

8′

7′

*

6 foot diameter hot tub

2

6′6″

26″

16′

4′

3′8″

12′

2′6″

5′6″

Fig. 14-45   *12 × 16 hot tub deck.*   California Redwood Association

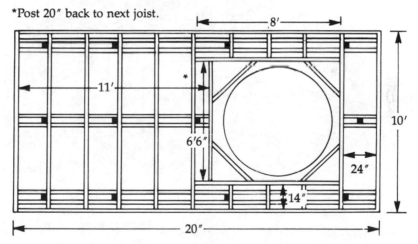

*Post 20″ back to next joist.

8′

11′

*

6′6″

10′

24″

14″

20″

Fig. 14-46   *10 × 20 hot tub deck.*   California Redwood Association

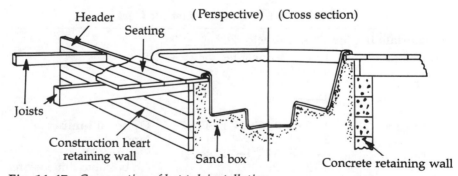

Header   (Perspective)   (Cross section)

Seating

Joists

Construction heart retaining wall   Sand box   Concrete retaining wall

Fig. 14-47   *Cross section of hot tub installation.*   California Redwood Association

Deck plans   **205**

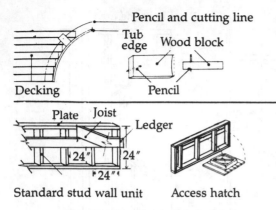

Fig. 14-48 *Hot tub deck detail.*

absorb the final weight of the deck. They can be poured in simple box forms. Posts are the vertical supports placed in or on the footings. They support the stringers solidly. Posts attach to footings with a variety of connectors. Stringers gather the load structurally and support the joists. Attach stringers to posts with lag screws or carrier bolts.

Joists support decking and are nailed (16d) to stringers. Headers, which stabilize the ends of joists, and angle bracing frame the top along with joists. Blocking is nailed between joists. Use 16d nails for all of this.

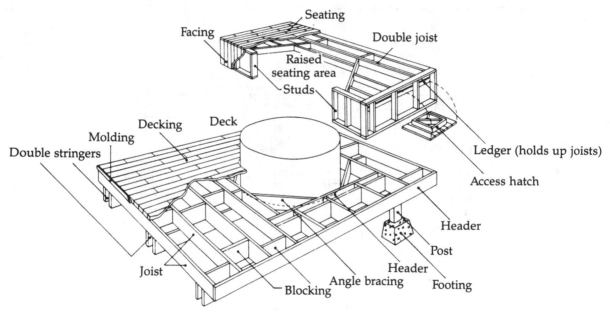

Fig. 14-49 *Raised seating area.* <small>California Redwood Association</small>

Table 14-6. Materials List for Deck

Materials list for 12′ × 16′ deck

Decking:	1×4—370 linear feet or 2×6—240 linear feet
Molding:	1×2, 56 linear feet
Posts:	9—4×4×height
Stringers:	4—2×10×16′, 2—1×10×7′, 2—2×10×2′
Joists:	6—2×6×12′, 1—2×6×6′, 6—2×6×26″
Blocking:	12—2×6×2′

Optional lumber lengths:
9—2×6×20′
(To be cut to dimensions. Cut longer lengths first.)

Table 14-6. Continued

Angle bracing:	4—2×6×3'
Headers:	2—2×6×8', 2—2×6×16'
Nails:	3# 16d Common, 8# 16d Box
	(galvanized, stainless)
Lag screws &	36—³/8×4"
washers:	(galvanized, stainless)

Materials list for raised seating area (12' × 16' deck)

Facing:	1×6	124 linear feet or
	1×4	194 linear feet
Decking:	2×6	124 linear feet or
	2×4	194 linear feet

Studwall units:

Plates:	2—2×4×12', 6—2×4×6'
Studs:	26—2×4×2'
Joists:	2—2×6×12', 2—2×6×4',
	2—2×6×3'
	1—2×6×3'8", 2—2×6×1'6"
Ledgers:	2—2×6×6'
Nails:	2# 16d Common, 4# 16d Box
	(galvanized, stainless)

Optional lumber lengths:

4—2×4×20'

4—2×4×8'
2—2×6×8'
1—2×6×20'
(To be cut to dimensions.
Cut longer lengths first.)

Materials list for 12' × 16' deck

Posts:	12—4×4×Height
Stringers:	4—2×10×20',
	2—2×10×2'
	2—2×10×11',
Joists:	8—2×6×20', 1—2×6×6'
	6—2×6×14"
Decking:	2×4=424 linear feet;
	2×6=274 linear feet
Blocking:	18—2×6×2'
Molding:	60 linear feet
Nails:	3# 16d Common,
	8# 16d Box
	(galvanized, stainless)
Lag screws &	48—³/8×4"
washers:	(galvanized, stainless)
Angle bracing:	2—2×6×3'
Headers:	2—2×6×8', 2—2×6×20'

Materials list for raised seating Area (10' × 20' deck)

Facing:	1×6=114; 1×4=178
Decking:	2×4=138 linear; or
	2×6=88 linear

Studwall units

Plates:	2—2×4×10',
	6—2×4×6'
Studs:	24—2×4×2'
Joists:	2—2×6×10',
	2—2×6×4'
	2—2×6×2',
	2—2×6×11",
	1—2×6×3'8"
Ledgers:	2—2×6×6'
Nails:	2# 16d c &
	4# 16d Box.
	(galvanized, stainless)

Footages are net; ask your redwood retailer how much to allow for trim.

Available lengths may vary. Longer lengths listed as options may be trimmed down to size. Posts should be Construction Heart, other members Construction Heart or Common. Decking should be of random length.

Decking rests on the joists. Predrill nail holes, then nail decking to joists with 16d nails. Allow 1/8-inch space for drainage between deck boards. Molding can be applied at the end of the job to give the sawn ends of the deck a finished appearance.

The raised seating area serves a number of useful purposes. Beyond seating and sunning it can be used to house the plumbing as well as store accessories. The basic element is the stud wall unit which rises 24 inches above the deck. The deck should be 1/2 inch below the tub trim. Build the five stud wall units first and then attach the other members, following standard nailing methods, in this order: ledgers, joists, blocking, facing, and then decking.

The access hatch consists of 2×4s or 2×6s attached to a simple box frame. The frame should measure approximately 22 1/4 × 20 3/4 inches so it fits securely into the stud walls. Although the hatch can be removable, a hinge is the easiest way to attach it to the stud wall unit.

The raised seating area of the 10×20-foot deck is structured the same as the 12×16, less 1 foot on either side.

Trimming the decking to fit around the tub can be simply accomplished by tracing the deck with a scribe made of a block that has a pencil secured to it. Cut the curve of the tub on the block with a jig or keyhole saw. Then rough-cut the decking so it almost touches the side of the tub. Trace with the scribe, then cut, nail, and finally trim.

Children's pool deck

Make a splash for the youngsters. Figure 14-50 shows a junior-size version of a standard swimming pool deck minus the posts and beams.

First choose a pool, then build the deck to fit. Make sure the surface of the deck is exactly the right height to fully support the lip of the pool without holding the pool bottom off the

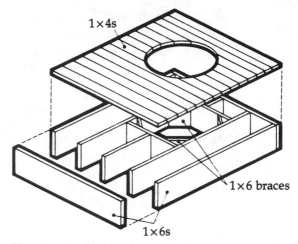

Fig. 14-50 *Children's pool deck.* Georgia-Pacific Corp.

ground. The pool sits loosely inside the cutaway. It can be removed easily for cleaning or storage. Materials include: 147 linear feet of 1×4 lumber; 56 linear feet of 1×6 lumber; and galvanized nails.

For this 42-inch-diameter pool, 1×6s are used for the understructure and 1×4s for the decking. Cut short pieces of 1×4s for the center portion of the deck. Nail these on either side of the pool location, then trim them with a saber saw.

Children's sandbox

This sandbox and deck (FIG. 14-51) are easy to construct and very enjoyable for the youngsters.

The sand sits in a 3×3-foot box that has walls made of 1×8s. This box also has a bottom made of exterior-grade plywood. Surrounding the box is a deck understructure made of 1×6s. Note the short 1×6s positioned at the centerline of the sandbox. They prevent the deck surface, made of 1×4s, from being too springy. Materials include: 95 linear feet of 1×4 lumber; 36 linear feet of 1×6 lumber; 12 linear feet of 1×8 lumber; and galvanized nails.

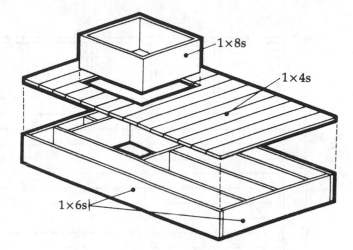

Fig. 14-51 *Children's sandbox deck.*
Georgia-Pacific Corp.

1×8s

1×4s

1×6s

Unusual deck plans

Now that you've seen how decks are built, let's look at a few unusual deck plans that might solve space and design problems. Of course, any of them can be easily modified to match your specific needs and resources.

Figures 14-52 and 14-53 illustrate the most basic of decks, the patio deck. This one is 12×16 feet in size with two small handrails. From this simple beginning you can add steps, planters, and even secondary decks to meet your requirements. The materials list for the patio deck includes 9 pieces of 2×6 by 12-foot floor joist; 2 pieces of 2×6 by 16-foot skirting boards; and 26 pieces of 3/4×6 by 16-foot deck planking.

All wood should be pressure-treated or decay resistant. Remember to use galvanized nails and hardware. Also remember that boards should not be butted snugly together; allow space for wood swelling in humid weather.

Maybe you prefer a free-form deck that suits your landscaping and your imagination (FIGS. 14-54 and 14-55).

Fig. 14-52 *Basic patio deck.*
Wolmanized pressure-treated lumber

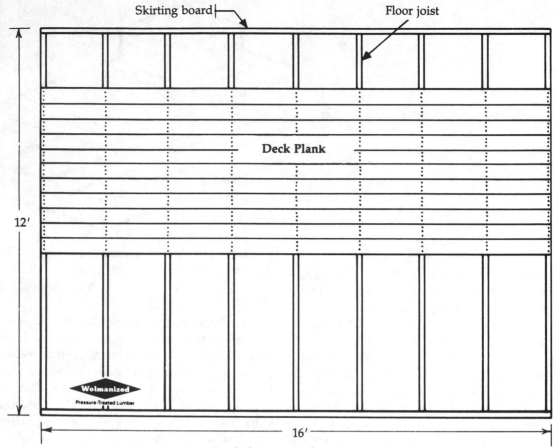

Fig. 14-53 *Basic patio deck construction.* Wolmanized pressure-treated lumber

Materials List for Free-Form Deck

- 12 pieces of 4×4 by 4-foot wood, cut to approximately fit the terrain of your deck.

For the ledger and ribbon boards:

- 6 pieces of 2×8 by 12-foot lumber
- 2 pieces of 2×6 by 12-foot lumber
- 6 pieces of 2×4 by 12-foot lumber
- 4 pieces of 2×8 by 10-foot lumber
- 4 pieces of 2×4 by 10-foot lumber

For the perimeter joists of fascia boards:

- 4 pieces of 2×8 by 8-foot lumber

- 2 pieces of 2×8 by 12-foot lumber

For the joists:

- 30 pieces of 2×8 by 8-foot lumber

For the decking:

- 96 pieces of 2×4 by 16-foot lumber

You'll also need nails and accessories as required. In addition, you will need materials for stairs, depending on the requirements of your free-form deck.

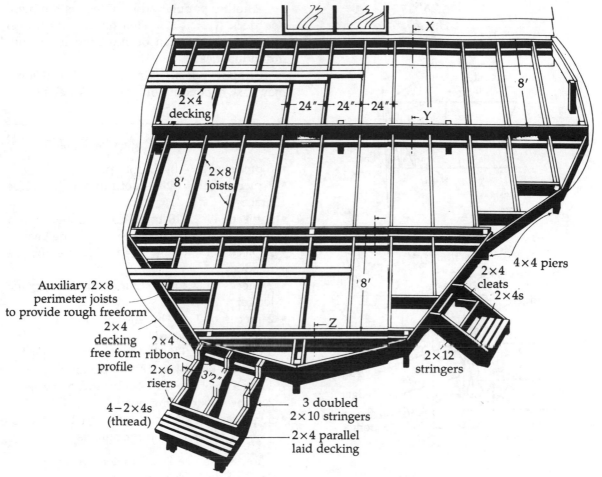

Fig. 14-54 *Free-form deck.* Wolmanized pressure-treated lumber

Sometimes the best place for a deck is on the roof of a garage or spare room. Figure 14-56 illustrates how to add a deck to such a roof. This one is 10 by 14 feet.

Materials for Roof Deck

- 16 pieces of 4×4 base posts cut to the slope of your roof
- 8 pieces of lumber, 4×4 by 3 feet 2 inches for railing posts
- 4 pieces of lumber, 2×8 by 14 feet for beams
- 8 pieces of lumber, 2×6 by 10 feet for joists
- 1 piece of lumber, 2×6 by 14 feet for the header (optional)

- 1 piece of lumber, 2×6, 14 feet long, and 2 pieces 11 feet long for the rail caps
- 2 pieces of lumber, 1×2 by 10 feet, 1 piece 14 feet long, 2 pieces 1×3 by 10 feet, and 1 piece 14 feet long for the railing strips
- 15 pieces of lumber, 2×4 by 14 feet and 10 pieces 2×6 by 14 feet for decking
- Nails and accessories as required.

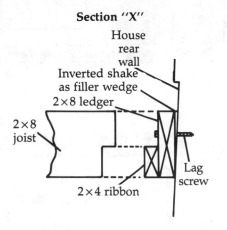

Section "X"

House
rear
wall
Inverted shake
as filler wedge
2×8 ledger
2×8
joist
Lag
screw
2×4 ribbon

Another popular add-on deck is the high-rise deck (FIG. 14-57). This one is 10×12 feet but, of course, it can be modified to fit your individual needs.

Support posts, estimated at 12 feet long, may vary depending on your deck height.

Materials for High-Rise Deck

- 6 pieces of 2×4 by 12-foot posts
- 1 piece of 2×4 by 10-foot lumber, 45-degree brace
- 2 pieces of 2×10 by 12-foot lumber, and 1 piece of 2×6 by 12-foot wood for the beam
- 2 pieces of 2×8 by 12-foot lumber for the headers
- 2 pieces of 2×4 by 12-foot lumber for the ledger
- 2 pieces of 2×10 by 10-foot lumber for the outside fascia boards
- 5 pieces of 2×8 by 10-foot lumber for joists
- 30 pieces of 2×4 by 12-foot decking
- 10 pieces of 2×6 by 4-foot and 5 pieces of 2×4 by 4-foot railing posts
- 50 pieces of 2×2 by 34-inch and 12 pieces of 2×6 by 48-inch wood for railings

You'll also need stair material, as required, from 2×4 by 12-foot lumber, as well as nails and accessories for the deck.

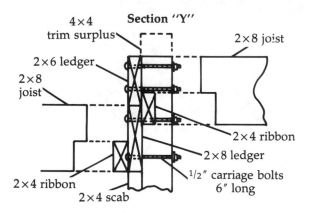

Section "Y"

4×4
trim surplus
2×6 ledger
2×8
joist
2×4 ribbon
2×4 scab
2×8 joist
2×4 ribbon
2×8 ledger
½" carriage bolts
6" long

Finally, one more deck that is easy to build and fun to use, is the 10×10-foot fire pit deck (FIG. 14-58). The deck is constructed of eight pieces of 4×4 by 10-foot and 27 pieces of 2×4 by 10-foot lumber. Benches (6 feet, 8 inches and 8 feet, 8 inches long) are made using five pieces of 4×4 by 4-foot, 5 pieces of 2×4 by 7-foot, and 5 pieces of 2×4 by 12-inch materials. The fire pit is constructed of 40 pieces of 4×4 by 16-inch lumber, two pieces of 2×6 by 6-foot lumber, and one bag of mortar. You'll also need nails and accessories as required.

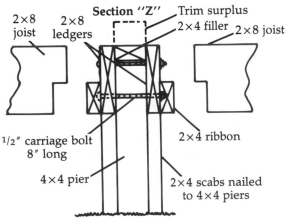

Section "Z"

2×8
joist
2×8
ledgers
Trim surplus
2×4 filler
2×8 joist
½" carriage bolt
8" long
4×4 pier
2×4 ribbon
2×4 scabs nailed
to 4×4 piers

Fig. 14-55 *Free-form deck construction details.*
Wolmanized pressure-treated lumber

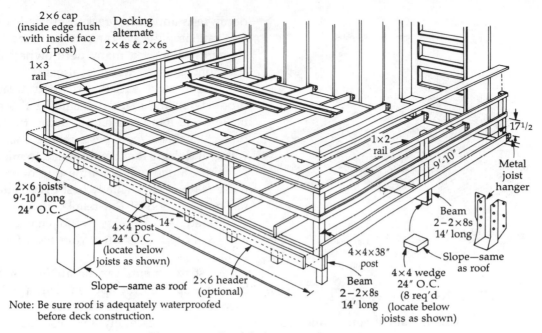

Fig. 14-56 *Roof deck.* Wolmanized pressure-treated lumber

Labels in figure:
2×6 cap (inside edge flush with inside face of post)
Decking alternate 2×4s & 2×6s
1×3 rail
1×2 rail
9'-10"
17½
Metal joist hanger
2×6 joists 9'-10" long 24" O.C.
Beam 2−2×8s 14' long
Slope—same as roof
4×4 post 24" O.C. (locate below joists as shown)
Slope—same as roof
2×6 header (optional)
4×4×38" post
4×4 wedge 24" O.C. (8 req'd) (locate below joists as shown)
Beam 2−2×8s 14' long
Note: Be sure roof is adequately waterproofed before deck construction.

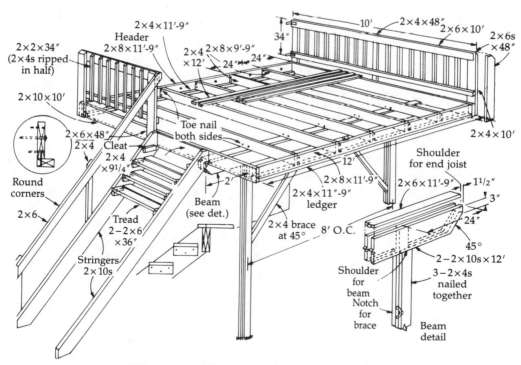

Fig. 14-57 *High-rise deck.* Wolmanized pressure-treated lumber

Labels in figure:
2×2×34" (2×4s ripped in half)
Header 2×8×11'-9"
2×4×11'-9"
2×4 ×12'
2×8×9'-9"
24"
34"
10'
2×4×48"
2×6×10'
2×6s ×48"
2×10×10'
2×6×48" / 2×4
Cleat 2×4 ×9¼"
Toe nail both sides
Round corners
2×6
2×4×10'
Shoulder for end joist
2×6×11'-9"
1½"
3"
24"
45°
Tread 2−2×6 ×36"
Beam (see det.)
2'
12'
2×8×11'-9"
2×4×11"-9" ledger
2×4 brace at 45° 8' O.C.
Stringers 2×10s
2−2×10s×12'
3−2×4s nailed together
Shoulder for beam Notch for brace
Beam detail

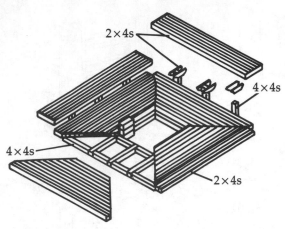

Fig. 14-58 *Fire pit deck.* _{Georgia-Pacific Corp.}

2×4s

4×4s

4×4s

2×4s

Finishing your deck

Once your deck is installed, you should consider how to best finish it. Of course, with decay-resistant and pressure-treated woods, you can simply leave them to be toned by the elements. However, many deck owners desire additional color or wood treatment.

There are a variety of wood treatment products on the market, including those that make wood more resistant to decay, those that protect against wood pests, those that repel water, and those that are designed to minimize warping. Some will combine one or more of these features. It's usually best to consider the recommendation of the retailer that sold you your materials, because wood characteristics and local conditions affect your need for these products.

Most treatments can be applied by being brushed, sprayed, or applied with a roller. In each case, follow the manufacturer's and retailer's directions carefully for best results and greatest safety.

15

Gazebos

Rain or shine, a gazebo is the ideal setting (FIGS. 15-1 and 15-2) for outdoor entertaining and family dining. In this chapter you'll learn how to plan and construct a traditional hexagonal garden gazebo, a latticework gazebo, a classic walkway arbor, an old fashioned rose arbor, and other outdoor structures for shade.

Each design can be modified to fit your backyard. They can be enlarged for larger families and yards, or they can be condensed for intimate yards. As none of these plans require roofs to carry heavy loads, designs can easily be modified without resorting to the help of an architect. But if you do make up your own plans, have an experienced building materials retailer look them over for functional safety.

Basic gazebo design

You can design your own gazebo once you know what the components are. The base can be simple, such as small concrete pads supporting concrete blocks that hold beams for the floor. You can pour a concrete slab, or erect a small deck.

The floor can be wood, concrete, brick, or tile. You may have a floor or deck in place on which you can build.

Structural supports must look good as well as do the job. A type of post-and-beam design makes sense because it has the necessary strength and few components to obstruct the view.

The cover can be closed or open. It can be tight for sun protection or loose for mixed sun and shade.

Decorative touches are optional, but they can add plenty of character to the design at little cost.

The cupola is added for appearance, or for increased ventilation if your gazebo is covered with a solid roof.

Garden gazebo

This garden gazebo design (FIGS. 15-3 through 15-9), with its decorative rails and high, steep-

Fig. 15-1 *Gazebos can become part of a backyard deck.* Wolmanized pressure-treated lumber

pitched roof, will enhance almost any yard. It can be built as a focal point of your backyard, or tucked into a cluster of trees. The garden gazebo is the perfect place to spend warm, lazy days or balmy evenings, or to escape rain showers. For children, a gazebo becomes a kingdom.

The generous floor deck, approximately 12 feet in diameter, provides ample room for tables, chairs, a portable barbecue, and chaise lounges.

Build your garden gazebo following the instructions and the illustrations in this chapter. Table 15-1 lists required materials.

Fig. 15-2 *Typical gazebo.* Georgia-Pacific Corp.

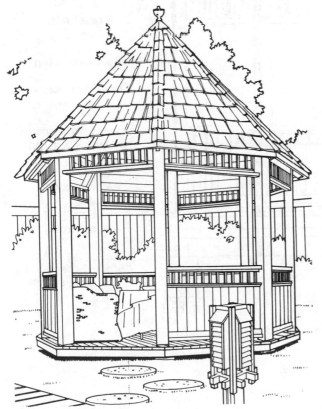

Fig. 15-3 *Garden gazebo.* Wolmanized pressure-treated lumber

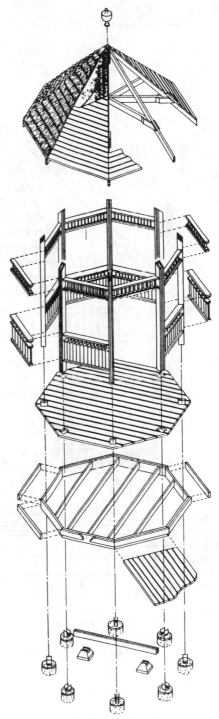

Fig. 15-4 *Exploded view of garden gazebo.*
Wolmanized pressure-treated lumber

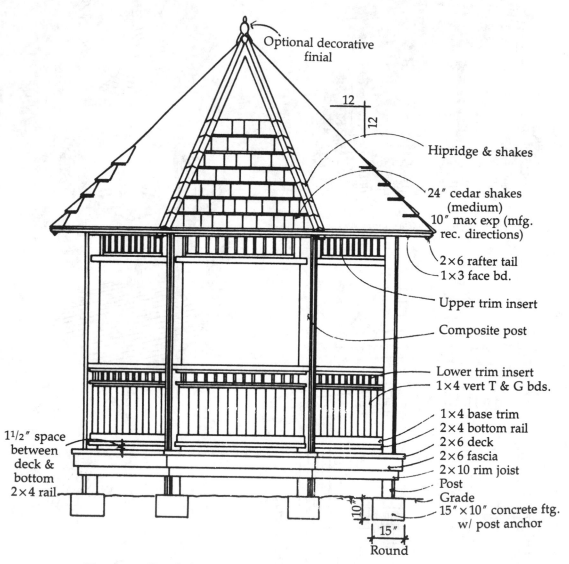

Optional decorative
finial

12
12

Hipridge & shakes

24″ cedar shakes
(medium)
10″ max exp (mfg.
rec. directions)

2×6 rafter tail
1×3 face bd.

Upper trim insert

Composite post

Lower trim insert
1×4 vert T & G bds.

1×4 base trim
2×4 bottom rail
2×6 deck
2×6 fascia
2×10 rim joist
Post
Grade
15″ × 10″ concrete ftg.
w/ post anchor

1¹⁄₂″ space
between
deck &
bottom
2×4 rail

10″

15″

Round

Fig. 15-5 Detailed cross section of garden gazebo. Wolmanized pressure-treated lumber

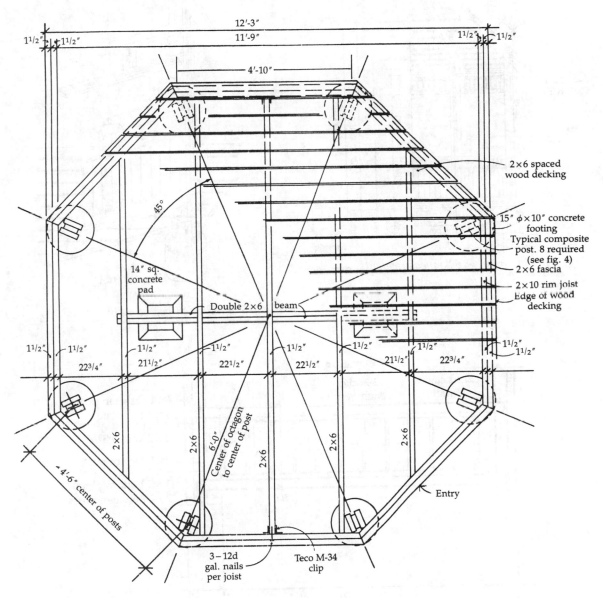

Fig. 15-6 *Flooring detail of garden gazebo.* Wolmanized pressure-treated lumber

Labels on figure:

12'-3"
11'-9"
1 1/2" 1 1/2"
1 1/2" 1 1/2"
4'-10"
2×6 spaced wood decking
45°
15" φ×10" concrete footing
Typical composite post. 8 required (see fig. 4)
2×6 fascia
14" sq. concrete pad
2×10 rim joist
Edge of wood decking
Double 2×6 beam
1 1/2" 1 1/2"
1 1/2" 1 1/2" 1 1/2" 1 1/2" 1 1/2" 1 1/2"
22 3/4" 21 1/2" 22 1/2" 22 1/2" 21 1/2" 22 3/4"
2×6 2×6 2×6 2×6 2×6
6'-0" Center of octagon to center of post
4'-6" center of posts
Entry
3–12d gal. nails per joist
Teco M-34 clip

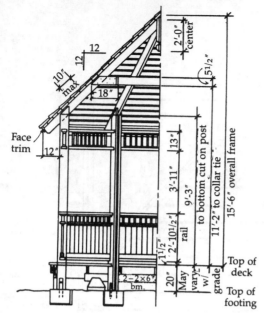

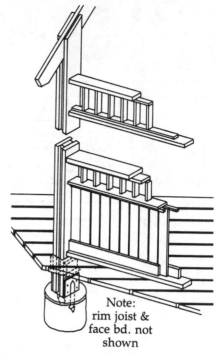

Fig. 15-7 *Garden gazebo measurements.* Wolmanized pressure-treated lumber

Fig. 15-8 *Garden gazebo railing detail.* Wolmanized pressure-treated lumber

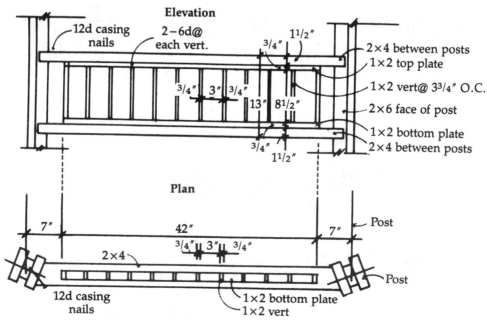

Fig. 15-9 *Railing construction.* Wolmanized pressure-treated lumber

Table 15-1. Materials List for Garden Gazebo

Foundation
8-12 bags premixed concrete
(8) 6×6 post anchors and galvanized nails or bolts
(2) precast pier pads, min. 14" base
Form material, such as 15" "Sonotube," available at masonry supply
14" stakes

Posts
(treated for ground contact, LP-22)
(8) 2×4, 12'
(16) 2×6, 12'
Moisture barrier (such as composition shingles)

Beam
(2) 2×6, 9', treated for ground contact

Deck framing
(treated to above-ground standards, LP-2)
(6) 2×6, 10'
(3) 2×6, 12'
(2) 2×6, 8'
(4) 2×10, 10'

Decking
(treated to above ground standards, LP-2)

(14) 2×6, 14'
(4) 2×6, 12'
(4) 2×6, 10'
(6) 2×6, 8'

Rafters
(8) 2×6, 12'

Centerblock
(1) 2×6, 8'
General purpose construction adhesive

Collar ties
(8) 2×6, 10'

Gusset plates
(2) 2×6, 12'

Straps
(3) TECO 16s, 16"
General purpose framing anchor: (4) TECO M-34

Roof decking
T&G select
(16) 2×6, 12'
(16) 2×6, 10'
(30) 2×6, 8'

Fascia board
(4) 1×3 (clear), 12'

Roof
15# felt paper, 2 rolls
Cedar shakes, 16 bundles
Hip & ridge shakes, 7 bundles

Finial in wood, copper or galvanized/painted

Top railings
(for 8 bays)
Top & bottom rail: (8) 2×4, 10'
Top & bottom plate: (8) 1×2, 8'
Verticals: (9) 1×2, 8'

Bottom railings
(for 7 bays)
Cap rail: (4) 2×6, 10'
Top & bottom plate: (7) 1×4, 10'
Verticals: (4) 1×2, 10'
Stop: (7) 1×1, 10'
Stop: (7) 1×4, 10'
Vertical boards: (21) T&G 1×4 (210 lineal feet in random 2' multiples)
Bottom rail: (4) 2×4, 10'

Nails
All hot-dipped galvanized
12d casing, 20 lbs.
12d common, 1 box
8d casing, 5 lbs.
3d finish, 2 lbs.
1" roofing nails, 2 lbs.
Shake/shingle nails

Wolmanized pressure-treated lumber

To begin drive a stake into the center of the proposed site. Drive a nail into the top of the stake and, with a tape or string, mark a circle with a radius of 6 feet (12-foot diameter) using powdered chalk or lime. Locate the gazebo entrance and drive a second stake on a line adjacent to the entry opening, placing it about 2 feet outside the circle you have marked. Then drive a third stake opposite the first, so a string tied between them will cross the center stake.

Drive two more stakes at right angles to the first. String a line between the stakes, making sure the string crosses the center stake. Divide the remaining quadrants with stakes and string to create eight equal spaces.

Finally, drive a second row of stakes at the point where each string crosses the circle. These should be 6 feet 0 inches on center from the middle stake. The space between stakes on this inner row should measure 4 feet 6 inches on center. These stakes need to be exactly right, because they mark the centers for each footing and post.

Next Dig a hole for each footing that is at least 12 inches deep and 15 inches in diameter. Install forms if needed, and pour footings, using a marker or board to make sure the tops of the footings are all at the same level. Accurately mark points where the string crosses the circle and install post anchors before the concrete sets. Remember that the post anchors must be set so that the center of your posts will all be 6 feet out from the center of the gazebo, and the on-center distance between posts will be 4 feet 6 inches. Recheck measurements and make adjustments if necessary. Check to make sure that all post anchors are level with one another.

When the concrete has set for two days, recheck all measurements and make certain the post anchors are all level with one another and the spacing is exactly right. A good gazebo starts with good footings.

The third step Posts are fabricated from pressure-treated lumber using two 2×6s on the outside with a shorter 2×4 sandwiched in the center to support the rafters. Before you cut all 16 2×6s and eight 2×4s required to make the eight posts, make one post as your sample and cutting pattern for the others.

Set post anchors using a composition shingle as a moisture barrier. Shim posts in position, using pressure treated lumber (anchor will be 1 inch larger than the post) and temporarily brace with scrap lumber. Check distances between posts: 4 feet 6 inches on center (o.c.) apart and 6 feet 0 inches o.c. from center stake, plus or minus 1/2 inch. Check level at top of posts and adjust if necessary. Fasten all posts to post anchors using nails or bolts.

Measure out 3 feet on either side of the center stake and set 14-inch pier pads in place. Pier pads are 6 feet apart o.c.

Fourth Mark the position of 2×10 rim joists on posts, making sure all marks are level. Then cut 2×10 rim joists to length, mitering ends at 22 1/2 degrees; nail to posts with 12d nails. Now cut 5 1/2 inch deck support blocks from 2×6 pressure-treated lumber. Predrill and nail blocks to both sides of posts so top is flush with the top of the 2×10. Additional blocking may be required in order to nail decking board securely around posts.

Set 2×6 floor joists in place and flush with the top of rim joist. Use framing anchors at both ends of the center joist. End-nail remaining floor joists to rim joist with three 12d nails, and to posts where possible. Install 2×6 fascia board flush with the top of the rim joist, mitering ends at 22 1/2 degrees. Apply 2×6 treated decking to floor joists, allowing about 1/4-inch space between boards. Fit decking around posts and trim ends of deck boards to a constant 1-inch overhang.

Fifth Moving to the roof, you can now install rafters and collar ties. For the center block, cut four 24 inch lengths of 2×6s. Using a construction adhesive, glue and nail to form a 6 inch block, then trim and notch, and set aside. Next place two opposing 12 foot 2×6 rafters in position, then use a plumbline bob to find the center and tack the rafters together temporarily.

Mark the position for the center block, allowing for 12 inches of overhang. Cut 45-degree angles on the ends next to the center block, and trim overhanging end. Use as a pattern and cut the remaining six rafters.

Temporarily toenail two opposing rafters to

the center block using 12d nails. Position on posts and check fit. Remove from posts and firmly toenail these first two rafters to the center block. Predrill holes to avoid splitting.

Sixth Position the continuous (8 feet of 2×6) collar tie across the first two rafters. Mark angles for trimming ends. Pieces should trim to approximately 7 feet 4 inches on the long side of the angle cut. Trim and toenail the collar tie into position with 12d nails.

Cut two 2×6 collar tie plates, mitering one end 45 degrees to match the rafter angle; the other end is beveled. Use this as a pattern for the remaining 14 plates required for the other seven collar ties. Cut the remaining plates and set them aside.

Next nail the first two plates into position using 12d nail, predrilling holes to avoid splitting. Set the roof truss on posts, making sure the center block is centered and overhang is equal. Nail rafters to the post through the outer 2×6s using 12d casing nails. Temporarily brace upper part of posts to keep dimensions rigid and true. Now anchor the remaining rafters to the center block and posts, toenailing to the center block with 12d nails and nailing to posts as discussed. Cut the remaining collar ties and assemble, toenailing them into position with 12d nails. Install the remaining collar plates and straps.

Seventh To begin constructing the roof, start the first course of tongue-and-groove roof decking flush with the ends of rafters, tongue up. Put the finished face of the decking down so it will be seen from below. Miter one end of the board and allow a little extra length at the other end. Face nail the first board to rafters with 12d nails. For the remaining boards, cut and miter in the same way, using two 12d nails per rafter—one toenailed through the tongue and one face nailed. After each triangle section is in place, snap a chalk line down the center of the rafter and trip the other end of the decking.

Make sure the boards line up between sections to produce the "coursing" effect of the grooves on the underside.

Apply 1×3 face trim to the end of the rafters, flush with the top of the decking, then miter the ends. Apply felt roofing paper according to manufacturer's directions, taking care to seal well around the peak. Apply cedar shakes according to standard roofing methods. Install the optional decorative finial on the peak.

Eighth The upper railing sections are installed on eight bays; lower railing is omitted on the entry bay. Before cutting horizontal boards, measure each opening to adjust for any variations in the widths between posts. When nailing smaller components together, make certain your nails are an appropriate length so that finished rails have a neat appearance.

Cut horizontal 1×2s and 2×4s to length, mitering ends of 2×4s at 22$\frac{1}{2}$ degrees. Each bay will require 12 vertical 1×2s, each 8$\frac{1}{2}$ inches long. End nail vertical 1×2s to horizontal 1×2 rails at the top and bottom, 3$\frac{3}{4}$ inches on center. Nail the rail section to the 2×4 base and cap using 6d casing nails. Then toenail the completed railing section to posts using 12d casing nails. Build identical rail sections for remaining seven bays.

Ninth For the upper trim, cut horizontal members to length, mitering ends at 22$\frac{1}{2}$ degrees. Toenail 2×4 bottom rail to posts, 1$\frac{1}{2}$ inches above the deck, with the inside 1×4 stop-nailed to the 2×4 with 12d casing nails.

End nail 1×2 verticals to the horizontal top and bottom 1×4s, 3$\frac{3}{4}$ inches on center, same as for the upper railing section. Toenail to post, in position, 24 inches above the bottom 2×4. Cut vertical 1×4 tongue and groove boards to 23$\frac{7}{8}$ inches (you will need 14 boards per section); cut 1×2 verticals to 6$\frac{3}{4}$ inches (12 per section).

Assemble the 1×4 verticals for the first section on a flat surface using a straightedge to keep edges square. Trim the last 1×4 to size. Using 3d finish nails, temporarily nail 1×4 bottom stops and 1×1 top stops in place on the panel and check the section for fit. Once fitted, secure in position with 6d casing nails. Build six more railing sections for the remaining bays.

Latticework gazebo

This is an interesting variation on the basic gazebo. Refer to FIGS. 15-10 through 15-15 and the materials list for the latticework gazebo.

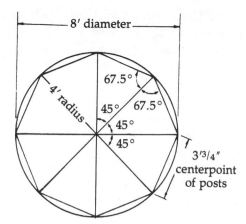

Fig. 15-11 *Measuring for postholes.* Georgia-Pacific Corp.

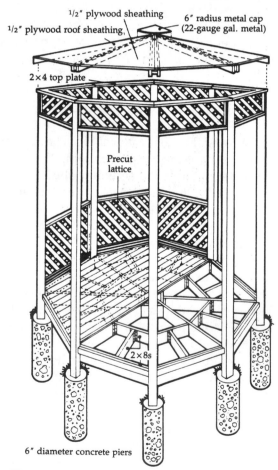

Fig. 15-10 *Latticework gazebo.* Georgia-Pacific Corp.

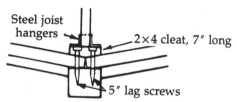

Fig. 15-12 *Setting joists.* Georgia-Pacific Corp.

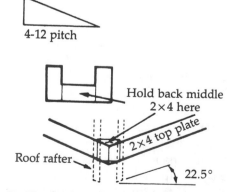

Fig. 15-13 *Setting top plate and rafters.* Georgia-Pacific Corp.

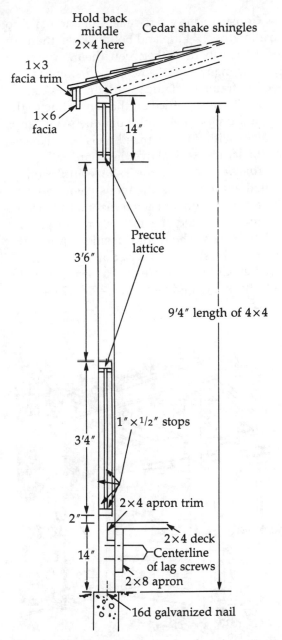

Fig. 15-14 Latticework gazebo elevation. Georgia-Pacific Corp.

Labels in figure: Hold back middle 2×4 here; Cedar shake shingles; 1×3 facia trim; 1×6 facia; 14"; Precut lattice; 3'6"; 9'4" length of 4×4; 1"×1/2" stops; 3'4"; 2×4 apron trim; 2"; 2×4 deck; Centerline of lag screws; 14"; 2×8 apron; 16d galvanized nail

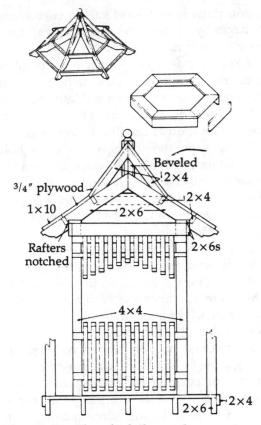

Fig. 15-15 Plans for lathe gazebo. Georgia-Pacific Corp.

Labels in figure: Beveled 2×4; 2×4; 3/4" plywood; 2×6; 1×10; Rafters notched; 2×6s; 4×4; 2×6; 2×4

- 62 pieces of lumber, 2×4 by 8 feet long
- 6 pieces of lumber, 1×6 by 8 feet long
- 4 sheets of 4×8 foot by 1/2-inch exterior plywood
- 32 2×8 joist hangers
- 16 5-inch lag screws with washers
- 12 pieces of 4×4-foot precut lattice panels
- 4 bundles of shingles
- Galvanized nails
- Wood filler
- Semitransparent stain

Latticework Gazebo

- 8 pieces of lumber, 4×4 by 10 feet
- 12 pieces of lumber, 2×8 by 8 feet long

For best results, choose pressure-treated lumber. This lumber is treated with a preservative that makes it particularly resistant to damage from moisture and insects.

You must have a level site for such a project. Begin by grading the selected area, if necessary, to level it.

First Locate a center reference point for the gazebo by driving a stake into the ground of the gazebo floor. Drive a nail into the center of the stake. Measuring from this nail, determine the location of the foundation piers.

Using a posthole digger, dig eight holes approximately 6 inches in diameter and $3^1/2$ feet deep. Fill the holes with concrete. While the concrete is still wet, embed a 16d nail, point up, in the center of each pier so the nail sticks out about $1^1/2$ inches.

Be sure to allow the concrete to cure for three or four days before proceeding.

Next Cut the posts to length. Find the center point at one end of each post and mark it with a pencil or small nail hole. Cut all eight pieces of the top plate from 2×4s.

Set the first post on the first concrete pier, making sure to line up the center of the post and the nail sticking out of the pier. Push the post down until it rests firmly atop the pier. Set the second post in the same manner. With these two posts in position, nail one section of the top plate in place. Continue until all eight posts are set and all sections of the top plate are in place.

Cut the apron frame from 2×8s and nail it in place with three 16d galvanized nails at either end. Cut the eight cleats from a 2×4 and temporarily nail them in place.

Predrill the holes for the lag screws. Counterbore so the screw heads will be flush with the surface of the wood. This will enable the joist hanger to lay flat against the cleat. Secure the cleats with the screws. Construct and nail in place the rest of the floor framing.

Third To lay the floor boards, first cut the 2×4 floor decking. Nail the 2×4s in place, taking care to allow approximately $1/2$ inch of space between each of them. Cut the apron trim and nail it in place.

Construct the guard rails. Cut and nail into position the 2×4 top and bottom rails, then cut the lattice to fit in between them. Rip from 2×4s as many 1-×-$1/2$-inch wood stops as you need to frame the lattice work on two sides.

Position the lattice on the center line of the top and bottom rails, then nail the wood stops in place with 3d galvanized nails. Do likewise for the lattice-work above the guard rail.

Fourth Start on the rafters and roofing. Note that the pitch of the roof shown here is 4-12—a 4-inch drop for each horizontal 12 inches.

You can build the rafters on the ground and then raise them into position. Make the rafters in the shape of a C by nailing three 2×4s together. Cut the middle 2×4 to 3 inches wide. Hold back the middle, 3-inch-wide 2×4 from one end.

Fig. 15-16 Classic arbor. Wolmanized pressure-treated lumber

Nail on the $1/2$-inch plywood sheathing and the 1×6 fascia board. Apply the shingles, then nail on the metal dome cap. Cut the 1×3 fascia trim from a 1×6 and nail it in place.

Finally Set all nail heads and fill all voids and cracks with wood filler. Stain the entire gazebo, if you like, with the semitransparent stain of your choice.

The last step is to get a good friend and a couple of glasses of cool lemonade, and share your latticework gazebo.

Classic arbor

The simple styling of this classic arbor is equally at home in contemporary or traditional settings (FIGS. 15-16 through 15-21). Used as an entry arbor, it will transform an ordinary walkway into a grand entrance. Located near the sidewalk or close to the front door it immediately adds dimension and interest to the entire front yard. In the backyard, the sturdy structure could serve as a generous-sized grape arbor, supporting several vines. An arbor can also be used to provide a dramatic focal point in a space-defining fence or hedge. Or you can add a couple of benches or outdoor chairs and make it your private retreat for reading and relaxation.

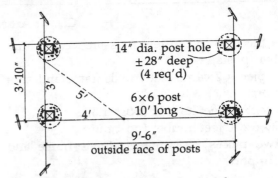

Fig. 15-18 *Post location for classic arbor.* Wolmanized pressure-treated lumber

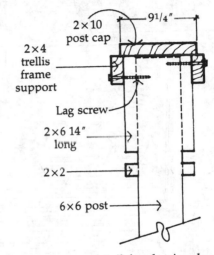

Fig. 15-19 *Post cap detail for classic arbor.* Wolmanized pressure-treated lumber

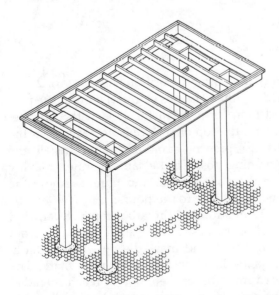

Fig. 15-17 *Framing for classic arbor.* Wolmanized pressure-treated lumber

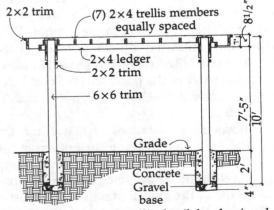

Fig. 15-20 *Post and trellis detail for classic arbor.* Wolmanized pressure-treated lumber

Classic Arbor Materials List

- 4 pieces 6×6×10 feet pressure-treated lumber (posts)
- 4 pieces 2×4×6 feet (trellis frame and support)
- 2×2×10 feet lumber (post trim)
- 2×6×10 feet lumber (post trim)
- two pieces 2×8×6 feet (trellis frame and support)
- two pieces 2×8×12 feet (trellis frame and support)
- 2×10×4 feet lumber (post cap)
- 2×10×10 feet lumber (post trim)
- galvanized fasteners: 8 2×4 joist hangers; 16 ¼×5 inch lag screws (or 20d nails); assorted box and casing nails
- cement, sand, gravel for post holes

Fig. 15-21 *The finished classic arbor.* Wolmanized pressure-treated lumber

The four 6×6 posts are 10 feet long and pressure treated for durability. Two feet of the 10-foot length will be set in the ground. With string and stakes, lay out the location of the four 6×6 posts. The string line should be along the outside face of the posts. Dig the post holes approximately 14 inches in diameter and 28 inches deep.

Shovel about 4 inches of gravel into the post hole—enough to bring the bottom of the hole up to 12 inches below grade level. Tamp the gravel firmly. Then place the post in position on top of the gravel. Make sure the post is in line with the string, then check for plumb on two sides of the post, using a carpenter's level.

Brace the post into position with 2×2s or 2×4s. Add another 2 inches of gravel around the post and tamp firmly. Fill the hole with concrete, sloping the top of the concrete away from the post to prevent standing water. Install the remaining posts in the same manner, making sure they are parallel and plumb. Allow the concrete to cure for 48 hours.

To ensure that the arbor top is level, find the shortest post and measure up 8 feet from ground level and mark the post. Temporarily tack a leveling board even with the mark. The board must be long enough to reach the adjacent post. Using a carpenter's level, adjust the other end of the board until it's level and mark the cutting line on the second post. Repeat the process for the other two posts.

For each post, you will need two lengths of 2×6 and two lengths of 2×10, each 14 inches long. Nail the 2×6s to opposite sides of the post, even with the top. Rip the 2×10s to 8½ inches wide and nail them to the remaining sides. Cut two lengths of 2×2, each 5½ inches long, and two lengths 8½ inches long for each post. Nail the 2×2s in place around the post, 1½ inches below the 2×6 trim.

For the trellis frame supports, cut four lengths of 2×4, each 6 feet long. Temporarily nail the 2×4s to opposite sides of the posts, flush with the top, using 12d casing nails. The 2×4s will extend beyond the posts 11½ inches at both ends. Make sure the 2×4s are level, then fasten with 2 ¼ inch × 5 inch lag screws or 20d nails on each side of the post, predrilling holes. Cut four lengths of 2×10 for the post caps, each 9¼ inches square. Center over the posts and nail in place.

For the trellis frame, cut two lengths of 2×8, each 12 feet long, and two lengths 6 feet long. End nail the 12 foot lengths to the ends of the 2×4 frame supports. The top of the 2×8s should be 1½ inches above the top of the 2×4s (flush with the top of the post cap) and extend 12 inches beyond the 2×4s at each end. Install a 2×4 joist hanger over the ends of the frame supports and nail it in place. Then nail the 6 foot end pieces in place with sides overlapping the ends.

For the ledger, cut two lengths of 2×4, each 10 feet 6 inches long, and two lengths 6 feet long. Center the longer lengths on the inside of the 2×8 frame, under the 2×4 trellis frame supports. The bottom of the ledger will extend 1¼ inches below the 2×8 frame. Position the 2×4 end pieces so they overlap the side pieces; end nail to the side pieces and toenail to the 2×8 frame.

Next, cut seven lengths of 2×4 for the overhead trellis members, each 6 feet long. Space them equally across the top of the ledger, on edge, approximately 8 to 9 inches apart. End nail them to the 2×8 frame.

For the top trim, cut two lengths of 2×2 12 feet long, and two lengths 6 feet 3 inches long. Nail them around the outside of the 2×8 at the top. For long-lasting good looks, finish the arbor with a good quality outdoor paint or stain.

Rose arbor

Here's a variation of the classic arbor, called a rose arbor (FIGS. 15-22 through 15-27). The primary difference is that the rose arbor is more closed and more ornate. It is a better choice for a smaller backyard or within a flower garden.

Fig. 15-22 *Rose arbor.* Wolmanized pressure-treated lumber

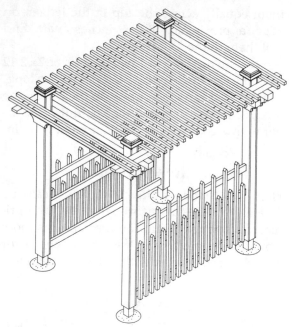

Fig. 15-23 *Framing for rose arbor.* Wolmanized pressure-treated lumber

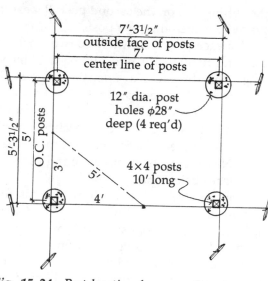

Fig. 15-24 *Post location for rose arbor.* Wolmanized pressure-treated lumber

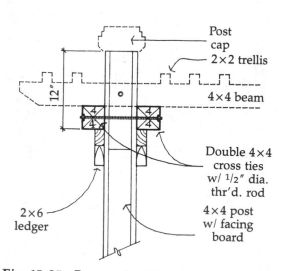

Fig. 15-25 *Post cap detail for rose arbor.* Wolmanized pressure-treated lumber

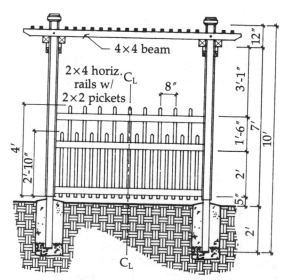

Fig. 15-26 *Post and trellis detail for rose arbor.* Wolmanized pressure-treated lumber

Fig. 15-27 The finished rose arbor. Wolmanized pressure-treated lumber

The illustrations give you the basic dimensions. Basic construction steps are the same as for the classic arbor. Pay special attention to the rails and pickets on the sides of the arbor as well as on the ornate post cap. And, of course, you can modify this design for your own unique arbor.

Sunshades

Sunshades are often called trellises. They can be light and airy and frequently are used to train vines upon. Essentially they are overhead constructions whose purpose is to filter the sun's rays, creating a pleasant, open atmosphere that contributes much to outdoor relaxation. The use of a deciduous vine as a cover makes sense because the plant affords maximum protection during summer months. After dropping its leaves, the plant allows more of the sun to come through when the weather turns cold.

A sunshade can project from a house wall and be situated over an existing patio or deck, or it can be a freestanding unit, isolated a bit so it serves as a private retreat. Location and placement affect how it should be erected. Study FIG. 15-28 and formulate basic consider-

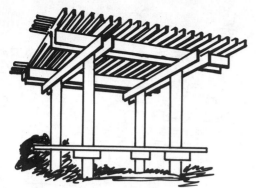

Fig. 15-28 *Easy-to-build sunshade.* Georgia-Pacific Corp.

ations for planning and building a sunshade.

Floor The sunshade can go over your existing patio or can be built together with it.

Main supports Supports or posts depend on the size, weight, and framing of the shading top. The most common are 2×4 posts for light

frame shades and 4×4 posts for heavy frame shades.

Joists Joists for a sunshade are chosen and attached much like those for a deck, except the sunshade doesn't need as much structural stability. The joists can be of smaller materials placed farther apart because they won't carry any weight.

Ledger Consider how you will attach the sunshade to your house. You may be able to lock it to the roof rafters with bolts, or spike a ledger into wall studs.

Cover How much filtration do you want? Your decision affects what you should use: 2×4s, lath strips, fiberglass panels, etc.

Sidewalls Not all sunscreens have sidewalls, but they should be considered as a windbreak or for privacy. They can be open or solid (see FIGS. 15-29 and 15-30).

Fig. 15-29 *Covered deck.* Georgia-Pacific Corp.

Fig. 15-30 *Structures for greater outdoor living: sunshade with benches, work area with enclosed trash cabinets, wood storage, and wooden planter.* Western Wood Products Association

Wall trellis

A simple wall trellis can be made in a very short time and will make an attractive addition to the home (FIGS. 15-31 and 15-32). You'll need: 2 pieces 2×4 by 7 feet 10 inches; 2 pieces 2×4 by 7 feet 6 inches; 8 angle irons; 15 pieces of 1×3¹/₂ inch dowels; and 85 feet of rope or plastic wash line or wire.

The framework is made out of 2×4 stock. Sand and plane down the wood so the finish is smooth enough to take paint.

The dimensions for the frame are 7 feet 6 inches by 8 feet 6 inches, but these can be varied to meet individual requirements. Do not, however, make the frame too wide; it could

become difficult to remove it when necessary to paint the house siding.

Joints of the framework are simple butts made with two 16d nails each and reinforced on the inside with angle irons. The framework is attached to the house siding with angle irons, too. Use only non-corrosive screws for attaching the angle irons; don't nail the framework to the house siding. The framework should be given a prime coat of paint or be coated with a preservative wood stain before it is attached to the exterior wall. Make certain the backside of the frame is adequately protected with a finish. The base of the frame should be kept at least 6 inches above ground level.

Two methods are suggested for attaching the cord to the frame. Dowels make a more professional-looking job, but take much more time to install than screw eyes. Also, non-corrosive wire staples will be required on each side of each dowel to prevent the cord from slipping off. Dowels are held in place by means of an 8d finishing nail driven in through the edge of the framework at an angle. Use some stout cord or wire attached to the doweling.

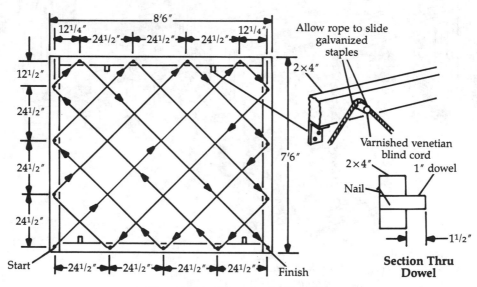

Fig. 15-31   Plans for wall trellis.

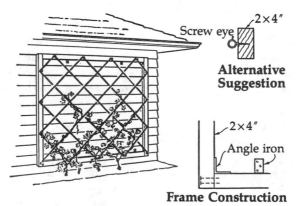

Fig. 15-32   Finished wall trellis.

16

Other outdoor structures

Today's family can use as many work and play areas outside the home as in. Storage spaces are needed for equipment and products the family uses in outdoor work and recreational activities.

This chapter gives general guidelines for recreation and storage areas. Any of these designs can be easily adapted to fit your specific needs. Work and recreational areas may include a garage, shed, yard and garden, outdoor cooking area, game and play areas. We'll first consider storage structures, then recreation structures.

A plan that provides adequate, handy work and storage space requires careful thought. To begin, develop a list of work area and storage needs, including your automobile and other vehicles. Keep in mind that needs change over the years and equipment items often are switched to newer and sometimes larger equipment. At other times, new interests are developed and are added to or substituted for initial interests and activities. Flexible, open areas can allow for changes.

One useful approach that can help you decide on size and arrangement is to study available plans and visit other families who have already built and are busily engaged in using outdoor structures.

Judging convenience

Convenient storage means the stored item is easy to see, reach, grasp, remove, and replace. Don't stack articles unless they are of similar nature, such as firewood or bags of mulch.

A half hour of garden work can be done conveniently if the machines and tools you need can be easily removed and replaced. If the machine or tools are hard to reach you're apt to put off the job.

Bicycles, wagons and other toys should generally be easy to get at because they are frequently used.

Machines removed from storage areas often require routine maintenance before being used. It is therefore a good idea to store the

235

maintenance products so they can be used between the storage area and outdoor work area.

Some machines and tools, such as lawn mowers, require space for maintenance or repair. There should be a space where they may be worked on, preferably in the workshop area.

Tools associated with the workbench should be stored in a locked cabinet above the bench. Seasonal equipment can be stored in a less convenient area in the off season and in a more accessible area during the season of use. Items can sometimes be interchanged seasonally in the same storage spaces. An example is lawn mowing and snow blowing machines. Skis and croquet sets are seasonally used and could justify more security in their storage.

Utility connections are needed to operate or service some machines, tools, or products. Locate them conveniently near where they are used. Make sure there is adequate lighting in work and service areas. Utilitarian lighting fixtures need not be expensive.

Storage areas should not be too deep. Most items do not require a storage area more than 12 inches deep.

Safety

Planning for safety in outdoor storage structures is important. Some articles require protection from the weather. Others need to be protected from extreme heat or cold. Some machines are heavy and require an adequate base for support. Outside and garage storage areas might need special security measures to deter theft and vandalism.

Electrical lighting and connections should enhance safety. Beyond general lighting needed for safety while handling equipment, special lighting is needed at work areas.

Adequate ventilation is needed in work areas where carbon monoxide, dust, or noxious fumes might be generated. An exhaust fan can be mounted in the wall or ceiling.

The garage

Before you begin building an outdoor storage structure, first look at your garage. It might, with remodeling, have sufficient storage and work space to fit your needs (FIGS. 16-1 and 16-2).

Your garage is important not only for the car, but for the variety of tools and power equipment associated with today's family residence. The garage needs to be handy, large enough, and designed and built for safety and security. Most homes in recent years have been built with attached garages large enough for two cars. A common size has been about 20×20 feet, which leaves little room for a work bench or for storing recreation equipment or power equipment popular for yard work.

A garage 24 feet wide and 28 feet deep would include useful work and storage areas, as well as ample room for driving in and out. Adding this space to your garage is less expensive than building the same space in a separate structure because the existing door, lighting, drains, etc. are used.

Whatever the size of your garage, however, you can use basic building techniques to add shelves, cabinets, workbenches, racks, wall hooks, and a variety of other storage units to increase storage space.

Adding a shelter

Sometimes building an outdoor structure to expand your home's living space is as simple as adding a shelter (FIGS. 16-3 through 16-9). This redwood shelter will shade your patio or decks, making it cool and comfortable. In fact, it can help your house stay cooler by shielding

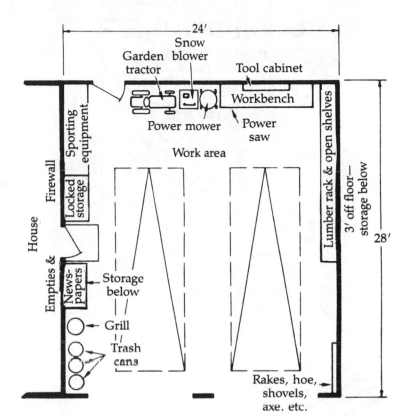

Fig. 16-1 *Designing your garage work area.*

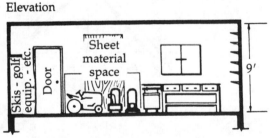

Elevation

Fig. 16-2 *Garage storage elevation.*

windows, walls, and sliding glass doors from sun and heat build-up.

The following explanation is for building an 8×12-foot shelter, but you can easily adapt it for other dimensions. To enlarge this design, use larger lumber for posts, beams, and joists, and consider additional posts for proper support. If you are in doubt, consult a building materials retailer, contractor, or landscape architect.

Economical garden grades of redwood will perform well in a deck shelter. Be sure to use a heartwood grade like Construction Heart for posts and the ledger. These members will need the decay and insect resistance provided by redwood's heartwood. Construction Common can be used for joists and louvers.

Materials List for Deck Shelter

- Posts: 2 pieces, 4×4 by 8 feet
- Ledger: 1 piece, 2×4 by 12 feet
- Beam: 1 piece, 4×6 by 12 feet
- Joists: 4 pieces, 2×6 by 8 feet
- Louvers: 24 pieces, 1×4 by 12 feet

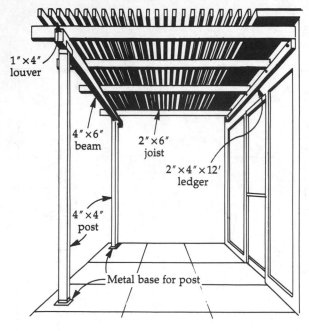

1" × 4"
louver

4" × 6"
beam

2" × 6"
joist

2" × 4" × 12'
ledger

4" × 4"
post

Metal base for post

Fig. 16-3 *Outdoor shelter.*
California Redwood Association

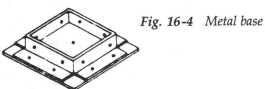

Fig. 16-4 *Metal base*

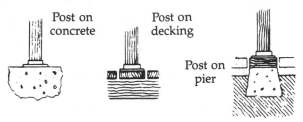

Post on
concrete

Post on
decking

Post on
pier

Fig. 16-5 *Footings for outdoor shelter.*

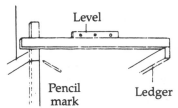

Level

Pencil
mark

Ledger

Fig. 16-6 *Leveling the deck.*
California Redwood Association

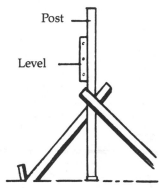

Post

Level

Fig. 16-7 *Leveling posts.*

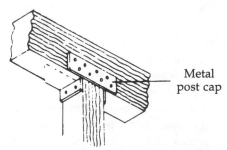

Metal
post cap

Fig. 16-8 *Metal post cap installation.*
California Redwood Association

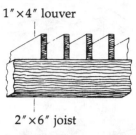

1"×4" louver

2"×6" joist

Fig. 16-9 *Installing louvers.* California Redwood Association

You'll also need two non-corrosive metal bases for the posts; two non-corrosive metal caps for the posts; four non-corrosive lag screws or bolts for the ledger; 8d nails for louvers, joists, and beam; 16d nails for attaching the metal bases to the wood deck or concrete nails for attaching the metal bases to a concrete patio. To avoid staining, all metal hardware should be stainless steel, aluminum, or top-quality, hot-dipped galvanized.

First step Anchor the ledger to the side of the house using lag screws or bolts. Screws should penetrate into studs or header to provide best support. Make sure there is room for 2×6 joists to rest on the edge of the ledger and pass under the eaves of your house.

Second Prepare the footings for posts. The bases for the posts will vary, depending on the construction of your patio or deck. If the 4×4 posts are to rest on a wood deck or concrete patio, a metal base can be anchored into the surface with 16d or concrete nails. In other situations, the post can sit on a precast pier block.

Trim the posts to the proper height. The top of the posts should be the same height as the ledger, minus the thickness of the beam. Measure the actual dimension of the lumber you are using. The actual dimension of a surfaced 4×6 will be close to 3¹/2 by 5¹/2 inches.

Also make allowance for the metal base and post cap.

Anchor the posts to their bases or footing with 8d nails. Plumb the posts with a bubble level and use temporary support boards to hold them in position while you complete the shelter's construction.

Attach the metal post caps and secure the 4×6 beam with 8d nails.

Third Install joists at 4-foot intervals and toenail to the ledger and beam with 8d nails. If your measurements were accurate, joists should be level. If possible, nail joists to part of the eaves because this will restrict lateral movement of the shelter.

Finally Toenail the 1×4 louvers in place. The distance between the louvers will determine the degree of shade or sun that penetrates. For moderate filtered sunlight, 3-inch intervals work well. If, after your shelter is completed, you find it needs more lateral stability, add corner braces from the beam to each post.

Outdoor planters

Planters can be easily built and installed to add beauty and function to your landscape and your garden. Let's consider the construction of a few outdoor planters and wooden structures.

The fresh lines of the planter shown in FIG. 16-10 will enliven a deck, garden, or patio. It can be built with preservative-treated wood or with naturally decay-resistant wood, such as redwood. For best results, measure and trim each piece as you build. Predrill holes, especially at the ends of boards, to prevent splitting. Use only top-quality, hot-dipped galvanized nails to prevent rust stains. If using redwood, Construction Heart grade is best for pieces in contact with the soil.

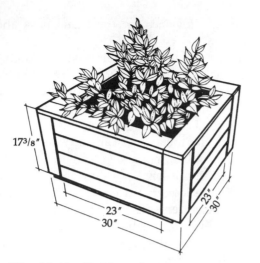

Fig. 16-10 *Outdoor planter.* California Redwood Association

Materials List for Planter

- 4 pieces of 4×4 by 15-inch lumber
- 16 pieces of 1×4 by 22¹/₂-inch lumber
- 4 pieces of 2×6 by 22¹/₂-inch lumber
- 2 pieces of 2×4 by 24¹/₂-inch lumber
- 16 pieces of 1×4 by 22¹/₂-inch lumber
- 4 pieces of 1×4 by 26¹/₂-inch lumber
- 8 pieces of 2×2 by 15-inch lumber
- About 60 galvanized 12d nails
- About 160 galvanized 6d nails

To make your planter (FIG. 16-11), first nail two 2×2s to adjacent faces of each 4×4 corner post, using 12d nails. Leave room for the 1×4 panels to fit flush with outer faces of the 4×4 posts. Attach 1×4 boards to posts with two 6d nails at each board end. The 1×4 boards should be evenly spaced along the post and flush with the bottom and outer face.

Complete two walls, inside and out, to form an L as shown in the illustration. Then construct the last two walls, completing the box. It might help to lay the project on its side when nailing the last wall.

For the base, turn the box upside down

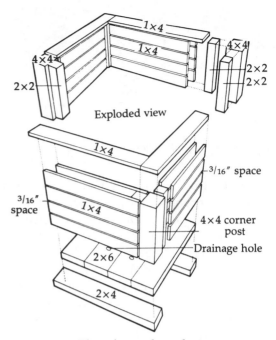

Fig. 16-11 *Plans for outdoor planter.* California Redwood Association

and place 2×4s on opposite sides, 1 inch in from the edge. With two 12d nails in each board end, attach the 2×4s to the 4×4 posts. Drill two 1-inch drainage holes in two of the 3×6s to be used for the bottom. Turn the box upright and lay all four 2×6s in place to form the bottom of the planter.

For the top trim, butt-join 1×4s flush with the planter's outer edge. Use two 6d nails at each board end, penetrating the 4×4 at one end and the 2×2 at the other. These nails can be countersunk and filled with non-oily wood filler. Interior surfaces should be lined with a polyethylene liner. Make sure to provide proper drainage by cutting holes through the bottom of the planter and the liner.

Figure 16-12 illustrates a modified and enlarged version of the planter used for raised bed gardens.

You could also use lengths of pressure-treated lumber, staked in place, as sidewall framing for the raised bed method of garden-

Fig. 16-12 *Enlarged planter used for raised bed garden.* Wolmanized pressure-treated lumber

ing (FIG. 16-13). It also makes moving the bed much easier because it can be dissassembled.

Pressure-treated or naturally decay-resis-tant woods can also be used in the garden to support sugar pea plants (FIG. 16-14) or tomato plants.

Fig. 16-13 *Simple raised bed garden.* Wolmanized pressure-treated lumber

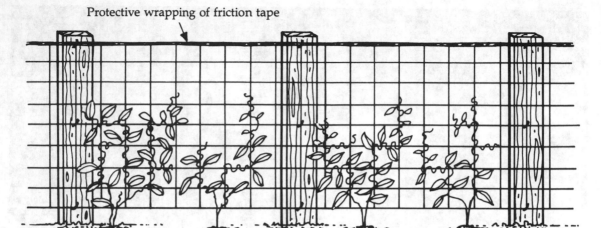

Protective wrapping of friction tape

Fig. 16-14 *Plant supports.* Wolmanized pressure-treated lumber

Outdoor benches

Benches can be a comfortable addition to your backyard garden or deck. Figures 16-15 and 16-16 illustrate the construction and finished product. It can be made of decay-resistant redwood or other treated woods. For best performance, use non-corrosive nails and hardware.

The butcherblock bench is made entirely of 2×4s for the seats and legs. Legs are built up

Fig. 16-16 *Finished butcher block bench.* California Redwood Association

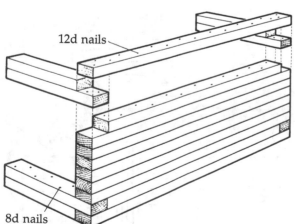

12d nails

8d nails

Fig. 16-15 *Construction of butcher block outdoor bench.* California Redwood Association

by nailing a long and short 2×4 together. First trim four pieces of 2×4 18 inches long and four pieces about 12½ inches long. (Subtract the actual width of your 2×4 from 18 inches for this measurement.) Assemble short and long pieces in pairs with six 8d nails and attach to each end of the seatboard, flush on the ends and edges.

Laminate seatboards, making sure they are level and even on the top seating area. Fit a short seatboard between legs and nail every 6 inches in a zigzag pattern. With 12d nails, laminate eight long seatboards, alternating zigzag nailing pattern, then nail remaining legs and the last short and long seatboards.

Figures 16-17 and 16-18 illustrate the construction of an open lattice bench. The open lattice bench is a variation of the butcherblock design, using 2×4 seatboards with alternating 1×4 spacers. Legs are made from 1×4 spacers sandwiched between two 2×6s.

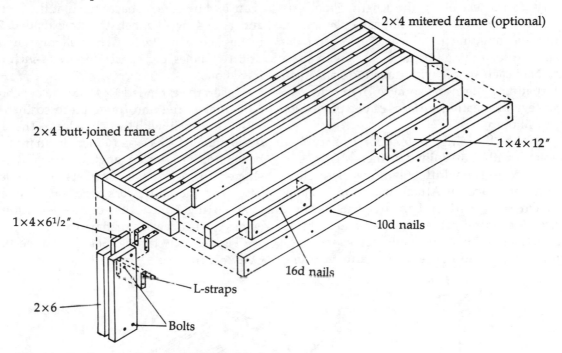

Fig. 16-17 *Construction of open lattice bench.* California Redwood Association

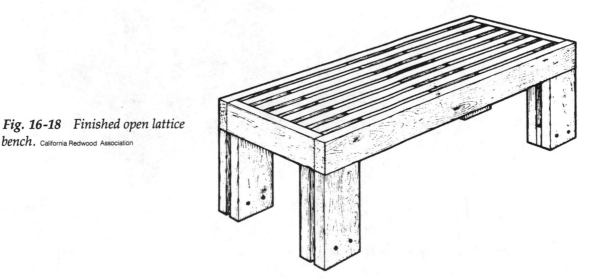

Fig. 16-18 *Finished open lattice bench.* California Redwood Association

For the latticework, precut all 1×4 spacers 12 inches long. Rough-cut six 2×4s to the desired bench length. Set spacers on each side of one 2×4, 4 to 6 inches from each end and every 2 to 3 feet along the length. From one side only, nail with three 10d nails per spacer. Continue building up the latticework on the nailing side, adding five more 2×4s with spacers. Nail each spacer with three 16d nails in an alternating pattern, as shown. Then trim 2×4 ends evenly. Seating surfaces can be planed for extra smoothness.

For the framing, outer 2×4 trim can be applied with butt-joined corners. Trim end frame pieces the width of latticework (including outer spacers). Attach with one 10d nail at each seatboard end in a zigzag pattern. Trim side frame pieces to cover end framing and attach with three nails per spacer. For optional mitered corners, trim and fit frame individually, then miter-cut the board ends 45 degrees.

To build bench legs follow these instructions: Between two 2×6 by 12½-inch boards, set a 1×4 by 4-inch spacer flush at the bottom and a 1×4 by 6½-inch spacer extended 2½ inches above the 2×6s. Clamp all together and drill two holes per spacer for ¼×4-inch carriage bolts.

Insert the extended 1×4 into the bench top tight against the end frame piece so that the 2×6s are flush with bench edges. The 1×4 insert should be recessed 1 inch down from the bench top. At inside angles, attach two L-shaped or right-angle brackets to the leg's 2×6s and the latticework seat. Attach one L-strap to the 6-inch side of the leg running across the latticework seatboards.

Figures 16-19 through 16-21 illustrate three other bench ideas.

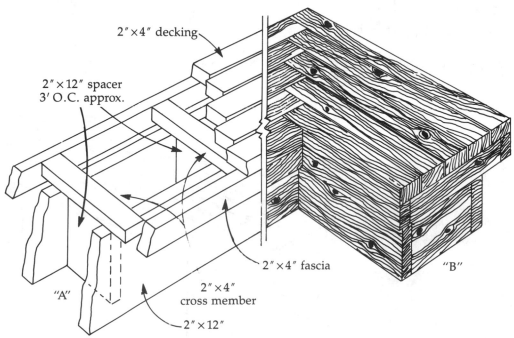

Fig. 16-19 *Deck bench construction.* California Redwood Association

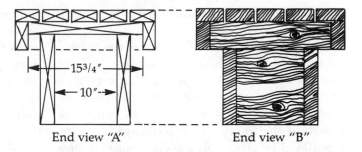

Fig. 16-20 *Side views of deck bench.* _{California} Redwood Association

End view "A"   End view "B"

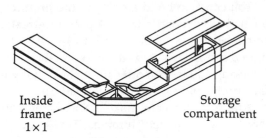

Inside frame 1×1

Storage compartment

Fig. 16-21 *Deck bench with storage compartment.* Georgia-Pacific Corp.

Outdoor nook

Figure 16-22 illustrates the construction of a unique outdoor structure for those who enjoy privacy. This curvy wall is sized to fit a table for two as well as a bench for watching the sun rise or set.

When planning your version of this project, first lay out a circle as large as the top of the table you intend to use inside it. Be sure also to make room for the chairs. The retreat shown is 5 feet tall at its highest point. It tapers down to roughly 3 feet. You'll probably want to adjust the height to suit your needs and surroundings.

Naturally, the amount of material you'll need will depend on the circumference and height of the unit you choose to build. The

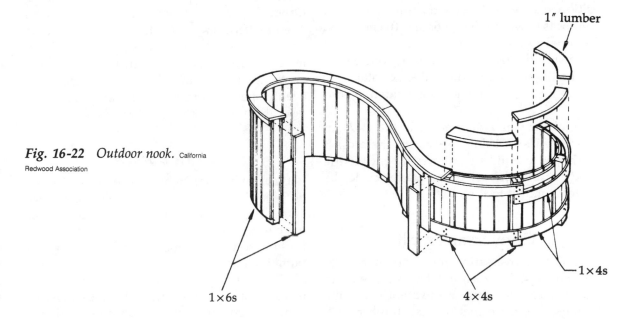

Fig. 16-22 *Outdoor nook.* California Redwood Association

1″ lumber

1×6s   4×4s   1×4s

running length of the wall shown here is 34 feet.

The circumference of a circle is the diameter times pi, which is approximately 3.14. So if you want to make a single wall that's roughly three-quarters of a circle and has an inside diameter of 6 feet—or 72 inches—figure the length of the interior wall this way: 72 multiplied by 3.14 gives you the circumference of a whole circle. That figure multiplied by .75 will give you the length of a three-quarter-circle wall.

To calculate the circumference of the exterior wall—assuming that the wall will be 6 inches thick—use 6.5 feet or 78 inches times 3.14, multiplied by .75.

Make similar calculations for the other arc of the nook. Next, add the four circumference figures together to get the total length of the surface to be covered.

Assuming that you'll use 1×6s to make the walls, divide the total by the actual width of a 1×6 (5.5 inches). That tells how many 1×6s you need to build the wall.

The reference drawing shows a 4×4 post positioned at every 3 feet of the wall. You'll also need 1×4s to which the 1×6s are attached, and additional 1×7 lumber for the cap.

Be sure to anchor the 4×4s in concrete by pouring the concrete around them or attaching them to metal post anchors embedded in concrete.

Once the wall is in place, add the 1×7 cap as shown. Use a saber saw to cut the arcs. If you choose to build a cantilevered bench to the outside of the shorter three-quarter circle, be sure to anchor it to the posts.

Conversation pit

An outdoor conversation pit is shown in FIGS. 16-23 and 16-24. The central table can be a cover for a fire pit for cooking or for warmth on chilly evenings. The main platform is a lumber deck constructed in conventional fashion but with vertical 2×6s nailed to joists to serve as supports for the bench tops. Use ³/8-inch nuts and bolts to attach 2×4s placed on edge. Frame the opening with 2×12s and then make a cover to fit. If you include a fire pit, it must be fireproof. Build a double-brick wall on four sides and then add a veneer of firebrick bonded with fireclay—this is one way to build a fire pit.

You can also build a deck on the ground if you nail deck boards to 2×4 pressure-treated lumber cleats placed flat on a 3- to 4-inch bed of tamped sand. This lends itself to prefabrication of decking squares (about 4×4 inches) that you place uniformly or in a parquet pattern.

Another idea is to make a grid frame with 2×6 pressure-treated lumber. This may be placed on a sand bed and then covered with deck boards placed parallel.

Engawa

An engawa is simply an outdoor corridor or passageway made of lumber (FIG. 16-25). The idea came from Japan and is very popular in Oriental garden landscaping, where it serves as a link between rooms that open onto a court or garden. A rail may also be part of this floor-level platform. Once the frame is built on short posts, 2×4s are turned on their edges and evenly spaced to make the decking. The 2×6 fascia boards are often used as trim.

Lattice walls

Lattice can be used tightly woven to screen out an objectionable view, or to shield a service yard or garden work center. With its spaces open wide, a lattice will let in a view, serve as a traffic director, or double as a display tier for potted plants.

Lattices may be used to support climbing roses or other vines. Such plantings must be kept pruned, or they will run away with the

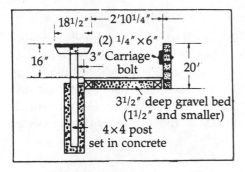

Materials List

1. Deck
   8 pieces required 4×4×10'
   27 pieces required 2=4×10'
2. Benches: (6'-8" long & 8'-8" long)
   5 pieces required 4×4×4'
   5 pieces required 2=4×7'
   5 pieces required 2=4×12"
3. Firepit
   40 pieces required 4×4×16"
   1 bag mortar
   2 pieces required 2×6×6'
4. Nails and accessories as required

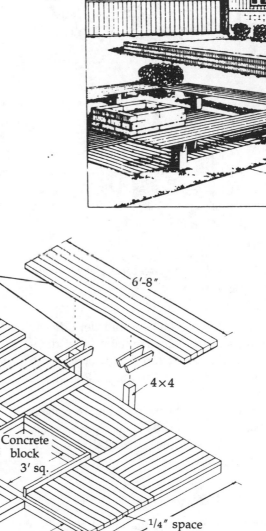

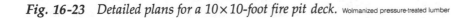

Fig. 16-23 *Detailed plans for a 10×10-foot fire pit deck.* Wolmanized pressure-treated lumber

Fig. 16-24 *Conversation pit.* Georgia-Pacific Corp.

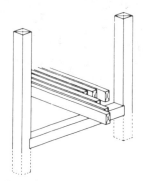

Fig. 16-25 *Details on an engawa or elevated walkway.* Western Wood Products Association

wall, and they have to be removed periodically to permit repainting. Because some vines damage wood by keeping it too damp, check with your nurseryman before planting alongside a lattice wall or screen.

The only construction tip for lattice walls is to use a basic post and rail frame. Space evenly the thin lattice slats either horizontally and vertically or diagonally.

Pavilion

A pavilion is simply a large gazebo that is often square or rectangular in shape rather than round. Pavilions can be used for shade in the garden, as an outdoor eating area, or as a cover for outdoor activities. Construction consists of setting posts and joists as you would with a sunscreen or deck and covering with an appropriate cover.

Aerie

An aerie is a small gazebo that usually contains two or four benches and a small table for eating. Aerie literally means a "nest." Construct as you would a gazebo. Aeries are often built just outside the kitchen door, so breakfast or lunch can be served in the outdoors during better weather.

Tree house

A tree house is simply a deck built around a tree (FIG. 16-26). Support for the structure comes from the tree itself, with a frame that girds the trunk, then joins the joists for the flooring.

Fig. 16-26 *A tree house without a tree.* Georgia-Pacific Corp.

The railing on a tree house is especially important. It must be strong and tall enough to contain children and discourage exit other than down the ladder or rope. Many tree houses have slanted top rails and lower bottom rails to help solve this problem.

Don't secure the house to the tree with too many nails. The nails open the trunk to infection. If possible, paint over any nails with tree paint.

Greenhouse

A greenhouse is a fun project that can be a source of year-round vegetables (FIG. 16-27). Whether you build a freestanding unit or a lean-to, a good construction technique is to prefabricate frames using 2×4 fir or pine with joints reinforced with 3/8-inch exterior grade plywood gussets attached with glue and nails. Space frames 16 to 24 inches on center and run 2×4s horizontally inside, at the ridge line, frame corners, and along the base. The covering can be polyethylene sheet, corrugated fiberglass, smooth rigid plastic, or double-strength glass. Polyethylene can be attached with staples, but a better way is to use lathe strips as battens so the material won't tear as easily. Corrugated or rigid plastic can be secured directly to the framing, but lay down a bead or two of caulking over the frame members first.

Fig. 16-27 *Solar greenhouse.* Georgia-Pacific Corp.

Backyard storage shed

Build the shed on a concrete pad as you would a small house, or make a foundation of precast concrete piers. Span with 4×6 pressure-treated lumber beams to which you nail 1¹/8-inch exterior grade plywood underlayment. Go up from there with sole plate, studs, double top plate, and then roof rafters. Do a simple design—a shed roof covered with mineral-surfaced roll roofing, or a gable covered with cedar shakes. Cover the exterior walls with plywood siding—textured, channel-grooved, or smooth. You can match it to the house or make the project of a different design (FIG. 16-28).

Fig. 16-28 *Storage shed.* Georgia-Pacific Corp.

Playhouse and toolshed

If space in your backyard is in short supply, you might not be able to have both a toolshed for storing garden equipment and a playhouse for children—unless you can piggyback the two.

Figure 16-29 illustrates the bi-level playhouse/toolshed. The 6-by-12-foot storage compartment of this dual-purpose project is large enough to hold all your garden equipment and the family's bicycles, too. It's topped with an overhanging playhouse with its own ladder.

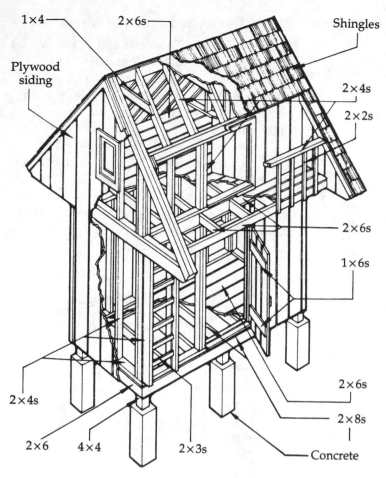

1×4

2×6s

Shingles

Plywood
siding

2×4s

2×2s

Fig. 16-29 *Playhouse and toolshed
plans.* Georgia-Pacific Corp.

2×6s

1×6s

2×6s

2×8s

2×4s

2×6   4×4   2×3s

Concrete

The kids can play safely and in comfort since windows on either end admit plenty of fresh air. The playhouse and toolshed can be built of cedar, redwood, or pressure-treated lumber.

Materials List for Playhouse/Toolshed

- 1 piece of lumber, 2×8 by 8 feet long
- 24 pieces of lumber, 2×6 by 12 feet long
- 2 pieces of lumber, 2×6 by 12 feet long
- 3 pieces of lumber, 2×6 by 10 feet long
- 30 pieces of lumber, 1×8 by 12 feet long
- 40 pieces of lumber, 2×4 by 7 feet, 3 inches long
- 8 pieces of lumber, 2×4 by 12 feet long
- 7 pieces of lumber, 1×6 by 12 feet long
- 16 pieces of lumber, 1×4 by 8 feet long
- 6 pieces of lumber, 1×4 by 12 feet long
- 1 piece of lumber, 1×2 by 12 feet long
- 4 pieces of lumber, 1×3 by 12 feet long
- 4 pieces of lumber, 2×2 by 12 feet long
- 6 4-by-8 foot sheets of 1/2-inch plywood
- 2 4-by-8 foot sheets of 3/8-inch plywood
- 13 4-by-8 foot sheets of plywood siding (or shiplap siding)
- Other materials include: 6-inch galvanized joist hangers, roofing felt, asphalt shingles, nails, aluminum Z flashing, windows, door pulls, strap hinges.

First, set the 4×4 posts in concrete footings and let them cure. Bolt pressure-treated 2×6s to the posts just above grade level to form band joists. Next install pressure-treated 2×6 joists with galvanized joist hangers. Top them with 1×8s.

Begin framing the wall by driving nails through a 2×4 sill plate into the joists under the perimeter of the floor. Nail the studs 24 inches on center. Add the top plate.

Attach the 2×6 ceiling joists to the vertical posts at either end of the structure. Extend the joists 4 feet past the storage shed, as shown in the drawing. For the cantilevered deck, install a 2×6 header 2 feet from the end of the joists. Attach 2×6 ceiling joists to the header so they rest on the top plate. Top the floor with 1×8s (leave an opening for the ladder).

Attach a 2×4 sill plate to the perimeter of the attic. Frame the attic with 2×4 studs, then attach the front top plate. Make the double end rafters from two 2×4s. Connect them with a 1×8 ridge beam. Install the 2×4 rafters. Top them with 1/2-inch plywood sheathing.

Finally, apply the siding. Build the railing. Add the ladder built of 2×3s, the window and door trim, and the roofing.

Now it's time to clear out the garage and call out the kids!

Roofing outdoor structures

Small outdoor structures, such as the playhouse/toolshed and the gazebos illustrated in this chapter, often require roofing. Let's look at how even the novice builder can easily roof or reroof such a structure.

Figures 16-30 through 16-32 illustrated how

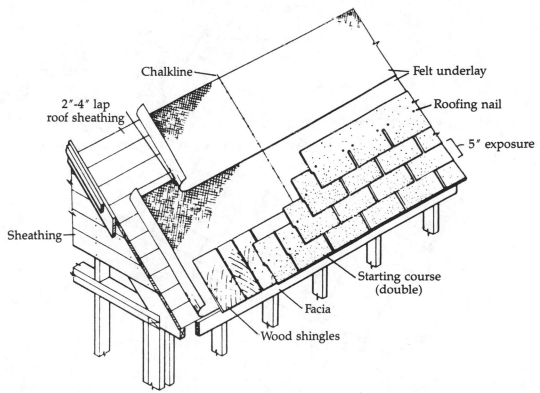

Fig. 16-30 Installing asphalt shingle roofing.

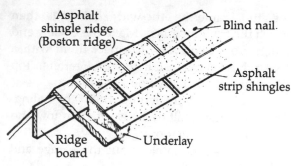

Fig. 16-31 *Installing asphalt shingle ridge or Boston ridge.*

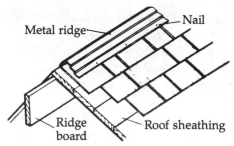

Fig. 16-32 *Installing a metal ridge.*

asphalt roofing is installed. The square-butt strip asphalt shingle is 12 by 36 inches, has three tabs, and is usually laid with 5 inches exposed to the weather. There are 27 strips in a bundle and three bundles will cover 100 square feet of roof.

The method of laying an asphalt shingle roof is shown in FIG. 16-30. A metal edge is often used at the gable end to provide additional protection. The first course of asphalt shingles is doubled; or, if desired, a starter course. This first course should extend downward beyond the edging about 1/2 inch to pre-

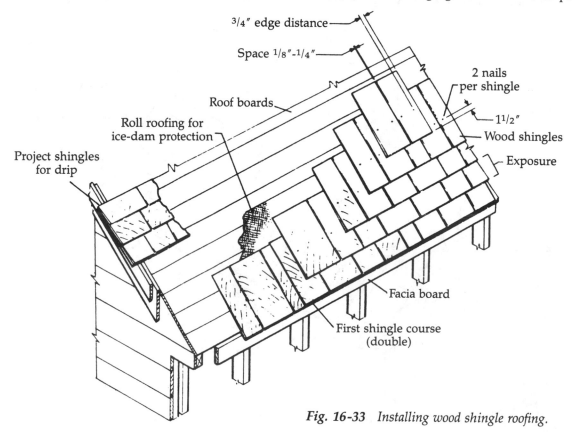

Fig. 16-33 *Installing wood shingle roofing.*

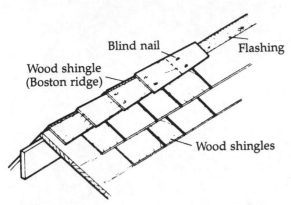

Fig. 16-34 *Installing wood shingle ridge or Boston ridge.*

Blind nail

Flashing

Wood shingle
(Boston ridge)

Wood shingles

vent the water from backing up under the shingles.

Several chalklines on the underlayment will help you align the shingles so that tab notches will be in a straight line for good appearance. Each shingle strip should be fastened securely, according to the manufacturer's directions. It is good practice to use six 1-inch galvanized roofing nails for each 12×36 strip. A sealed tab or asphalt sealer will also help prevent wind damage during storms.

Figure 16-31 illustrates how asphalt shingles are added to the ridge to cap your roofing job.

Installing wood shingles (FIG. 16-33) is similar to installing asphalt shingles, except that wood shingles come in single units rather than tabs. Make sure a small space is allowed between shingles for expansion during rainy weather. Figure 16-34 shows how a wood shingle roof is capped.

Enjoy your outdoor structures.

Appendix A
Grading lumber and boards

This appendix will assist buyers and users to properly specify and identify the grades of western softwood dimension lumber and boards that best suit their needs. The material is adapted from *Western Wood Product Species Book, Vol. 1: Dimension Lumber* and *Vol. 2: Select-finish/Commons-Boards*, courtesy of the Western Wood Products Association (WWPA), Yeon Building, Portland, OR 97204.

Western softwood species commonly manufactured into dimension lumber include western hemlock, Engelmann spruce, larch, western cedars, and all pines and firs. Many of these species are grown, harvested, manufactured, and marketed together. They have similar performance properties that make them interchangeable in use, grading, and grade marking. Douglas fir and larch are grouped together as "Douglas fir-larch." Western hemlock combines with true firs as "hem-fir." The "white woods" include Engelmann spruce, all true firs, hemlocks, and pines. "Ponderosa pine" is an individual species.

Specifications

Dimension lumber is surfaced lumber of nominal thickness from 2 to 4 inches. It is used for structural support and framing including studs, joists, and rafters.

National grading rules classify dimension lumber in three width categories and four use categories. Structural Light Framing and Light Framing are 2 to 4 inches wide. Studs are 2 to 6 inches wide. Structural Joists and Planks are 5 inches and wider.

The Structural Light Framing and Structural Joists and Planks categories each contain four grades, covering a range of characteristics and manufacturing imperfections that affect strength, stiffness, and appearance.

Select Structural is the highest grade in the Structural Light Framing and Structural Joists and Planks category. Lumber in this grade must look good as well as be strong and stiff.

The No. 1 grade is recommended where good appearance is desired but is secondary to strength and stiffness. The No. 2 grade is recommended for most general construction uses. The No. 3 grade is appropriate for general construction where great strength is generally not a factor.

The Light Framing category contains three grades. Construction is the highest grade in Light Framing. This indicates a piece suitable for general framing, with a good appearance but graded primarily for strength and serviceability. Some pieces in this grade would be No. 1 or better in Structural Light Framing.

Standard grade is customarily used for the same purpose or with construction grade, providing good strength and excellent serviceability.

Utility grade is recommended for economy: uses include studding, blocking, plates, and bracing.

Stud grade is a separate grade. Pieces are suitable for all stud uses including load-bearing walls. Restrictions on crook, wane, and edge knots make this one of the most popular grades for wall construction. Lengths, however, are limited to 10 feet.

Economy grades are also available in the Structural Light Framing, Light Framing, and Structural Joists and Planks categories.

Grade stamp

The Western Wood Products Association grade stamp contains five elements that identify the manufacturer, grade, species, moisture content, and certification (FIGS. A-1 and A-2).

Fig. A-1 Typical grade stamp. Western Wood Products Association

Fig. A-2 Grade stamp from structural light framing lumber. Western Wood Products Association

Manufacturer The originating mill is identified by an assigned number or by the firm's name or brand.

Grade The grade is shown by the grade name or its abbreviation. Dimension grade names include: CONST (Construction), STAND (Standard), UTIL (Utility), STUD (Stud), SEL STR (Select Structural), 1 (No. 1), 2 (No. 2), and 3 (No. 3).

Species mark Species or species grouping is indicated by an appropriate symbol.

Moisture content Moisture content at the time of surfacing is shown by an appropriate abbreviation: S-GRN (Surfaced Green, Standard size unseasoned lumber with moisture content of 20 percent or more); S-DRY (Surfaced Dry, Standard size lumber dried to moisture content of 19 percent or less); MC 15 (Moisture Content 15 percent, Standard size lumber dried to a specific moisture content of 15 percent or less).

Certification A piece bearing this mark has been graded under supervision of the Western Wood Products Association.

Characteristics

Grades are determined primarily by the natural characteristics of the log that has an effect upon the lumber's strength, stiffness, and appearance. Manufacturing imperfections, no matter what the cause, also affect the grade.

The grade is calculated on a complex formula that considers type, size, closeness, frequency, and location of all characteristics and imperfections within the piece. It is the responsibility of the grader to visually judge the total effect of these considerations according to limitations set forth in the grading rules for each grade and species.

Knots are the most frequently encountered characteristic. Knot terms include: round, sound, encased, intergrown, spike, tight, and watertight.

Wane is the presence of bark or lack of wood on the edge or corner of a piece of lumber.

Shake is a lengthwise separation of the wood that usually occurs between or through the annual growth rings.

White speck and honeycomb are caused by a fungus in the living tree. White speck is small white pits or spots. Honeycomb is similar, but the pits are deeper or larger. Neither is subject to further decay except under wet conditions.

Decay is a disintegration of the wood due to the action of wood-destroying fungi. It may also be called dote, rot, or unsound wood.

Checks are separations of the wood fibers. They may occur across or through the annual growth rings and usually as a result of seasoning.

Splits are similar to checks except the separations of the wood fibers extend completely through a piece, usually at the ends.

Bow is a deviation from a flat plane of the wide face of a piece of lumber from end to end.

Crook is a deviation from a flat plane of the narrow quality, with one hole per linear foot.

Twist is a deviation from the flat planes of all four faces in a spiraling or torsional action. It is usually the result of seasoning.

Cup is a deviation from a flat plane, edge to edge.

Manufacturing imperfections include chipped, torn, raised, or loosened grain, skips in surfacing, undersizing, mismatch, wavy

dressing, and machine-caused burns, chips, bite, or knife marks.

Other characteristics include burl, compression wood, pitch, slope of grain, pitch streak, pith, pocket, sapwood, and stain.

Dimension lumber grades
Structural light framing (DF-L, Hem-Fir, PP)

- Select Structural—Sound, firm, encased and pith knots are limits to up to $7/8$ inch and are tight and well-spaced. Unsound or loose knots or holes are limited to up to $3/4$ inch, one per 4 linear feet.
- No. 1—Knots must be of the same type as in the Select Structural grade, up to $1 1/2$ inches. Unsound or loose knots or holes are limited up to 1 inch, one per 3 linear feet.
- No. 2—Well-spaced knots of any quality are allowed up to 2 inches, with one hole per 2 linear feet.
- No. 3—Knots can be up to $2 1/2$ inches of any widths to $1 1/4$-inches on 14-inch widths, one per 4 linear feet.

Structural joists and planks (DF-L, Hem-Fir, PP)

- Select Structural—Knots are limited to sound, firm, encased, and pitch knots, if tight and well-spaced, with one unsound or loose knot or hole per 4 linear feet. Center line knots range from maximums of $1 1/2$ inches on 5-inch widths to $3 1/4$-inches on 14-inch widths. Edge knots range from maximums of 1-inch on 4-inch widths to $2 3/8$-inches on 14-inch widths. Unsound or loose knots or holes range from maximums of $7/8$-inch on 5-inch face of a piece of lumber from end to end.
- No. 1—Knots must be of the same type

as in Select Structural grade. They can be slightly larger with one unsound or loose knot or hole permitted per 3 linear feet.

- No. 2—Well-spaced knots of any quality are allowed and no more than one hole from any cause per 2 linear feet.
- No. 3—Well-spaced knots of any quality are allowed and no more than one hole from any cause per linear foot.

Light framing (DF-L, Hem-Fir, PP, WW)

- Construction—Sound, firm, encased, and pith knots are tight and limited to no larger than $1^1/2$ inches. Unsound or loose knots or holes are limited to 1 inch, one per 3 linear feet.
- Standard—Knots are not restricted as to quality up to 2 inches anywhere on the wide face. Holes are limited up to $1^1/4$ inches, one per 2 linear feet.
- Utility—Knots are not restricted as to quality up to $2^1/2$ inches anywhere on the wide face. Holes are limited up to $1^1/2$ inches, one per linear foot.
- Stud—Knots are not restricted as to quality, but they must be well-spaced. Sizes are up to what is allowed in Utility grade. Lengths are limited to a maximum of 10 feet.

Board lumber

Western softwood species commonly manufactured into board lumber include Douglas fir, western larch, Ponderosa pine, lodgepole pine, sugar pine, Engelmann spruce, Idaho white pine, western red cedar, incense cedar, western hemlock, and true firs.

Many of these species are grown, harvested, manufactured, and marketed together. Some have similar appearance and performance properties that make them interchange-able in use. This applies to western hemlock and the five true firs that are grouped together as hem-fir. Similar marketing groups include western cedars (incense and western red cedar) and white woods (Engelmann spruce, any true firs, any hemlocks, and any pines).

Softwood from other parts of the country will have similar groupings and classifications.

Grade classifications

Select and Finish grades of western woods are used for many applications where appearance is important. Grading is based on a 1×8 by 12-foot piece with the number and extent of characteristics in larger or smaller pieces varying in proportion.

Select grades are determined from the better side, or face, and are separated into three grades: B and BTR, C Select, and D Select.

B and BTR Select grade is the ultimate in appearance. It is the highest quality of Select grade lumber. Many pieces are absolutely clear.

C Select grade is recommended for all finishing uses where fine appearance is essential. Its appearance ranks only slightly less than B and BTR grade.

D Select grade has many of the fine appearance features of C Select grade. It is suitable where the finishing needs are less exacting.

Finish grades are determined from the side or face and from both edges on pieces 5 inches and narrower, and from the better side or face and edge on pieces 6 inches and wider. Finish grades are Superior, Prime, and E.

Superior is the highest grade of Finish lumber. Many pieces are absolutely clear.

Prime grade exhibits a fine appearance, although it is less restrictive than Superior grade.

E Finish can be ordered when pieces can be crosscut or ripped to obtain cuttings of Prime or better quality.

There are five grades of boards referred to as Commons and five Alternate Board Grades. Grade levels of boards referred to as Commons are not identical to those of Alternate Board Grades. Overlapping levels provide customers with a broader choice of grade variations.

Common board grades, determined from the better face, are 1 Common, 2 Common, 3 Common, 4 Common, and 5 Common. The usual practice is to combine 1 Common with 2 Common and market the mixture as 2 and Better Common.

The No. 1 Common grade is not usually carried in stock in large quantities, but may be ordered when the ultimate in fine appearance of knotty material is required.

The No. 2 Common grade is intended primarily for use in paneling, shelving, and other uses calling for knotty lumber with fine appearance.

The No. 3 Common grade is widely used for shelving, paneling, and siding as well as fences, boxes, crating, sheathing, and industrial applications.

The No. 4 Common grade is more widely used than any other grade for general construction, such as for subfloors, roof and wall sheathing, concrete forms, low-cost fencing, crating, etc.

The No. 5 Common grade is intended for use in economical construction where appearance and strength are not basic requirements.

Alternate Board Grades, determined from the better face, are: Select Merchantable, Construction, Standard, Utility, and Economy.

Select Merchantable grade is intended primarily for use in housing and light construction where it is exposed as paneling, shelving, and where knotty-type lumber with the finest appearance is recommended.

Construction grade is recommended and widely used for subfloors, roof and wall sheathing, concrete forms, and similar types of construction.

Standard grade is most widely used for general construction purposes where it is seldom left exposed.

Utility grade is judged primarily on serviceability instead of appearance, and provides an inexpensive lumber for general construction purposes.

Economy grade is suitable for low-grade sheathing, crating, bracing, temporary construction, and similar uses.

Appendix B
Specifications for galvanized steel chain-link fence materials

These standards and specifications are offered by the Chain-link Manufacturers Institute and by the International Fence Industry Association.

1. Purpose

1.1 The purpose of these specifications is to provide a nationally recognized standard of quality for galvanized steel chain-link fence fabric.

2. Scope

2.1 This specification gives the nomenclature, definitions, and general requirements for galvanized steel chain-link fence fabric.

3. Definitions

3.1 Chain-link fence fabric Chain-link fence fabric is a fencing material made from wire helically wound and interwoven so as to provide a continuous mesh without knots or ties, except in the form of knuckling or of twisting the wire's ends to form the selvage of the fabric.

3.2 Knuckling Knuckling is the term used to describe the type of selvage obtained by interlocking adjacent pairs or wire ends and bending the wire ends back into a closed loop.

3.3 Twisting Twisting is the term used to describe the type of selvage obtained by twisting adjacent pairs of wire ends together in a close helix of $1^1/_2$ machine turns, which is equivalent to three full twists.

4. Requirements

4.1 Materials

4.1.1 Base metal The base metal of the fabric shall be a good commercial quality steel wire of the gauges specified in TABLE B-1. The wire shall withstand the following breaking loads: No. 6 gauge, 2,170 pounds; No. 9 gauge, 1,129 pounds; and No. 11 gauge, 850 pounds. The break strength of the wire shall be determined in accordance with the requirements of 5.5.1.

4.1.2 Zinc coating The fabric shall be zinc-coated by the hot-dip process after fabrication, or it shall be fabricated from wire zinc-coated by the electrolytic or hot-dip process. The weight of zinc coating shall be not less than 1.2 ounces per square foot of

Table B-1. Common Chain-link Fence Parts

Materials you will need	What size	How many
Posts—corner, end and gate posts	1⅞″ or 2⅜″ outside diameter, 24″ to 30″ longer than the height of the wire.	1 for each end and corner, and 2 for each gate.
Line (intermediate) *posts*	1⅝″ outside diameter, 18″ to 24″ longer than the height of the wire.	1 for every 10′ of fence line.
Top rail (swage end)	1⅜″ outside diameter, 21′ lengths	The same linear footage as fence line.
Chain-link wire (fabric)	36″, 42″, 48″, 60″, or 72″ height	The same linear footage as the fence line.
Post caps	The same size as the outside diameter of the corner and end or gate post.	1 for each end, gate, and corner post.
Rail ends	1⅜″ outside diameter.	1 for each brace band.
Top rail sleeves (connectors)	1⅜″ outside diameter, 6″ long. *(Required only if swage end toprail is not used)*	1 for each length of toprail.
Gate hinge	Included with gate.	
Brace bands	The same size as the outside diameter of the corner and end or gate post.	1 for each end or gate post, and 2 for each corner post.
Eye-top	1⅜″ eye; 1⅝″ base.	1 for each line post.
Tension bars	2″ shorter than wire height.	1 for each end or gate post, and 2 for each corner post.
Tension bands	The same size as the outside diameter of the corner and end gate post.	3 for 36″, 42″, and 48″ end/gate post; and 4 for 60″—5 for 72″. Double quantities for corner posts.
Tie wires	Pre-cut aluminum.	1 every 24″ of toprail and 1 every 12″ of line posts.
Gate latch	Included with gate.	
Scroll	Included with gate.	
Post hinge	The same size as the outside diameter of the gate post.	2 for each walk gate; 4 for each drive gate.
Nuts and bolts	5/16″ diameter; 1¼″ long.	1 for each brace and tension band.

the actual surface covered when tested in accordance with 5.5.2. The zinc used for the coating shall conform to the grades specified in ASTM Designation B6 Standard Specifications for slab zinc.

4.2 Fabric sizes The height, size of mesh, and wire diameters of chain-link fabric shall be as given in TABLE B-1. The methods of measurement and tolerances are given in 4.2.1, 4.2.2, and 4.2.3 respectively.

4.2.1 Height of fabric The height of the fabric shall be the overall dimension from ends of barbs or knuckles. The tolerance on the nominal height shall be plus or minus 1 inch.

4.2.2 Mesh sizes The size of mesh shall be determined by measuring the minimum clear distance between the wires forming the parallel sides of the mesh, measured in either direction. The tolerance in the size of $1^3/_4$- and 2-inch mesh shall be plus or minus $1/_8$ inch, and for 1-inch mesh it is plus or minus $1/_{16}$ inch.

4.2.3 Wire diameter The diameter of the coated wire shall be determined as the average of two readings measured to the nearest 0.001 inch taken at right angles to each other on the straight portion of the mesh's parallel sides. The tolerance in the diameter of the coated wire shall be plus or minus 0.005 inch.

4.3 Selvage Fabric 60 inches high and under in 2-inch mesh shall be furnished with knuckling at each selvage. Fabric over 60 inches high in 2-inch mesh shall be furnished with knuckling at one selvage and twisting at the other. All fabric less than 2-inch mesh shall be furnished with knuckling at both selvages. Special selvages may be specified by the purchaser.

4.4 Workmanship The chain-link fence fabric shall be made of high-grade materials and with good workmanship. The zinc coating shall be applied in a continuous process and shall not be applied to the fabric in roll form. Excessive roughness, blisters, sal ammoniac spots, bruises, and flaking shall be noted. These and other obvious defects, if present to any considerable extent, may provide a basis for rejection.

5. Inspection and testing

5.1 General The tests given herein are intended primarily for use as production tests in conjunction with manufacturing processes, inspection methods, and with other tests if needed, according to 5.2, so as to ensure the conformity of the chain-link fabric with the requirements of this specification.

5.2 Production inspection and testing The manufacturer shall make such inspections and tests during the manufacturing processes as are needed to maintain the quality of the product so as to be consistently in conformity with this specification. The inspection and tests given herein (see 5.3 and 5.5) shall be made regularly during production for all chain-link fabric furnished as being in conformity with this specification.

5.3 Inspection The chain-link fabric shall be visually inspected to determine its conformance with the workmanship, design, and dimensional requirements of this standard.

5.4 Sampling One roll from every 50 rolls or fraction thereof shall be selected at random for test purposes, but in no case shall less than three rolls be selected from a shipment. The specimens for test purposes shall consist of individual pieces of wire taken from the outside end of the sample rolls.

5.5 Test procedures

5.5.1 Breaking strength The break-strength of the fabric shall be determined in accordance with the method described in ASTM Designated E8 Tension Testing of Metallic Materials, using one specimen from each sample roll. Specimens to establish conformance to this requirement shall constitute individual pickets from a section of the fence fabric to a sufficient length so as to measure 15–18 inches after straightening. The straightened portion of the specimen shall be inside the jaws of the tensile testing machine, so the actual test is performed on the underformed section between the jaws. If fracture takes place other than between the grips, the test shall be discarded.

5.5.2 Weight of zinc coating The weight of zinc coating on the fabric shall be determined in accordance with the method described in ASTM Designation A90, Weight of Coating on Zinc-Coated (Galvanized) Iron and Steel Articles, using one piece of wire removed from the fabric of each sample roll. The specimen tested may be on any continuous length over 12 inches, but it preferably should be about 24 inches long.

5.6 Noncompliance If any specimen tested fails to meet the requirements specified, two additional specimens shall be taken from the sample roll and tested. Both shall meet the requirements in every respect. Otherwise, the material represented by that sample roll shall be considered as not being in compliance with this standard.

Industrial steel specifications for fence posts, gates, and accessories

1. **Materials** Posts, gate frames, braces, rails, stretcher bars, and truss rods shall be of steel. Reinforcing wires shall be of high-carbon steel. Gate hinges, post caps, barbed wire supporting arms, stretcher bar bands, and other parts shall be of steel, malleable iron, ductile iron, or similar material, except that ties and clips may be of aluminum (TABLE B-2).

   Posts, gate frames, rails, and braces shall conform to the dimensions and weights shown in TABLE B-3.

2. **Zinc coating** All steel and iron parts shall be zinc-coated after fabrication, using zinc grade "E" in accordance with Federal Specification QQ-Z-351.

   The weight of the zinc coating per square foot of actual surface area shall average not less than 1.2 ounces. No individual specimen shall show less than 1.0 ounce.

3. **Gates** Gates shall be swing or sliding as specified, complete with latches, stops, keepers, hinges or rollers, and roller tracks, and

Table B-2. Fabric Sizes.

Height of fence fabric (inches)	Size of mesh (inches)	Gauge, coated wire (number)	Nominal diameter of coated wire (inch)
36, 42, 48, 60, 72, 84, 96, 108, 120, 144	2	6	0.1920
36, 42, 48, 60, 72, 84, 96, 108, 120, 144	2	9	.1483
36, 42, 48, 60, 72, 84	2	11	.1205
96, 108, 120, 144	1³/₄	11	.1205
36, 42, 48, 60	1	13	.0915

Table B-3. Dimensions and Weights

Use and section		Outside diameter or dimensions, nominal (inches)	Weight per foot, nominal (pounds)
End, corner, and pull posts (tubular) for fabric heights:			
6 feet and less:	Round	2.375	3.65
	Square	2.00	3.60
Over 6 feet:	Round	2.875	5.79
	Square	2.50	5.70
Gate posts for nominal width of gate, single, or one leaf of double			
6 feet and less:	Round	2.875	5.79
	Square	2.50	5.70
Gate width 13 feet and less:	Round	4.00	9.10
	Square	3.00	9.10
Gate width over 13 feet to 18 feet, incl.:	Round	6.625	18.97
Gate width over 18 feet:	Round	8.625	24.70
Gates: exterior frames for fabric heights: 6 feet and less, and leaf widths not exceeding 8':	Round	1.660	1.806
	Square	1.50	1.90
Over 6 feet, or gate leafs over 8' width:	Round	1.90	2.72
	Square	2.00	2.10
Internal gate bracing:			
	Round	1.660	1.806
	Square	1.50	1.90
Rails and post braces (tubular):	Round	1.660	1.806
Intermediate posts for fabric heights:			
6 feet and less:			
Tubular (round)		1.90	2.72
H-Section		$1.875 \times 1.625 \times .113$	2.70
Over 6 feet:			
Tubular (round)		2.375	3.65
H-Section		$2.25 \times 1.95 \times .143$	4.10

Note: Where no tolerances are specified in this table or elsewhere in this specification, standard commercial tolerances shall apply. Note #4 of ASTM A-120 shall apply to weight tolerances.

when so specified, with provision for three strands of barbed wire above the fabric.

3a. Gate frames shall be constructed of tubular members (round or square) welded at all corners or assembled with fittings. On steel, welds shall be painted with aluminum-based or zinc-based paint. Where corner fittings are used, gates shall have truss rods of 3/8-inch nominal diameter to prevent sag or twist. Gate leaves shall have vertical intermediate bracing as required, spaced so that no members are more than 8 feet apart. Gate leaves 10 feet or more shall have a horizontal brace or one 3/8-inch, diagonal truss rod. When barbed wire top is specified (see 6.2), the end members of the gate frames shall be extended 1 foot above the top horizontal member to which three strands of barbed wire, uniformly spaced, shall be attached by use of bands, clips, or hook bolts. Dimensions and weights of gate frames shall be as shown in TABLE B-2. Gate filler shall be of the same fabric as specified for the fence and shall be attached securely to the gate frame at intervals of 15 inches.

3b. Fabric shall conform to the current CLFMI specification and shall be the same type as used in the fence construction. The fabric shall be attached securely to the gate frame at intervals not exceeding 15 inches.

3c. Hinges shall be of adequate strength for the gate and with large bearing surfaces for clamping in position. The hinges shall not twist or turn under the action of the gate. The gate shall be capable of being opened and closed easily by one person.

3d. Latches, stops, and keepers shall be provided for all gates. Latches shall have a plunger bar arranged to engage the center stop, except that for single gates of openings less than 10 feet wide a forked latch may be provided. Latches shall be arranged for locking. Center stops shall consist of a device arranged to be set in concrete and to engage a plunger bar of the latch of double gates. No stop is required for single gates. Keepers shall consist of a mechanical device for securing the free end of the gate when in the full open position.

4. **Posts** Posts shall be of the lengths specified and shall be tubular, except that line posts may be H-beam (FIG. B-1).

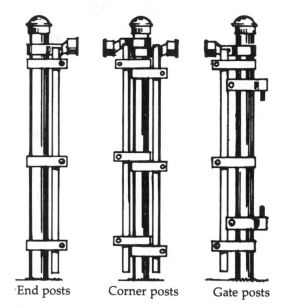

End posts   Corner posts   Gate posts

Fig. B-1   Kind of posts. Builders Fence Co., Inc.

5. **Post braces** Post braces shall be provided for each gate corner, pull, and end post for use when the top rail is omitted or with fabric 6 feet or more in height. A post brace shall consist of a round tubular brace extending to each adjacent line post at approximately mid-height of the fabric, and a truss consisting of a rod not less than 3/8 inch in nominal diameter from the line post back to the gate, corner, pull, or end post, with turnbuckle or other equivalent provision for adjustment.

6. **Post tops** Post tops shall consist of ornamental tops or combination tops with

barbed wire supporting arms as specified. When so specified or when a top rail is to be provided, the top shall be provided with a hole suitable for the through passage of the top rail. The post tops shall fit over the outside of posts and shall exclude moisture from tubular posts.

7. **Barbed wire supporting arms** When specified to be furnished, these arms shall be at an angle of approximately 45 degrees or vertical as specified. They shall be fitted with clips or other means for attaching three strands of barbed wire. With 45-degree arms the top wire shall be approximately 12 inches horizontally from the fence line, and the other wires are spaced uniformly between the top of the fence fabric and the outside strand. The barbed wire arm shall be of sufficient strength to withstand a weight of 200 pounds applied at the outer strand of barbed wire. Six line barb wire V arm may be specified if desired.

8. **Top rails** Top rails shall be round (tubular), in lengths not less than 18 feet, and shall be fitted with couplings for connecting the lengths into a continuous run. The couplings shall be not less than 6 inches long, with .070 minimum wall thickness, and they shall allow for expansion and contraction of the rail. Open seam outside sleeves shall be permitted only with a minimum wall thickness of .100 inch. Enough suitable ties or clips shall be provided for attaching the fabric securely to the top rail at intervals not exceeding 2 feet. Means shall be provided for attaching the top rail to each gate, corner, pull, and end post.

9. **Stretcher bars** These bars shall be no less than $3/16 \times 3/4$ inch and no less than 2 inches shorter than the full height of the fabric with which they are to be used. The stretcher bars shall be arranged for attaching the fabric to all terminal posts by threading through the fabric, by bands, or by other positive mechanical means. One stretcher bar shall be provided for each gate and end post, and two bars are for each corner and pull post.

10. **Tie or clips** Ties or clips of adequate strength shall be provided for attaching the fabric to all line posts at intervals not exceeding 15 inches.

11. **Bands or clips** Bands or clips of adequate strength shall be provided for attaching the fabric and stretcher bars to all terminal posts at intervals not exceeding 15 inches. Tension bands and brace bands shall be formed from flat or beveled steel and shall have a minimum thickness of $.115 \pm .005$ after galvanizing with a minimum width of $7/8$ inch $\pm .015$.

12. **Tension wire** If the top rail is not specified, a top tension wire shall be provided. Spiraled or crimped tension wire shall be not less than No. 7 gauge ± 0.005 inch in diameter. Ties or clips shall be provided for attaching each wire to the fabric at intervals not exceeding 2 feet. Zinc coating shall be a minimum coating of .80 ounce per square foot of surface area.

13. **Barbed wire** Barbed wire shall consist of two strands of $12^{1}/_{2}$-gauge wire with 14-gauge, four-point barbs spaced approximately 5 inches apart. All wire shall be zinc-coated with a minimum coating of .80 ounce per square foot of surface area on $12^{1}/_{2}$-gauge wire and .60 ounce per square foot of surface area on 14-gauge wire.

Commercial standard for industrial aluminum alloy chain-link fencing

1. **Purpose**

   1.1 The purpose of this commercial standard is to provide a nationally recognized standard of quality for aluminum alloy chain-link fencing to promote fair marketing practices and a better understanding between manufacturers, distributors, and users of this fencing. It will also assist ultimate users in determining the types and sizes of fencing that are standard within the industry.

2. **Scope and classification**

2.1 **Scope** This standard covers the design, construction, and the minimal chemical and mechanical requirements of the component parts and accessories for industrial aluminum alloy chain-link fencing intended primarily for installation on the premises of any dwelling, building, or structure as a boundary line or for the protection of property.

3. **Requirements**

3.2 **Materials**

3.2.1 **Fabric** Aluminum alloy chain-link fence fabric of 1-inch mesh size shall be made of wire conforming to the requirements of Alloy 6061-T94 of ASTM Designation B211. Fabric of 1³/₄- and 2-inch mesh size shall be made of wire conforming to the requirements of Alloy 6061 or of any alloy having equivalent strength and corrosion resistance of the same specification, except that the minimum tensile strength of the wire after weaving shall be 50,000 psi.

3.2.2 **Pipe** The aluminum alloy pipe shall conform to the requirements for Alloy 6063, Temper T6, of ASTM Designation B241.

3.2.3 **Extruded shapes**

3.2.3.1 **Square tubing** The aluminum alloy square tubing shall conform to the requirements for Alloy 6063, Temper T6, of ASTM Designation B235.

3.2.3.2 **H-Beam** The aluminum alloy H-beam sections shall conform to the chemical and mechanical property requirements of ASTM Designation B221. The sections shall comply with dimensional tolerance requirements of this specification as applicable.

3.2.3.3 **Accessories** The accessories shall be made of aluminum alloy materials specified in TABLE B-4.

3.3 **Construction.**

Table B-4. Nomenclature, Size, and Material of Fencing Accessories

| Accessories | | Diameter of dimensions (nominal) (inches) | Aluminum alloy | |
Nomenclature	Type or material		Alloy & temper (No.)	ASTM designation (No.)
Tension bars	Bar	$1/4 \times 3/4$[1]	6063-T5 or T6	B221
	Bar	$3/16 \times 1/2$ or $1/4 \times 3/8$[2]	6063-T5 or T6	B221
Brace and tension bands	Bar	$1/8 \times 7/8$	6063-T5	B221
			3003-H14	B221
Extension arms			3105-H14	
Arm-line post	Bar	0.080 (thick)	6061-T4	B221
			5052-H34	B209
Arm-corner & end post[3]	Castings	To fit posts & bases	SG70A, ZG61A	B26
			ZG61B, ZC81A	B26
Bases	Castings	To fit posts	ZG70A	B108
			SG100B, S12B	B85
Rail and brace ends, post tops, and turnbuckles	Castings	To fit posts & rails	Same as for above castings	Same as for above castings

Accessories Nomenclature	Type or material	Diameter of dimensions (nominal) (inches)	Aluminum alloy Alloy & temper (No.)	ASTM designation (No.)
Rail couplings— outside	Pipe	6×0.078	6063-T6	B241
Rail couplings— inside	Pipe	6×0.062	6063-T6, 5052-H34, 3105-H18	B241 B241 B241
Truss rods	Rod	0.375	6061-T6 6063-T6	B221 B221
Barbed wire— double strand	Wire	0.110	5052-H38	B211
Barbed wire—barbs	Wire	0.080	5052-H38	B211
Tension wire	Wire	0.192	6061-T6 5052-H38	B211 B211
Hog rings	Wire	0.105	6061	B211
Fabric ties	Wire	.144	3105-EC-F or 1100-H14	B211
Bolts and nuts	Wire	5/16	2024-T4, 6061-T6	B211 B211
Rivets	Wire	5/16	1100-F	B211

[1] Intended for use with 1 3/4 and 2 inch mesh.

[2] Intended for use with 1 inch mesh.

[3] Bar 0.105 inch thick (nominal) of Alloy 6061, Temper 4, of ASTM Designation B221 may also be used for arm.

3.3.1 Chain-link fabric The chain-link fabric shall be made from wire helically wound and interwoven so as to provide a continuous mesh without knots or ties, except in the form of knuckling or of twisting the selvage of the fabric.

3.3.1.2 Fabric sizes The height, size of mesh, and wire diameters of the chain-link fabric shall be as given in TABLE B-5. The methods of measurement and tolerances are given in 3.3.1.3 and 3.3.1.4 respectively.

3.3.1.3 Height of fabric The height of the fabric shall be the overall dimension from ends of barbs or knuckles. The tolerance on the nominal height of 1 3/4- and 2-inch mesh

size fabric shall be + 1 inch, and for 1-inch mesh size it is + 1/2 inch.

3.3.1.4 Selvage Fabric 60 inches high and under in 2-inch mesh shall be furnished with knuckling at each selvage. Fabric more than 60 inches high in 2-inch mesh shall be furnished with knuckling at one selvage and twisting at the other. All fabric less than 2-inch mesh shall be furnished with knuckling at both selvages. Special selvages may be specified by the purchaser.

3.3.2 Posts, top rails, and braces The fence posts, top rails, and braces shall be made of aluminum alloy pipe (see 3.2.2) or extruded shapes (see 3.2.3) of the sizes shown in

Table B-5. Fabric Sizes

Height of fence fabric (nominal) (inches)	Size of mesh (inches)	Nominal wire[1] diameter (inches)
36, 42, 48, 60, 72, 84, 96, 108, 120, 144	2	0.192
36, 42, 48, 60, 72, 84, 96, 108, 120, 144	2	.148
96, 108, 120, 144	1³/₄	.120
36, 42, 48, 60	1	.095

[1] Tolerance, plus or minus 0.0015 inch.

TABLE B-6 for the specified height of fabric and application (see TABLE B-5).

3.3.3 Gate posts and frames The gate posts and gate frames shall be made of aluminum gates shall have intermediate members and/or diagonal truss rods as necessary to provide rigid construction of ample strength that is free from sag and twist.

Table B-6. Sizes of Pipe and Extruded Shapes for Posts, Top Rails, and Braces

Fabric height	Application	Pipe sizes[2]		Square tubing sizes		H-beam sizes	
		Nominal size[1]	Outside diameter (nominal)	Dimensions (nominal)	Weight per foot (nominal)	Dimensions (nominal)	Weight per foot (nominal)
feet		*inches*	*inches*	*inches*	*pounds*	*inches*	*pounds*
6 to 12, incl.	End, corner, & pull posts	2¹/₂	2.875	3.00 × 3.00	2.00	–	–
6 to 12, incl.	Line posts	2	2.375	–	1.26	2.25 × 1.95	1.253
6 to 12, incl.	Top rails, braces	1¹/₄	1.660	–	78	–	–

[1] Limiting values for the nominal dimensions and weights are given in the applicable ASTM specifications.
[2] Schedule 40, nominal weight. Standard commercial tolerances shall apply.

alloy pipe (see 3.2.2) or square tubing (see 3.2.3.1) of the sizes shown in TABLE B-7 for the specified opening and swing of gate.

3.3.3.1 Gates

3.3.3.1.1 Gate frames Assembly of gates shall be accomplished by using properly designed fittings or by welding. Gates shall operate freely through a minimum arc of 180 degrees. Where corner fittings are used,

3.3.3.1.2 Hinges, latches, center stops, and holdbacks Hinges shall be aluminum alloy castings conforming to the latest issue of ASTM Designations B108 or B26 or made of malleable iron or steel and hot-dip galvanized. Hinges shall be designed not to twist or turn under gate action. They shall not allow the gate to swing a full 180 degrees to lie along and parallel to the fence line.

Table B-7. Size of Pipe and Square Tubing for Gateposts and Frames

Application	Gate opening		Pipe sizes[2]		Square tubing sizes	
	Single swing	Double swing	Nominal size[1]	Outside diameter (nominal)	Dimensions (nominal)	Weight per ft (nominal)
Gateposts	*feet* 6 and under	*feet* 12 and under	*inches* 2½	*inches* 2.875	*inches* 3.00 × 3.00	*pounds* 2.00
	Over 6 to 12, incl.	Over 12 to 24 incl.	3½	4.000		3.15
	Over 12 to 18, incl.	Over 24 to 36, incl.	6	6.625		
	Over 18 to 32, incl.	Over 36 to 44, incl.	8	8.625		
Gate frames	All	All	1½	1.900	2.00 × 2.00	0.94

[1] Limiting values for the nominal dimensions and weights are given in the applicable ASTM specifications.
[2] Schedule 40, nominal weight. Standard commercial tolerances shall apply.

Latches, stops, and keepers shall be provided for all gates. Double gate latches shall be a combination fulcrum-type latch with center drop rod or of the plunger bar of the latch of double gates. Keepers engage the gate stop. Single gate openings may be furnished with a fulcrum type of latch or other suitable type latch. Center stops shall consist of a device arranged to be set in concrete and to engage a plunger bar of the latch of double gates. Keepers shall consist of a substantial mechanical device for securing and supporting the free end of the gate when in full open position. All latches, stops, and keepers shall be made of aluminum alloys as specified for hinges or galvanized malleable iron or pressed steel.

3.3.5 Workmanship All parts of the aluminum fencing shall be uniform in quality and temper. The exterior and interior surfaces of parts and pipe shall be clean, smooth, and free from slivers, laminations, folds, grooves, cracks, and other injurious defects within the limits consistent with best commercial practice.

4. Inspection and testing

4.1 Production inspection and testing The manufacturer shall make such inspections and tests during the manufacturing process of all components as are needed to maintain the quality of the product consistently in conformity with this standard.

4.2 Inspection All parts of the aluminum fencing shall be visually inspected to determine their conformance with the workmanship, design, and dimensional requirements of this standard.

Standards for chain-link fence installation

Installation All materials and workmanship shall be first class in every respect and done in a neat, workmanlike manner.

Post spacing Line posts shall be spaced at intervals not to exceed 10 feet on the average when measured from center to center between terminal posts. In determining the post spacing the measurement generally will be made parallel to the slope of the natural ground. All posts shall be placed in a vertical position except where designated otherwise by the owner or the owner's representative.

Post setting All posts shall be set in holes of appropriate diameter and depth. After the post has been set and plumbed, the hole shall be filled with 2,000 psi (four-sack mix) concrete. The exposed surface of the concrete shall be crowned to shed water.

Using mechanical devices for the setting of fence posts is acceptable under this specification, provided the mechanical device develops a strength in the ground equal or superior to the strength developed by the concrete settings as specified earlier.

Where solid rock is encountered without an overburden of soil, line posts shall be set a minimum depth of 12 inches. End, corner, gate, and pull posts shall be set a minimum of 18 inches into the solid rock. The hole shall have a minimum width of 1 inch greater than the largest dimension of the post section to be set.

After the post is set and plumbed, the hole shall be filled with grout consisting of 1 part Portland cement and 3 parts clean, well-graded sand. Other grouting materials may be used if they are approved or specified by the owner. The grout shall be thoroughly worked into the hole so as to leave no voids. The grout shall be crowned to carry water from the post.

Where solid rock is covered by an overburden of soil or loose rock, the posts shall be set to full depth unless the penetration into solid rock reaches the minimum depths specified earlier, in which case the depth of penetration may be terminated. Concrete footings shall be constructed from the solid rock to the top of the ground. Grouting will be required on the portion of the post in solid rock.

Terminal post End, corner, gate, and pull posts shall be set as shown heretofore. They shall be braced to the nearest post with a galvanized pipe horizontal brace used as a compression member, and a galvanized $3/8$-inch steel truss rod and truss tightener used as a tension member. On fences 3–5 feet in height where a top rail is required, no braces are needed. Bracing will always be required on all fences 6–11 feet high. If the center rail is omitted, two truss braces will be required in lieu of one at each terminal. Regardless of height, all fences installed without a top rail must have braces on all terminals. All changes in direction of the fence line of 30 degrees or more shall be considered corners. Pull posts shall be used at all abrupt changes in grade.

Chain-link fabric It shall be placed on the side of the fence as designated by the owner or his representative. The fabric shall be cut, and each span shall be attached independently at all terminal posts. Fastening to terminal posts shall be with stretcher bars and fabric bands spaced at maximum 15-inch intervals. Fastening to the line post shall be with tie wire, metal bands, or other approved material attached at maximum 15-inch intervals. The top edge of the fabric wire shall be attached with wire ties at intervals not exceeding 24 inches. The bottom edge of the fabric shall be fastened to the bottom tension wire with wire ties at intervals not exceeding 2 feet. Rolls of wire fabric shall be joined by weaving a single strand into the ends of the rolls to form a continuous mesh.

Insurance and permits The fence contractor shall provide and pay for workmen's compensation insurance; public liability insurance; bonds, where required; permits; and other requirements of national, state, and local governments.

Glossary

air-dried lumber Lumber that has been dried naturally by air and with a minimum moisture content of 12 to 20 percent.

anchor bolts Bolts to secure a wooden sill plate to concrete or masonry patio or foundation.

batten Narrow strips of wood used to cover joints or as decorative vertical members over wide boards, such as on fences.

beam A structural member transversely supporting a load.

blind nailing Nailing in such a way that the nailheads are not visible on the face of the work.

Boston ridge A method of applying asphalt or wood shingles at the ridge or at the hips of a roof as a finish.

brace An inclined piece of lumber applied to a wall or fence section to stiffen the structure. Often used as temporary bracing until framing has been completed.

butt-joint The junction where the ends of two timbers or other members meet in a square-cut joint.

concrete plain Concrete either without reinforcement, or reinforced only for shrinkage or temperature change.

corner braces Diagonal braces at the corners of frame structures to stiffen and strengthen the wall.

d See penny.

deck paint An enamel with a high degree of resistance to mechanical wear, designed for use on porch floors and similar surfaces.

direct nailing To nail perpendicular to the initial surface or to the junction of the pieces jointed. Also called face nailing.

expansion joint A bituminous fiber strip used to separate blocks or units of concrete to prevent cracking due to expansion as a result of temperature changes. Often used on large concrete patio slabs.

footing A masonry section, usually concrete, in a rectangular form wider than the bottom of the foundation wall or pier it supports.

frostline The depth of frost penetration in the soil. This depth varies in different parts of the country. Fence footings should be placed below this depth to prevent movement.

grain The direction, size, arrangement, appearance, or quality of fibers in wood.

grain, edge Edge-grain lumber that has been sawed parallel to the pith of the log and approximately at right angles to the growth rings.

grain, flat Flat-grain lumber that has been sawed parallel to the pith of the log and approximately tangent to the growth rings.

heartwood The wood extending from the pith to the sapwood, the cells of which no longer participate in the life process of the tree.

kiln-dried lumber Lumber that has been kiln-dried, often to a moisture content of 6 to 12 percent. Common varieties of softwood lumber, such as framing lumber, are dried to a somewhat higher moisture content.

lattice A framework of crossed wood or metal strips.

lumber, boards Yard lumber less than 2 inches thick and 2 or more inches wide. Most commonly used for fencing.

natural finish A transparent finish that does not seriously alter the original color or grain of the natural wood. Natural finishes are usually provided by sealers, oils, varnishes, water-repellent preservatives, and other similar materials.

o.c., or on center The measurement of spacing for studs, rafters, joists, and posts from the center of one member to the center of the next.

penny As applied to nails, it originally indicated the price per hundred. The term now serves as a measure of nail length and is abbreviated by the letter d.

pier A column of masonry, usually rectangular, used to support other structural members. Often used as support under decks.

plumb Exactly perpendicular; vertical.

plywood A piece of wood made of three or more layers of veneer joined with glue, and usually laid with the grain of the adjoining plies at right angles. Usually constructed with an odd number of plies to provide balanced construction.

run In stairs, the net width of a stem or the horizontal distance covered by a flight of stairs.

sapwood The outer zone of wood, next to the bark. In the living tree it contains some living cells, as well as dead and dying cells. In most species, it is lighter colored than the heartwood. In all species, it is lacking in decay resistance.

sealer A finishing material, either clear or pigmented, usually applied directly over uncoated wood for the purpose of sealing the surface.

square A unit of measure (100 square feet) usually applied to roofing material.

stud One of a series of slender wood or metal vertical structural members placed as supporting elements in walls and partitions.

toenailing To drive a nail at a slant with the initial surface in order to permit it to penetrate into a second member.

water-repellent preservative A liquid designed to penetrate into wood and impart water repellency and a moderate preservative protection.

Index